The Forever Rule

CARRIE ANN RYAN

NEW YORK TIMES BESTSELLING AUTHOR

The Forever Rule

THE CAGE FAMILY
BOOK ONE

CARRIE ANN RYAN

The Forever Rule

The Forever Rule
A Cage Family Romance
By: Carrie Ann Ryan
© 2024 Carrie Ann Ryan

Before I Knew © 2023 Carrie Ann Ryan
Cover Art by Sweet N Spicy Designs

This book is licensed for your personal enjoyment only. This book may not be re-sold or given away to other people. If you would like to share this book with another person, please purchase an additional copy for each person or use proper retail channels to lend a copy. If you're reading this book and did not purchase it, or it was not purchased for your use only, then please return it and purchase your own copy. Thank you for respecting the hard work of this author.
All characters in this book are fiction and figments of the author's imagination.

All content warnings are listed on the book page for this book on my website.

NO AI TRAINING: Without in any way limiting the author's [and publisher's] exclusive rights under copyright, any use of this publication to "train" generative artificial intelligence (AI) technologies to generate text is expressly prohibited. The author reserves all rights to license uses of this work for generative AI training and development of machine learning language models.

For my Family

Praise for Carrie Ann Ryan

"Count on Carrie Ann Ryan for emotional, sexy, character driven stories that capture your heart!" – Carly Phillips, NY Times bestselling author

"Carrie Ann Ryan's romances are my newest addiction! The emotion in her books captures me from the very beginning. The hope and healing hold me close until the end. These love stories will simply sweep you away." ~ NYT Bestselling Author Deveny Perry

"Carrie Ann Ryan writes the perfect balance of sweet and heat ensuring every story feeds the soul." - Audrey Carlan, #1 New York Times Bestselling Author

"Carrie Ann Ryan never fails to draw readers in with passion, raw sensuality, and characters that pop off the page. Any book by Carrie Ann is an absolute treat." – New York Times Bestselling Author J. Kenner

"Carrie Ann Ryan knows how to pull your heartstrings and make your pulse pound! Her wonderful Redwood Pack series will draw you in and keep you reading long into the night. I can't wait to see what comes next with the new generation, the Talons. Keep them coming, Carrie Ann!" –Lara Adrian, New York Times bestselling author of CRAVE THE NIGHT

"With snarky humor, sizzling love scenes, and brilliant, imaginative worldbuilding, The Dante's Circle series reads as if Carrie Ann Ryan peeked at my personal wish list!" – NYT Bestselling Author, Larissa Ione

"Carrie Ann Ryan writes sexy shifters in a world full of passionate happily-ever-afters." – *New York Times* Bestselling Author Vivian Arend

"Carrie Ann's books are sexy with characters you can't help but love from page one. They are heat and heart blended to perfection." *New York Times* Bestselling Author Jayne Rylon

Carrie Ann Ryan's books are wickedly funny and deliciously hot, with plenty of twists to keep you guessing. They'll keep you up all night!" USA Today Bestselling Author Cari Quinn

"Once again, Carrie Ann Ryan knocks the Dante's Circle series out of the park. The queen of hot, sexy, enthralling paranormal romance, Carrie Ann is an author not to miss!" *New York Times* bestselling Author Marie Harte

Before I Knew is the prequel to The Cage Family. While you don't need to read it before The Forever Rule, and can find it on it's own as a free thank you, I'm including it within Aston and Blakely's book. This way you don't miss a thing, in case you didn't pick up the prequel before this.

Thank you so much for reading and I cannot wait for you to join The Cage Family!

~CARRIE ANN

Before I Knew

Before I Knew

It all began with a wrong number.

When Blakely gets added to the Cage family group chat, chaos ensues. What she doesn't expect is to have a side chat with the eldest brother.

What was supposed to be a simple sign off, turns into a mild flirtation and invitation to lunch.

Only Aston Cage has his secrets.

And perhaps they should've left their conversation on read.

Before I Knew is the prequel to the Cage family series. Learn how Blakely and Aston met, before they finally get their happily ever after in The Forever Rule.

Chapter One
ASTON

ME:
Wait. Why did we make a group chat? I thought we already had a group chat? One with a name and everything.

FLYNN:
We had to make a new one because somebody ruined the last one.

DORIAN:
I feel like there was a little sarcasm in your pointed tone.

HUDSON:
How do you hear tone in a text message?

THEO:
Oh, we read tone.

FORD:

Seriously though, why the new group chat? Do you understand how many group chats I have?

FLYNN:

It's not our fault that you decided to marry two people who had large families.

HUDSON:

Greer's is a large family with three brothers and a bunch of spouses. Noah's family? Calling the Montgomerys large is like saying the earth is part of the solar system.

DORIAN:

That wasn't even a good analogy. You should have said something like water is wet.

THEO:

Oh, so are we making fun of Hudson's bad analogy here? Because I'm here for it.

ME:

I still want to know why we have a new group chat. Why we're even starting with the group chat.

FLYNN:

Because Dorian added his ex to the previous group chat, and I didn't know how to quietly remove her without notifying her.

BEFORE I KNEW

ME:
Are you serious? She was in there the whole time.

HUDSON:
You don't just add someone to the group chat. You make a separate group chat.

THEO:
That's the whole rule of group chats. What is said in group chat, stays in group chat.

HUDSON:
Until you take a screenshot of your chat and then you put it in the other chat hoping that the person that you're talking shit about doesn't actually see it. And now I've confused myself.

ME:
I hate all of you.

FORD:
You love us. Seriously though, do not add spouses to the family group chat. Or parents. We have a family group chat with the parents, and then a family group chat with just Mom, and then one with just Dad. Hence why I'm very confused why we continue to have more of them. We need to name this one.

ME:
Let's just call it the Cages.

FLYNN:

Yes, because we don't have anything called the Cages in the Cage family group chat. You're the CEO of this family, what the hell's wrong with you?

HUDSON:

He's the president of Cage Enterprises. Not the CEO of the family.

FLYNN:

For a man that doesn't work with the company, you do sound a little testy.

DORIAN:

Those sound like fighting words to me.

JAMES:

I have been in a meeting this entire time. Are we seriously just going to have a fifty-message long group chat about the efficacies and rules of group chat? This isn't Fight Club.

THEO:

All the more reason to actually speak about the group chat, as we're allowed to talk about it. Like you said, this isn't Fight Club.

FORD:

I thought we weren't supposed to talk about fight club.

HUDSON:

That movie came out what, fifty years ago at this point?

FLYNN:
Let's not let Hudson do math anymore.

ME:
Seriously. Now that we know we have a new group chat, we can come up with a name later.

FLYNN:
Fine by me. Did you start this discourse for a reason, eldest brother of ours?

ME:
I wanted to ensure we were all ready for family dinner on Friday. You know, our favorite thing to do.

HUDSON:
Groan.

DORIAN:
I'm busy.

JAMES:
New phone, who's this?

THEO:
Yes, because that totally works, James. Wait. Does it work? I need to know. For reasons.

FORD:
I will probably have dinner with the Montgomerys. In fact, I'll make sure I'll have dinner with the Montgomerys.

ME:
Dad won't be there. He's on a work trip.

THEO:

I'm in.

HUDSON:

Friday night at six again?

DORIAN:

I might not make it until six thirty.

JAMES:

I'll be there. We can hitch a ride together, Flynn.

FLYNN:

What if I have a date?

DORIAN:

You guys, I can't laugh so hard that I pee myself in public. Flynn. A date.

FLYNN:

Your urinary tract problems aren't my problems.

FORD:

I might have a Montgomery dinner, but I'm going to try to make it.

ME:

Dinner is at seven. Drinks begin at six. I suppose it's my turn to host. Unless we'd like to go to The Teal Door?

THEO:

Do not ruin my restaurant with a family dinner that will surely be loud and rowdy.

JAMES:
We are elite businessmen. We are not rowdy.

DORIAN:
I'd rather go to the restaurant.

THEO:
You are not allowed to date any more of my waitresses. One quit already.

ME:
Dorian, what the hell did you do?

DORIAN:
I didn't do anything. Laura said she was moving to be near her mom because she got sick. I may like women, but I don't fuck with them.

HUDSON:
Sure, Dorian. Whatever you say.

DORIAN:
I'm offended.

THEO:
You really aren't.

JAMES:
You really, really aren't.

ME:
We'll pick the place soon. But Theo, is it okay if we use your place instead? I'd rather not have to deal with a caterer. I could cook, but I don't have time.

THEO:

Fine. However, just know I'm going to charge you out the ass.

ME:

Charge the company.

DORIAN:

Wait, you're not even going to cook for us, Aston?

ME:

I'm not in the mood to search for a middle finger emoji.

FLYNN:

My God, how old are you?

JAMES:

We don't ask those types of questions.

UNKNOWN NUMBER:

Hello? Do you know how to exit a group chat? Not that this hasn't been enlightening, but I don't think I'm supposed to be here.

I LEANED BACK AND STARED AT MY PHONE AS IF IT WERE a snake ready to strike. I did not recognize the number. It wasn't Dorian's ex. And now I was wondering why we had a complete stranger in our family group chat. Damn it. I picked up the phone as soon as it rang, Flynn's name appearing on the screen.

"Do you know who that is?" Flynn asked, his voice sounding slightly panicked.

"Is it weird that I hope it's someone that Dorian met

and accidentally put her number in?" Because having it be a complete stranger would be worse. At least we hadn't shared company and family issues within the chat. So far.

"We don't know if it's a *her*."

That was true. We didn't know if it was a her. And here I was, acting as if it could be. Weird.

"Hell, no one else is texting, so they're probably waiting for me to handle it?" I ask, pinching the bridge of my nose.

"Sounds about right. But you are the big brother. It's what you're used to. Handle it."

"At least we didn't discuss company secrets."

"No, we just said our names often enough that now someone has our numbers. Hopefully it's not the press. Or a rival. Fuck."

I could practically see Flynn pace his office. We weren't working in the same building today. Flynn was off in the small town that we had purchased over two generations ago, while I was in our high-rise in the city of Denver. I liked running Cage Enterprises. Our grandfather, and later our father, had built it from the ground up, and while they had made some questionable business choices along the way, we had changed the game. We worked with gaining financing and worked with ethical and environmentally friendly building. Hence why we worked with Ford's family, the Montgomerys so often. We worked with real estate development, small business backers, and environmental research. Meaning we had way too many NDAs to begin with, and people were constantly trying to reach us.

And now, we were adding random people to group chats.

Again, the group chat went completely silent, and I copied the person's number before starting a new chat.

ME:
> Sorry about that. Wrong number I assume?

The three little dots flared for a moment, before they went away, and I had to hope that that was for the best.

UNKNOWN NUMBER:
> I wouldn't know. You're the one now texting me outside the group chat. Where did you get my number?

I studied the number, then quickly went through my contacts, and cursed under my breath. It was one away from Dorian's. Meaning, when Flynn had made the group chat, he had somehow typed in Dorian's number. Which didn't make any sense to me because you could just go through the contact list. I quickly called up Flynn again.

"How did you make the group chat?"

"My phone was giving me problems, so I just typed in everyone's numbers. I have them all memorized."

I rolled my eyes. "Of course you do. But you added one more you shouldn't have."

Flynn cursed under his breath. "Apparently I was tired."

"Apparently I have to clean up your messes."

"It's a chat. We'll delete it. Breathe."

I rolled my eyes at the fact that it was Flynn telling me to calm down now. That was rich. "You were the one panicking before. Because now this person has our numbers, our names, and where we'll be on Friday."

"Yes. Because she could be a sniper. We've just alerted our own demise where we'll be. It'll make it easy for them. But hopefully I'll have wine beforehand."

"I hate when you get all quick-witted after you're done panicking because you know I'll handle it."

"It's like you know me. Got to go. Meeting's starting."

I sighed, then gestured for James to come in as he walked across my office and set down a stack of papers. He raised a brow, and I sighed, gesturing toward the phone.

"I'll handle it."

"It's not anything to handle. But I'll see you soon."

"Yeah. You will."

I liked the fact that James and Flynn worked with me. I didn't feel like I was constantly searching to find my large family. I had way too many brothers to count. Okay, I had six brothers. With Flynn and Hudson as twins, Ford was the youngest, and I was the oldest. And yet Ford was the one who was married and happy and settling in his life. The rest of us were figuring out what we wanted. That was fine though, it wasn't as if my end of days were here. But I was busy with work, far too busy to deal with something like a relationship. Flynn and James worked hours just as long as I did.

And I knew Theo as a chef and a restaurant owner worked off hours, to the point that we rarely got to see him. Dorian was on the same hours as Theo since he owned a bar and grill that went for high class clientele even though the place was called The Cage of all things. I rolled my eyes at that.

Hudson and Ford were the only two that really didn't work for the company anymore. With Ford working for a security company that he owned with his spouse and his spouse's family, and Hudson painting for a living. It was odd to think that there was even an artist in our family, since it wasn't something that our father had really subscribed to. But Hudson had always gone his own way. After all, he had done his stint in the Army, spending far too many years overseas where we couldn't get ahold of him.

But now we were all here, doing something as casual as family dinner.

And apparently had just invited this stranger.

ME:
> We're sorry for bothering you. You can just remove yourself from the group chat by hitting the information button.

UNKNOWN NUMBER:
> Hmph. I should have thought of that.
> Sorry it's been a long day. But you guys sound hilarious. Brothers I take it?

I frowned, wondering why this person wanted the information, and why I wanted to answer.

> ME:
> Yes. Should I ask your name since you know mine?

UNKNOWN NUMBER:
You say that as if I could figure out who was who from the texts. There were a lot of them.

My lips curled into a smile.

> ME:
> Hazard a guess.

UNKNOWN:
I'm afraid to. But I assume you're the eldest from the way you're trying to take care of everything and texted me outside of the chat.

I frowned, wondering how this person could know this.

That was a little too intuitive and it made me uncomfortable.

> ME:
> And what's your name?
>
> ME:
> It seems only fair to ask.

UNKNOWN NUMBER:
Well, since you haven't asked for my location yet, I guess I can't be too worried about you being a serial killer.

> **ME:**
> I feel like I should be the one worried.

> **UNKNOWN NUMBER:**
> Blakely. My name's Blakely.

> **ME:**
> Well, Blakely. It is nice to meet you.

> **BLAKELY:**
> Nice to meet you as well. Although this isn't how I usually talk to men on phones or even on the internet. I don't like things like that. In fact, I should probably put my phone down before I realize you're a scam.

My lips twitch, and I did the one thing I should have done this whole time, I Googled the number.

And because the internet always showed everyone's secrets unless you knew how to hide them, I found it far too easily.

Blakely Graves.

I didn't look beyond the first page, but I wanted to make sure that she wasn't a scammer or anything. But Blakely Graves was a real person. And the photo attached to her profile that came from a job search site made my breath catch.

Gorgeous light eyes, blonde waves falling past her shoulders. And hell. Now I felt like the stalker here. Maybe I was the one asking for too much.

ME:
> Anyway, I have to get back to work. But sorry for interrupting your day.

BLAKELY:
> I've had a long and tedious day. So thanks for making me laugh. And you should totally cook for them. Not just do catering. At least one time.

I rolled my eyes.

ME:
> Did you see how many of them there are? No thanks. Plus I don't want to poison them.

BLAKELY:
> Good to know. Have a good day and I'll remove myself.

I looked at the chat and saw the notification that she had indeed removed herself from the chat. I didn't know why I felt a little sad about it. But I ignored it, and ignored the rest of the group chat as the brothers continued to talk now that they felt a bit safer after she left. Instead, I went back to work, my gaze looking at my phone every once in a while.

I didn't want her to text back. I didn't even know this person. I was just a little too tired.

I had been working too many long hours and knew the chaos was because I was trying to clean up a few messes my father had set to the side when he'd decided to retire. He was good at that. Making big promises and working on a few of them so they shone, and then letting everything else fall by the wayside. And I cleaned them up. Along with Flynn and the others, but it was mostly me.

And it wasn't as if Mom wanted anything to do with the company, or anything that came along with owning the town.

Because the Cages didn't just work in downtowns and across the world in high rises. No, we owned a whole town.

One in the mountains of Colorado, that was just for the Cages.

I had always thought as a child it was fun to have a town named after us, the one that held our legacy.

I just hadn't realized how much paperwork came with such an accolade.

Because we were not small town people. At least I didn't think so. My brothers on the other hand, they fit in a little bit more. Me though? I needed my suit and tie and martini. I wanted my Mercedes, and not the off-roader. I didn't want to deal with snow where we also had to be the ones who plowed.

I had too many other things on my mind.

Didn't that make me sound like a pompous ass.

I picked up my phone again, knowing I was distracted.

ME:
So do you think it's going to snow tomorrow?

I set down the phone again, wondering why I was even asking. It was ridiculous. But I couldn't get those eyes out of my head.

> **BLAKELY:**
> Probably. And then it'll be eighty degrees by the end of the day. It's Colorado. It's how we do weather.

> **ME:**
> So are you from here then?

I paused, wondering how to word it.

> **ME:**
> You have a Colorado number, so I just assumed you were local. But that doesn't mean anything anymore because we all have cell phones all over the world.

> **BLAKELY:**
> As soon as I typed my response, I realized the same thing. I don't even know why I replied.

> **BLAKELY:**
> But no, I'm from here. Born and bred. I wouldn't know where west is if I left. I need the mountains.

As the Rocky Mountains in Denver were always on the west, you always knew where north was. It did help with directions.

> **ME:**
> I got lost when I was in Central Pennsylvania once. We were in a valley, and I couldn't figure out where north was. It didn't help that it was overcast, and I couldn't see the sun.

> **BLAKELY:**
> You know our phones have compasses on them. And GPS.

> **ME:**
> Yes, but I couldn't look down when I was driving. And I couldn't figure out the rental car. It was a thing.

Now I felt embarrassed, like an idiot for even saying anything. I ran a multi-million-dollar corporation and several businesses, and I couldn't figure out a rental car. Or at least that one day had been a nightmare. I never showed weakness. That's how people took advantage of you. But apparently it was easy to do so over a single chat where neither of you knew the other in real life.

> **BLAKELY:**
> No it's okay. I'm the same way. I have to get into a meeting though, okay? Talk to you later?

> **BLAKELY:**
> Or not. Since we're strangers.

I smiled then, typing right back.

ME:
> Talk to you later.

But we didn't, at least not that night. The next morning I was working, dealing with a thousand meetings and papers on my desk, and when the snow began to fall in earnest, I smiled and picked up my phone.

ME:
> Well, it is indeed snowing.

BLAKELY:
> Good thing I dressed in layers. I wonder what the weather will be like later today.

A few hours later, my phone buzzed.

BLAKELY:
> It is 75 degrees outside. I do not understand this weather.

A few days later, I picked up the phone again when it buzzed.

BLAKELY:
> Did you see that score last night?

ME:
> Only a few glimpses of it. I didn't see the last save.

BLAKELY:
> The Avs are my team for a reason.

> **ME:**
> Well, brand loyalty helps. Although I used to be a Penguins fan as well.

> **BLAKELY:**
> I can't believe you just said that. I think I'm going to have to delete your number.

> **ME:**
> That would be a horrible reason for you to do that.

> **BLAKELY:**
> Okay true. But tell me you're at least a Broncos fan.

> **ME:**
> I can neither confirm nor deny. But I do like going to the games.

We had box seats for the Avs as well, but I only got to go to those when we had to bring in partners and clients. I rarely got to enjoy myself with things like going to games and having fun. Maybe I did need a weekend out in the town. Cage Lake had a little inn where you could rest and relax—though Flynn was the only one of us who had stayed there as of yet. The Cages owned the resort and many of the buildings in town, but we didn't tend to live there. We each had homes along the lake though, so I could just head there. Though I knew Flynn was renting his out right now.

Maybe I needed a break. Maybe I needed to go to a game.

The next day, I was the one who texted first.

> **ME:**
> Did you see that game?

> **BLAKELY:**
> No I missed it. Deadline.

I didn't know what she did for a living, nor was I sure she knew that I was Aston Cage. It wasn't that I was famous or anything, but in certain circles, people knew who our family was. That's why we were always careful about who we let in. Dorian may have played around, but he was still damn careful.

Hence why a group chat could change things.

> **ME:**
> It was a good game. I wish I could have gone.

> **BLAKELY:**
> Maybe someday.

The next day I texted again.

> **ME:**
> Let's meet for coffee.

I hadn't even realized I was typing it until the bubble exclaimed it was sent and there was no going back.

I just wanted to know who this woman was. I could have Googled more. I could have asked someone to look into her. The information was at my fingertips. But I couldn't get past my curiosity about the woman who made me laugh with just a few text messages.

> **BLAKELY:**
> I'm still not sure you're not a serial killer.

I grinned, grateful she was at least a little cautious. I sure as hell wasn't right then.

> **ME:**
> Public place and all. I promise I won't take you to a secondary location.

I wasn't sure if that sounded creepy or like a come on, but when she gave me a laughing emoji, my shoulders relaxed.

> **BLAKELY:**
> I shouldn't.

> **ME:**
> We should do it anyway.

> **BLAKELY:**
> Okay, that sounds like a good argument.

I straightened in my chair, my hand tightening around my phone.

> **ME:**
> Okay then. Tomorrow? Just coffee. No murder.

> **BLAKELY:**
> Okay. I can do that. Not the murder thing. Although all I know about you is that you live in Colorado. You could be hours away.

ME:
> Meet me at Taboo. Do you know that place? It's downtown.

I could see the chat bubble light up again before she answered.

BLAKELY:
> I know the place. And I work downtown. Coincidence.

Yeah, coincidence. Or maybe *she* was a serial killer.
I had a date with a wrong number.
And I didn't want to be wrong about *this*.

Chapter Two
BLAKLEY

"I'M DEFINITELY GOING TO BE MURDERED, RIGHT?" I asked as I paced my bedroom.

My best friend Isabella stared at her phone while perched on the edge of my bed, her legs crossed, and a small frown on her face.

When she didn't say anything, I cleared my throat and asked again. "Am I really going to get murdered if I do this?"

Isabella put down her phone and looked up at me, a small smile playing on her face now. I had known Isabella for years and she was one of my best friends. She was also one of the most beautiful people I knew. Her whole family was, if I were honest. She had three gorgeous sisters, and her brother was a man who apparently made people swoon when he walked into a room. I had always thought of him as Isabella's younger brother, so that hadn't been a thing in my eyes. But now as I stared at my friend, I had to wonder if I'd lost my mind about the decisions I'd made.

"No. Maybe. I hope not."

"Not helpful." We grinned at each other before she shook her head.

"Honestly, a group chat? So they just entered your number and suddenly you were part of their meeting? That sounds a little suspicious."

"I know, right? But it does happen. You've heard of it happening. There was that whole viral moment where a grandma texted the wrong person inviting him to Thanksgiving, and then it turned into this heartwarming thing."

"I remember that. It's just all that had happened with a group chat. You usually have to add contacts."

"Maybe he typed it in. Who knows. But I was in there, and all of the people sounded like they were joking around and they were a family who cared about each other. A real family with sarcasm as their love language."

"And so the real family is why you're going to go on this coffee date?"

I ran my hands down my dove-gray slacks, and immediately went to take them off, knowing I needed to wear something different. Maybe a skirt. Yes, a skirt would be good.

"Are you getting naked for me for a reason?" Isabella asked, and I flipped her off before putting my pants back on. "I was thinking about wearing a skirt, but then that seemed a little too forward."

"You mean one of your A-line pencil skirts? No, that wouldn't be too forward. And we're going to be late and hit every ounce of rush hour if you don't make a decision. You look gorgeous, Blakely. Live in it. Be in it."

I held back a smile since she sounded like the trainer in the classic *Miss Congeniality*. "Thank you for coming over. I know you're busy and you don't have time to deal with my insecurities and the fact that I'm going on a blind date with a man I'm randomly texting about the weather and Avalanche games."

"I still can't believe he said he was a Penguins fan." Isabella held up her hand. "It's okay. We all have a thing for Crosby."

I gave her a wry smile as I met her reflection in the mirror. "I'm sure there are other guys on the team you know."

My best friend shrugged. "Well, I don't really pay attention to them unless they are my team. It's not like I have time."

"You work more hours than I do."

"Maybe. But it's what I do. It's life. Now, you look wonderful, for work, and for a simple coffee. I like Taboo. They have great sandwiches, and I go in for a different type of coffee every time. They seem to fit my moods. It's a little creepy actually."

"I'm going to a creepy coffee place to go meet a serial killer," I blurted, and Isabella let out a deep breath, calming herself while I did the same. She knew I was on a downward spiral, and I needed to lift myself out of it if there was any way for me to make it through the day.

"You've been to Taboo. You like their coffee. You also like the look of the very hot tattoo artist next door."

I bit my lip and inhaled before letting out a long breath. "That is true. And there's a bookstore that I love nearby. In fact, I love that whole street. It's like a little oasis in the middle of downtown. This is fine. It's just coffee. It's a public space."

"Do you know his name?" she asked.

I froze, realizing that I didn't. That seemed like a little oversight and yet I knew it was for a reason. Being strangers in a text chain was easier to lean into than knowing who this man was. However I was about to meet him. "I don't. I don't even know what he looks like. I'm just going to meet some guy holding a phone in a coffee shop. I could sit next to anyone. This is so unlike me."

"Just Google his phone number and figure out who it is." Isabella reached for my phone, and I snatched it back, feeling a little protective of it. When she raised her brows, I winced.

"I don't know if I want to know."

"What are you worried about? That he is married? Someone you know? A ninety-year-old man?"

I put my face in my hand and groaned. "This is ridiculous. I should just look up his number."

"You should have done it weeks ago."

However, I did what I should and typed the number into my search engine.

"Do you really have it memorized?" Isabelle asked and I tried to ignore the humor in her tone.

I didn't look at her face, my cheeks burning. "We've been talking. It's been nice. And I've been looking at the number instead of a name because I couldn't add him to my contacts."

Yet everything changed with a single page load on my browser. I shouldn't have been surprised that the world was a little ironic. Because as soon as the page loaded, I stood in my room, mouth agape as Isabella sucked in a breath.

"Aston Cage?" I blurted, my voice going high-pitched. "Aston Cage. Of the Cage family? *Cage Enterprises*?"

"Your voice is getting a little high-pitched."

My hands gripped my phone so tightly, my knuckles went white. "It should be. Aston Cage. I know this man."

Isabella's eyes shot up to mine. "You've met him before?"

I shook my head. "No, my boss just hates him. Because a lot of times we go for the same developments, and they win."

"Because the Cages are a little savvier than your boss. You know that. That's why you work for your boss. You're always fixing everything he messes up."

I held up my hand. "I don't have time to worry too much about that. But look at him. *Look at him.*" I held up my phone to her and waved it around.

"What am I supposed to be looking at? He looks like a dude. With hair. That seems to be a little dark. Sometimes he has a beard in these photos, sometimes not. And he looks to do a lot of galas. That sounds boring."

I turned the phone back to me, and scrolled, realizing that he was indeed on the arm of a different woman in practically each one. Gorgeous statuesque women and variety of color of dresses. All for galas. "Oh, this is so stupid. This is Aston Cage. That means I was in the group chat of the *Cage family*."

"They aren't gods. Though your boss would've loved that."

My gaze shot to hers. "He can never find out. No wonder they all ghosted the chat right before I left. They had to be freaking out."

"It's not like they're going to divulge family and business secrets in a group chat. At least I would hope not. They seem smarter than that."

"But it's *Aston Cage*."

"Is he a playboy or something? I'm an accountant. I don't know these things," Isabella said with a sigh.

"You're a brilliant accountant, and no, I don't think so. Maybe. That doesn't matter. He's gorgeous."

"He's a man."

I laughed at that, shaking my head. "Maybe you're the one who needs to go out and meet somebody."

"The next time I get added to a family group chat, maybe I will. But I have enough in my life to deal with. Especially because we're going to be late. Now go to this coffee thing. Let one of us live a little. You're going to be fine."

"I can't believe you of all people are the one pushing me into this."

"I'm living vicariously through you. Your job is more fun, your life is more fun, and you're going to meet a CEO who could take over the world. I don't see the problem here."

"I see a very big problem here."

"What's the worst that can happen?" she asked, sounding so much unlike Isabella, I was afraid we had somehow switched places.

"Are you kidding me right now?"

"I have your phone tracked, and I'll put an AirTag on you. I'll know where you are at all times."

"That sounds a little more like the real Isabella," I said with a laugh, as I hugged her tightly. She patted my back, and then pushed off me.

"Now let's go. I'm not in the mood to deal with assholes on the highway. Which is every day."

"Thank you for getting here before the sun even rose."

"It's because I love you. And I needed to make sure that our tracking is going well."

I laughed at her, and we made our way to our respective jobs, that tension writing the back of my mind the entire time.

Work seemed to go at a slog all day. I enjoyed my job. I enjoyed strengthening businesses and figuring out which player was best for which position, but my boss of Howard Enterprises didn't play well with my ideas. But it was my job to make sure that we didn't go under and break the rules.

I wasn't a CEO. I wasn't a CFO. I was someone who had to have my hands in a thousand pots at once. And I enjoyed it. That meant I had to keep my mind on task, and I wasn't doing it very well because I was sitting here wondering what the hell I was going to do.

"Blakely, do you have the report?" Mr. Howard said

from my doorway, and I smiled at him. The man didn't specify which report and could have just emailed me. He didn't have to walk across the office just to ask me about a report that was probably already in his inbox and printed out in triplicate because that's how he liked things. Who needed to save trees?

"Which report?" I asked.

He scowled at me, and I knew that was probably the wrong thing to say. "You know, the report. The one I've been waiting on."

"It should be in your inbox." Again, I had no idea what report he was talking about, because *he* didn't know what report he was talking about, but I was up to date on what he needed from me, so it would be in his inbox. His team of assistants should have already handled it, but he liked to look grumpy and in charge on the floor. It lent a sense of control that I didn't understand, but he said it worked.

I had to remind myself I really loved my job when people did what they were supposed to do. Even though it wasn't my biggest fan right now.

"Good, good. You're still on for the gala this weekend?"

"I'll be there. It's a lovely charity event."

"Yes, but we have to make sure we don't let the Cages outshine us. You know them. They always like to walk around like little peacocks, pluming their little feathers."

I wasn't even sure that was true, but I did my best to keep a straight face. Because I was about to go on a coffee date with the head peacock.

Oh, God. This was such a bad idea.

"I will do my best to not let them take over."

"Good. It's a charity event, and we need to make a stand."

It was a charity event and that meant we should probably give to charity and raise awareness, but sure, making a stand worked. With that, Mr. Howard stomped off, probably to go growl at someone else, and I looked down at my phone, and realized I had fifteen minutes to get to Taboo. I quickly set everything as idle, nodded at my assistant, and made my way down the high-rise.

I loved living in Denver, I loved the view, the air. I even loved the insane weather that never made any sense. I lived in a suburb like most people who drove into the city, not downtown, but I didn't even mind the commute. When I had lived on the east side of town, I had been able to take the light rail in, but the west side of town didn't have everything I needed yet. But they were working on it, *so they said.*

I let out a deep breath. I spent so much time these days trying to live in my head rather than in the reality of the job I hated. So focusing on the commute and my family meant I didn't dwell on the day-to-day life that was slowly sucking the life from me.

Everything was fine. I loved this.

I loved my job.

The fact that I kept having to say that worried me, but it was a dream job. I sort of made it up as I went along and excelled in a business that stressed me out—when they powers that be allowed me.

And now I was meeting with my boss's rival. This was going to go lovely.

But he didn't know who I was. Unless he googled my number like I should have done this whole time. That seemed like a very big lapse in judgment.

I walked the two blocks toward the center of town, and finally made my way to the main street that I loved. There were little cafés and small businesses everywhere. Nothing looked too commercialized or downtrodden. People seemed to like each other on this particular street. It was always surprising since most of the time people tended to ignore each other.

Taboo had been located here since before I started working, and probably years before that. I loved the coffee and the pastries and needed to come down here for sandwiches more often, but I ate at my desk more than I should.

I looked down at my gray pants and soft pink top, and realized I looked like a business professional, not someone off to get afternoon coffee with a man I didn't even know.

Except for the fact I knew his name and what he looked like.

This was insane.

"Get over it, Blakely. It's a cup of coffee," I muttered to myself before opening the door to walk in.

There could have been tables around or even cute decorations. There could have been a thousand people in there, begging for coffee and pastries, but I didn't see them.

Instead, I only saw him.

Aston Cage.

All six-foot-something of him in a dark gray suit that fit him to a tee. Clearly bespoke or tailored perfectly for him. His piercing blue eyes caught me in a web, and I couldn't stop looking at him.

He was built, broad shouldered, but it narrowed down at the waist, so almost like a swimmer's body. His hair was dark, longer on the top than the sides, and perfectly coiffed as if he spent far too long in the mirror.

Or maybe he just woke up like that. Perfect and amazing.

Somebody bumped into me, and I moved to the side, realizing that I was blocking the door.

"I'm sorry."

"It's okay. If I had someone looking at me like that, I'd stand there too," the stranger said before she waved her fingers at me and him and moved back.

I moved to the side then, as Aston came forward.

"Hi," I whispered.

"Hi," he said right back, his voice deep, intoxicating.

What was with this? We hadn't even said anything.

When his lips quirked into a smile, I blinked, telling myself to snap out of it.

"I see you also Googled me," he said softly.

"I'm sorry. Hi, I'm Blakely," I said, awkwardly holding out my hand.

Aston looked down at it, that smile still on his face, and slid his hand over mine. "Aston. Can I get you a cup of coffee?"

"That would be lovely," I said with a laugh, and then he did the silliest and most attractive thing ever, and lifted my hand to his lips, and I knew there was a problem.

"Oh wow," another woman said as she walked by, fanning herself.

I blushed and took my hand back. "Now that I'm done making a scene. I'd love coffee. Though I am more of a latte girl."

"We can do a latte."

"Should I ask if you do this often? I feel like I should ask if you do this often."

"I have never asked a wrong number out for coffee before. Though I have been here before. Not with another woman though."

"Oh. That's good."

"It is."

We ordered our coffees, talking of weather and sports like we were good at, and I had to wonder if we would talk about anything else.

But it was just coffee after all.

The place was full, so we ended up sitting outside at a little table, nerves running through me.

"So. I would ask what you do, but I sort of know what you do."

"My brother who works in security would probably want to know if you knew that before you Googled me."

I blinked. "As in I somehow entered myself into your life through a random text message? Like I'm the one who typed it in?"

"That's what he would want to know. I assumed that

you didn't somehow secretly break into my other brother's house to type in your phone number."

My lips quirked, my shoulders immediately relaxing.

"Yes, it was all an accident. And I actually didn't Google your name until this morning."

Heat crossed my cheeks, and Aston leaned back and blinked at me. "Really? So you didn't know my name this whole time?"

"It was an oversight. But you didn't ask why."

"Because I Googled you that day," he mumbled, looking a little contrite. "Should I have waited?"

"No, you were the smarter one. Plus, you know, you have the whole family business you need to protect. But I'm not going to be a danger to any of that."

Though I did work for a man who hated him. However, that wasn't going to be a problem. This was just coffee, and Mr. Howard didn't care. They ran in different circles after all.

"I feel like I really should have asked your name."

"Maybe, but it was fun figuring out who you were just through text messages. I mean, I know that you don't like the Penguins."

I rolled my eyes. "I don't not like them. But you have to have loyalty. You're from here."

"I am. But sometimes I travel. And I can't get to an Avs game. Or a Broncos game."

"That is true. And honestly, I have no idea how you even got time away to have lunch today. You have to be too busy to have coffee today. What I know of your business is insane. You guys do so much."

He shrugged, tapping his finger on his mug. "True, and I have a good team and family that works with me. However, I'm allowed to have coffee with a beautiful woman."

I rolled my eyes. "That's a lie."

"It is not. I'm sorry to say, but you are beautiful."

"Well, I could say the same to you, but I'm pretty sure the two women that literally swooned next to you while we were talking in there answered that for both of us."

He snorted and finished his coffee. "I can't say that happens often."

"No you just don't notice it."

"So you didn't notice the man looking at you?"

"I only noticed you." I put my hand over my mouth and groaned. "Pretend I didn't say that."

"If it helps, I hadn't even realized I was standing there gawking at you until that woman said something," he whispered.

"Oh."

Oh.

"I really have to go back to work," I said after a moment, and he nodded.

"Same. I have meetings. But I'd like to do this again?"

My cheeks warmed. "Coffee in the middle of a workday?"

"Or dinner."

"Dinner. Dinner could be good."

He stood up and took my hand. "I'll text you?" he asked, the light in his eyes dancing.

I wanted to know this man. This enigma. "Okay. Text

me." Texting him felt familiar in such an unfamiliar situation.

He kissed my hand again, and I rolled my eyes. "I'm sorry, I've never met someone who actually did that."

"I don't think I've ever actually done that," he said, squeezing my hand. "It just felt apropos."

"I'm busy this weekend," I blurted. "But maybe next weekend?"

"Next weekend can work, and as it happens, I'm busy as well."

"Well, this was nice, I'll talk to you soon?" I asked, knowing I was babbling at this point.

"Yes, Blakely, I'll talk to you soon. It was lovely to meet you in person. Especially for a wrong number." And then he walked away, and I did my best not to watch him do so.

Oh, I was in so much trouble.

Chapter Three
BLAKELY

"I cannot believe I'm back here at your house helping you choose what to wear. I don't think we've ever done that and yet here I am. Again."

I rolled my eyes at Isabella before taking a long look in the mirror. I wore a coral pink dress that had pockets and flared a bit. I was comfortable and it was one of my favorites, but it went to my knees, and looked a little too casual.

Isabella studied me in the mirror and tilted her head. "This is more of a sundress, right?"

"Not quite a sundress, but maybe like a day dress in the spring?"

She smiled. "And on a quiet first date in high school."

"Okay, so this dress is a no."

I quickly stripped out of my dress, and without even offering, Isabella took it from me. She immediately hung it up, and I picked up the next one.

"Okay, this one should work." It was a light blue chiffon sort of dress that went to my ankles, with a high slit. It had this lacy overlay that looked a little bit like tulle but really wasn't. The one strap was thin around my neck, and the other one was thick and made a bow at the neck.

"Is that a bridesmaid's dress?" Isabella asked.

I flushed, realizing I looked like Cinderella on a bender in this outfit.

"Yes. They make you buy these things and then say you can wear them again. But when can I wear this again? Do you see how much tulle-like fabric this has?" I asked, fluffing at the bow.

"I bet you my sister could fix it."

"She could?" I asked, eager.

"Of course. She's had to sew her costumes all the time. However, your gala is tonight. I don't think she's going to be able to rescue this in a few hours. Maybe for another event. Lord knows you go to enough of them."

I sighed and then stripped off the dress, getting tangled in the extra bow, and was grateful when Isabella turned her face from me so I couldn't see her laugh. "This isn't funny. I'm panicking."

"Don't panic. You have plenty of time."

I raised a brow and then looked at the clock on my bedside table. "I have three hours. Three hours to shower, figure out what I'm supposed to do with my hair, do my makeup, and make sure that I have the right shoes and bag for this. I don't think three hours is enough."

"Yes, because you're such an old hag it's going to take you forever."

"Thank you for understanding my pleas."

"Blakely, my best friend. You're going to be fine. You have so many dresses in here. We'll find you something. And I brought you a few as well."

"And I'm grateful. But I don't think my boobs are going to fit in it."

"Are you calling me small-chested?" Isabella asked, in her most prim of ice queen voices.

To most people Isabella was standoffish, a little rude, and very much protective of her family. She was literally called the ice queen by people at her job, and straight to her face. They didn't even bother to whisper the nicknames behind her back. However, my best friend reveled in it. Because it kept people at a safe distance, and they treated her with respect at work. Maybe a little fear, maybe a little reverence, but respect.

I didn't mind that about her and found it more real and endearing than anything.

"Okay, what about this one?" I asked, picking up an A-line sage green dress.

"No. The slit's too high and I think there's a stain on it."

"Damn it. I thought I went to the dry cleaners with this. Maybe I forgot?"

"Maybe. You are busier than me most days."

I crossed my eyes, a little annoyed. "I have to remind myself that I like my job. But some days it's so hard."

"You don't like your job, you like what you're doing,

and you just don't like the place of business. Hence why you had to work late today even though your boss wasn't there, and everyone's expecting you to be there tonight. All dressed up and fancy-free."

"What does fancy-free mean?" I asked, staring at her in the mirror as I held up my stained sage dress.

"I'm not sure. Let me look it up."

"Oh good. We can get lost in this. We can forget that I have to meet with humans tonight."

"You're great meeting with humans. I mean, you're always so personable, and everyone likes seeing you. Don't stress. You've got this."

"I have to go and schmooze so that way the boss can get more clients."

"That's what these events are for. But you've got this. We'll find you something to wear. You're beautiful, you have things to work with, and like I said, you're not too much of an old hag."

"Seriously, the love that I feel from you? I don't think I can hold back my yearning."

"One day we'll finally take each other wildly in the barn and no one will know our secrets."

We met gazes, before each bursting out in laughter, and she handed me a soft pink dress.

"What's this one?" I asked.

"It's mine. And it might not fit you in the boobs, mostly because you have a lot more than me."

"You're no slack there," I teased.

"You can talk all about them in the barn later," she whispered, wiggling her eyebrows.

"It's beautiful," I whispered, holding up the soft pink dress that would flow down to my ankles, barely brushing the floor if I wore the right heels.

"I've never seen you in this."

"I bought it for an event I never went to. So it's just been sitting in my closet. I should have given it to one of my sisters, since I figured they would wear it more than me, but I just haven't. So I get to give it to you. My other sister."

"Calling me your sister after saying you'll take me in the barn adds a whole new level to our fan fiction."

She cringed and gestured for me to try it on. "Let's see how it is on you. Hag."

I flipped her off, even as I began to slide on the dress. It fit perfectly in the waist, a heart-shaped neckline that accentuated my breasts. It had tiny straps that held the dress up and for that I was grateful.

"Well, it seems the dress was meant for you," she whispered.

I met her gaze in the mirror and swallowed hard. "It's gorgeous. But I don't want to take away the first time you ever wear it."

"It didn't look as good on me. We have different coloring. Honestly now, it should just be yours. I might take the sage green dress though. And see if I can get out the stain."

"You don't have to do that."

"It's my nemesis. Now, go take off that dress, and take a shower."

"Aw, I thought you were asking me to take off the dress for other reasons."

"We do not have time to learn all about our hidden places, Blakely. We have to get you ready for a gala. So do you think Mr. Cage will be there?"

I tripped over my own two feet, and she raised a brow at me, and I shook my head. "I'm sure *a* Cage will be there. His family does own one of the largest corporations in the city."

"I don't know too much about them, to be honest."

"Well they run in my circles. Or at least, in my boss's circles. And he hates them."

"Really?"

"I don't know why. But he always gets annoyingly growly about them, and he wants to beat them."

"So I take it you're not going to do lunch with him when he asks officially? Or dinner?"

"My boss or Aston?"

Isabella snorted. "Yes, Aston."

"I don't know. He's only texted a hello, but we've been busy. Nothing more."

"Well that's not fun."

"We have lives." I tried not to let the disappointment pepper my tone. He had said that he was busy all weekend, and so was I. Hence this event. It wasn't like I wanted to continue to flirt over texts with him. I didn't even know if I was going to go out with him. Although it had already come up as something we were going to do. A week from now.

"Well, just have fun. And what will you do if he is

there though?" she asked, her voice soft as I stripped and got into the shower. I let the hot water run over my body as I thought about what I would do, and I didn't have an answer. That should have worried me more than anything.

"I'll say hello and be cordial. But this is a work event."

"So socializing with the Cages isn't in your repertoire?"

I washed my hair quickly, looking for more answers. "He probably won't even be there."

"If he was, would he bring a date?"

I nearly slipped in the shower, and glared at her as I looked around my shower curtain. "Really?"

She winced. "Sorry. I'm in a weird mood."

"Are you okay?" I asked, worried.

She waved me off and smiled. "I'm just fine. Promise. We were talking about you. If he's there, you should dance. You said there was a spark."

"And my boss would absolutely hate it."

"So a win-win," she teased.

I shook my head. "Not so much if I want to keep my job."

"He can't fire you for flirting with a Cage."

"I'm sure he'd find a way about competing interests, or just any other way. He's not a nice man." My contract was year by year and though I was one of his best employees, I also outshone some of his "Yes Men" on occasion. I stood up to him, but there were always company politics. Therefore we had a dance and charity gala this evening. None of the others on staff were required to go. But the boss wanted to show off his employee in a dress so he could show the world how modern he was. Oh, he'd never say that, and no one would never outright point it out—but we all knew it was the case.

"Then why do you work for him?"

That was the question. And I wish I had better answers. "Because it's the best job I can get. And I'm sure a Cage will be there, but it's not going to be him. It's going to be one of his countless brothers."

"Okay, let's hope it's that way so you don't have to make a choice. At least in front of everyone."

I rinsed the conditioner out of my hair. "Nothing's ever easy."

"No. But that's life. Unending pain and suffering until you die."

I toweled off my hair, pausing to stare at her. "Is everything okay, Isabelle?" I asked, worry etched in my tone. "We don't have to talk about me all the time."

"I'm perfectly fine. I'm just razzing you. Now, let's get your hair done. And you know we talk about my family more often than not."

"Are you sure you have time for this?"

"I have time to help my best friend look hot in a dress for whoever might show up."

"He's not going to be there," I warned.

"Fine, I have time to help my friend look hot in a dress for herself. How about that?"

"Yes. Let's go with that."

It took an hour, but drying my hair, straightening it

so I could curl it, and then doing a full face of makeup took time. Thankfully I had my grandmother's jewelry that I could make work with the dress, and when I finished the final clasp on my bracelet, I sighed in the mirror.

"Well, I don't look too shabby."

"You look beautiful. And don't stain my dress."

"I thought that I was being gifted this and you were taking the sage one?"

She smiled far too sweetly. "No, I'm just fixing the stain, and we can share both dresses. How about that?"

"You are a riot."

"I try. Now go knock them dead."

"Or at least try to win over clients. All in the name of finance," I said, sighing when Isabella rolled her eyes at me.

I drove myself to the event, because I was planning on only having one glass of champagne if that. I didn't want to deal with a ride-share or wait on anyone else. Thankfully there was a valet at the hotel, so I didn't have to find a way to park in this dress.

Holding my small clutch, I made my way into the hotel ballroom, smiling at a few people as I made my way around the room.

I saw a few familiar faces, though it was mostly strangers. When I caught the eyes of my boss's wife, she smiled softly at me and waved. I did not know how that sweet woman was married to that monster of a man, but then again, maybe he was only an asshole at work, and saved all his goodness for home.

The boss in question gave me a once-over and a tight nod, and I figured I'd passed some test.

A waiter passed by with a glass of champagne, and I milled about, holding my drink, barely taking a sip, and speaking with potential clients. I had already done research on the people that I knew I should talk to at the gala, the ones who had RSVP'd. But I hadn't seen a Cage on the list. Mostly because they were always invited, and they didn't have to RSVP to things like this.

That wasn't ominous at all.

"Well, small world."

It indeed was a small world. My hand squeezed on the stem of my champagne flute, and I turned around slowly, to stare into the eyes of Aston Cage.

"Oh. You're here."

He tilted his head and gave me that smile. The one that made my thighs clench, and I had to count backward from ten so I could catch my breath. "Yes, I'm here. The foundation is one that's close to my mother's heart. So we take turns attending different events. And it's my turn. Fancy that."

"I didn't know you'd be here."

He raised a brow. "And I didn't know you'd be here."

"Is it okay?" I shook my head. "Of course it's okay. This is work."

"You work for Howard, don't you?" he asked, his voice low. People really weren't paying attention to us other than the fact that their gazes would catch on Aston's. Because that's what the Cages did. They pulled in attention even when they weren't trying.

"I do."

"Is that going to be a problem?" he asked.

"Is what going to be a problem?" I asked, purposely obtuse. It wasn't as if we were making promises to each other or doing anything. I was just standing and speaking to a man at a gala, with a respectable distance between us. That's all that needed to be said.

"Well then, I'm glad that I'm the one who came, and not James."

"Which one was James on the text?" I asked, teasing.

"Probably the one trying to order us all."

"Wouldn't that be you?" I asked.

"That's what James would say," he replied, laughter in his gaze. Then a small pause. "Dance with me, Blakely," he whispered.

I shook my head. "I really shouldn't."

"There's many people on the dance floor, you can say you are schmoozing me."

"I don't think my boss would like that."

"Well, you should dance with me anyway. Please? I don't want to wait for a dinner date."

I couldn't see my boss anywhere, but I knew that this would probably get out. Because everything with the Cages did.

I set down my champagne flute on the table next to me anyway and placed my now free hand in his open one.

"Okay."

"Good." He clasped his hand over mine, and I was lost.

Chapter Four
ASTON

Getting hard in the middle of a ballroom while standing near many of my trustees, backers, and business rivals probably wasn't the best idea. But as soon as I saw Blakely across the dance floor, everything in me shifted.

And it wasn't just her beauty—those sharp cheekbones, those light eyes that shone underneath the soft lighting of the room. She'd even put her hair up in a half-do thing, so it framed her face, but still looked elegant. I used to be better about knowing what those were called, or even what kind of dress she wore. It had been a long time since I had been with anyone for that matter.

But no, it wasn't any of what she looked like, it was the aura that seemed to surround her and others could feel it too. She may not have even realized they did. They stopped what they were doing to glance over at her, as if they wanted to know her. She'd catch everyone's attention, whether it be to judge her or to admire her.

Or in my case, to barely hold back from falling down on my knees in front of her.

And now she was mine. If only for this dance.

"So, I didn't realize this is what you would be doing this weekend," she said softly as we glided across the dance floor. She had her hand on my arm, her other clasping my own, and I smiled down at her.

I hadn't done this much smiling since my brother's wedding when they had all danced and partied and looked as if they actually were going to have a great time.

It was a little odd to think I was doing so now.

"We try to represent the family."

"Are you the only one here?"

I shook my head before I looked over hers to see both of my brothers raising their brows. Flynn and James had curious expressions on their faces, nearly identical even though neither one of them were the twins.

It must be odd to see me dancing with someone since I usually did not dance at these things. I smiled, spoke to those I needed to, did a speech if required, and wrote a check. I never got out on the dance floor when I came alone.

And yet here I was, with Blakely, losing my mind.

"Two of my brothers are here, they're behind you, staring at me and wondering why I'm dancing."

"You don't dance? You seem to be good at it."

The heat of her seared me through her dress and my tuxedo, and I had to swallow hard not to do anything that would shame us both. "I don't dance. I can, but I don't."

"Then why with me?" she asked, her voice a little breathy.

"I think you know, Blakely."

"So how many brothers do you have here?" she asked, changing the subject. I didn't mind, both of us needed to take a step to breathe if the way that her pulse fluttered against her neck was any indication.

"James and Flynn are here because it was our turn. My parents are out of town, or my mother and father would be here. Mother enjoys attending these events."

I hoped the bite wasn't in my tone at that, considering she liked all of her sons at these things so she could show us off.

"So three of you. That's a good number then."

I shook my head as I twirled her during the next song, both of us not having realized the song had even changed. "It's not even a full fifty percent. There are a lot of us."

"I knew you had a few brothers, but I hadn't really paid attention too much beyond that."

"There's more than a few of us. Not all of us work with Cage Enterprises though. However we do all have a stake in the company because it's our family. If that makes sense."

"Not in the slightest," she said with a laugh, her eyes shining.

"Understandable. We are here as a family to show our support, to donate, and to do what our family requires."

"I would say that sounds annoying, but you get to eat some decent food, and probably make business deals along the way."

I raised a brow at her but nodded. "Yes. That is always a perk. What about you? You're here with Howard Enterprises?"

I could feel eyes on me, and I knew it wasn't just those who were curious who I was dancing with. No, the proprietor of Howard Enterprises was probably not happy about the woman who worked for him dancing in my arms. But there was nothing I could do about that. Nothing I wanted to do about that.

"Yes. Dancing with you is probably a mistake."

"He doesn't hate me that much, does he?" I asked, honestly curious.

"No. I don't think so. I think he just wants to one-up you."

"So does you dancing with me have anything to do with that?" I asked, oddly curious.

Her eyes narrowed, and she stopped dancing. I cursed under my breath and was grateful we were at the edge of the dance floor.

"I'm sorry. I didn't mean that."

"No you did. He didn't *ask* me to dance with you. You're the one who asked me to dance. And I knew it was going to be a mistake. He wants to beat you in everything all the time. So me dancing with the enemy probably isn't a good idea."

"I'm the enemy, am I?" I asked, my voice low.

She swallowed hard and shook her head. "No. It's not so dramatic as that."

"Good."

I lifted her hand up to my lips and kissed it again, a

bare brush of my mouth against her skin, and her intake of breath was all I needed to hear.

"You need to stop doing that."

"I don't know if I want to."

Nobody was paying attention to us now, as the emcee was making their rounds, so I tugged on her hand and pulled her around the corner.

"Aston," she said with a laugh, and I did what I had been wanting to do since I first saw her. I pressed my lips to hers.

She didn't pull away, didn't freeze. Instead wrapped her fingers under the lapels of my jacket and pulled me closer.

Groaning, I deepened the kiss, my tongue sliding along hers.

"We need to stop. Someone can come around the corner at any minute."

"I'll stop. Soon." I kissed her again, needing her taste, craving her, and when I knew that it would be too much if I continued, I wrenched myself away, my chest rising and falling in deep pants.

"Holy hell," I growled.

"Oh."

I looked over at Blakely, her hand over her bruised lips, her eyes wide. "Are you okay? Did I hurt you?"

"Not at all. I don't think I've ever been kissed like that before. Which probably isn't something I should say." I had barely any control when it came to her.

I felt like a cat who caught the canary, and a smile slid across my face. "That sounds like a compliment."

"Maybe. Or maybe I need to get out more." She grinned up at me.

Her eyes danced, and I wanted to know more. I wanted to know everything.

Who was this woman? And why did she do this to me?

"Sorry to interrupt, but they need you." I cursed at Flynn's timing, and Blakely's face drained of color, while she tried to hide behind a potted palm.

"It's just my brother. Everything's fine."

"I'm so embarrassed. I'm *working* for God's sake."

"It's okay, nobody saw. James and I had the exits covered."

"Should it worry me that it sounds like you guys have a plan for this sort of thing?" she asked, slight frost in her tone.

I cursed my brothers and everything they stood for, while I glared at him and James who walked up from behind him. "No, this is new. But we protect our family."

Flynn looked over my shoulder and winked at Blakely. "I'm Flynn. The quiet one here is James. It's good to see you."

"Hi. I'm going to go fix my face. And then I have to...work."

"You look wonderful," James said softly, and I glared at him before turning my back to them and looking at Blakely.

"I have to go be The Cage," I said with a roll of my eyes.

"I love the title." I heard the humor in her tone—even above the slight panic.

"I don't," I said softly. "I want to see you again."

Her eyes widened marginally. "Okay. Maybe not in the middle of a hallway?"

"No. Let's not. I'll call you."

When she let out a soft laugh, I relaxed. Marginally. "Good. And then I'll have my wits about me."

"I need to go." Long before this.

"He really does," Flynn called out.

"Then go," she whispered.

And then I pressed my lips to hers again before letting her walk away, presumably to go fix the blush of her face. But I thought she looked gorgeous.

"So, have you lost your mind?" Flynn asked as we stepped out of earshot.

"Stop it. I don't want to hear it."

Flynn clucked his tongue. "I think you've lost your mind."

"I think you're more like Dorian than we thought," James whispered, and I flipped them both off, before straightening my jacket.

"Let's go be Cages and do what we need to."

"So that's the girl from the chat?" James asked.

I nodded tightly. "We're done here."

"Oh, I think you've just begun," Flynn said with a laugh.

I rolled my eyes at my two brothers, and moved toward the ballroom, knowing we had people to meet, and there was work to be done. My phone buzzed in my pocket however, and I couldn't help but hope it was her.

However it wasn't Blakely calling, it was my mother.

"Answer it, or we're all going to have to deal with that," Flynn said with a roll of his eyes.

I sighed but answered anyway. "Hello, Mother. You're missing a great gala."

"Aston. It's your father."

Ice slid up my spine, and I swallowed hard. I must have looked as if something was wrong, because both my brothers stopped teasing me, and stood still, staring at me.

"What's wrong?"

"Your father is dead. And I need you here. Call the others. We need you." She hung up without saying anything else, and I stared at my brothers knowing everything had changed.

Chapter Five
BLAKELY

He hadn't called.

He should have called. But he hadn't.

I waited by my phone for four days, waiting for a call. The weekend had passed, and then the holiday where there was no work, just me waiting by a phone as I sat at home alone.

But he hadn't called.

I had picked up my phone countless times to call him, but he had said he would call me. And he was Aston Cage, man of business. I wasn't going to be the one who called first. Right?

Phone in hand, I knew I just needed to put on my big-girl panties and do it. I looked up his texts, pressed his icon, and called.

It rang once and went straight to voicemail. I frowned but didn't leave a message.

He had sent me straight to voicemail. Maybe he was in a meeting? Or maybe he just wasn't calling.

I knew I needed to get to work, and I had to stop stressing over the fact that a man hadn't called me after he had kissed the daylights out of me in the middle of a work function.

That was so unprofessional it wasn't even funny. I had gone right back to work, spoken to the clients I needed to, and made a few business deals for my boss. I had done what I was supposed to do, and yet everything felt different.

I felt different.

I sighed and went to finish my breakfast as I turned on the morning news. I needed to leave soon so I wouldn't be late, but everything felt off.

This just in, Dorian Cage the patriarch of the Cage family is dead at age sixty. He was the former president of Cage Enterprises and Businesses, a worldwide and billion-dollar firm of real estate development, small business backers, environmental research, including dozens of other subsidiaries. And while he wasn't at the helm of the business at the time of his death, with his eldest son Aston Cage taking that position, he was still the man on the mountain for many. However it seems that his death, while of natural causes, did not come without a scandal of its own.

There's more to come on this once we have all of the information, but according to inside sources, the Cage family has its secrets.

Everything froze within me as I stared at the TV and tried to understand what I was hearing.

Aston's father was dead.

No wonder he couldn't call or text. His father was dead.

And a scandal? I didn't even want to know exactly what that was, but I couldn't even imagine.

I picked up my phone again and knew that he was far too busy for me, but I needed to text. Needed to say something. Anything.

ME:
> I'm so sorry, Aston. I can't imagine your loss. My thoughts are with you and your family. And if there's anything you need from me, ever, let me know. I'm sorry.

I sent the text, hoping it was enough, even though it would never be. Maybe he would see it and remember. But I was just the girl from the texts, a woman that he saw on the dance floor and kissed.

No wonder he hadn't called.

Tears pricked my eyes, as emotions washed over me, but I knew that it was silly.

This wasn't about me. He had the most obvious reason not to call.

I gathered my things and headed to work, and knew that I was going to have to find a way to either get over Aston Cage, or make sure he wasn't alone. Because from what I could tell, as the eldest, he had the weight of the world on his shoulders.

Or maybe I was thinking too hard, and I had nothing

to do with it. It was all just a dream. Before I knew who he was.

I walked into work, and I realized that people were staring at me. It was odd, to feel the weight of a thousand stares, but I ignored them, and made my way to my desk.

"Blakely, come inside my office," Mr. Howard ordered, his voice deep, commanding. Ice slid down my back, but I swallowed hard, sitting my bag on the table, and wondering why he was here so early, and why he could want me first thing.

I lifted my chin, and ignored the stares of others, as I made my way to his office.

"Hello, Mr. Howard, good morning. What can I do for you?"

"You're fired."

I blinked at him, caught off guard. "What?"

"You're fired for working with the competition. We lost the Meridian account to the Cages, and that happened right after your little dance with him. We can connect the dots and have done so."

I schooled my features, hoping my racing heart didn't beat out of my chest. "What? I have nothing to do with that."

"Oh? So it's just a coincidence that we lost the biggest account that we have to the Cages right after you went on a little dance break and whatever else with the head of the company? What else did you say when you were sleeping with him?" he spat before his lawyer shut him up.

Rage filled me, as bile crept up my throat. "I didn't do anything…"

"We have evidence to say different," one of the lawyers said, and I glared at him, and realized that they were going to find any reason to get me out. They were going to lie and twist the narrative, and I wouldn't be able to fight back. I could sue. I could plead my case. And yet no one would listen to me.

Because I had danced with Aston Cage, and I had apparently made a fool of my boss.

"I didn't do this," I repeated.

"And I don't believe you," Mr. Howard said before gesturing to his lawyers and security to escort me out.

People continued to stare, as I realized this was my reality.

I had made one mistake—dancing with a gorgeous man who made me smile.

And even though I could find my own lawyers, and I could find a way to get out of a wrongful termination suit, they would find another way to push me out.

Out of a job I hated—out of a job that broke me.

And somehow this was Aston Cage's fault.

Because this was before I knew. Before I knew him. Before I knew how much I could feel.

And before I knew how much I could break.

Aston Cage was out of my life. Only the scars of that one dance with a Cage would shroud my life and my future.

I hoped he never called.

I had made enough mistakes when it came to Aston Cage.

And I would never make them again.

Start the Cage Family series and find out what happens with Aston and Blakely in:
The Forever Rule

The Forever Rule

The Forever Rule

What happens when the man you'd thought could be the one turns out to be your new boss?

Blakely

The moment I met Aston Cage, I knew my life had changed. A single dance later, we're both all in. Until he ghosted me.

Then my boss fires me for dancing with the enemy.

Three months later, working for the Cages is my last resort. Now I'll work beside him day by day, trying not to let my feelings take control. It's heaven and hell. Except I'm starting to think there's a part of this story I'm missing...

Aston

I made myself walk away from Blakely after my family's dirty laundry hit the news. My father's secret family complicates everything. In order to keep our inheritance intact, we're forced to do monthly dinners with both sides of the family—the brothers I grew up with and the new set of siblings we never knew about.

An additional obstacle: Blakely is my new sister's best friend.

Meaning the moment I give into temptation, I not only risk the woman I'm falling for, but the family legacy just starting to reveal itself.

But Blakley is worth it. I just have to prove I am as well.

Chapter One

ASTON

The Cages are the most prestigious family in Denver—at least according to the patriarch of the Cage Family.
And the Cages have rules.
Rules only they know.

I ALWAYS KNEW THAT ONE DAY MY FATHER WOULD DIE. I hadn't realized that day would come so soon. Or that the last words I would say to him would've been in anger.

I had been having one of the best nights of my life, a beautiful woman in my arms, and a smile on my face when I received the phone call that had changed my family's life.

The fact that I had been smiling had been a shock, because according to my brothers, I didn't smile much. I was far too busy being *The Cage* of Cage Enterprises.

We were a dominant force in the city of Denver when it came to certain real estate ventures, as well as being one of the only ethical and environmentally friendly ones who tried to keep up with that. We had our hands in countless different pots around the world, but mostly we gravitated in the state of Colorado—our home.

I had not created the company, no, that honor had gone to my grandfather, and then my father. The Cage Enterprises were and would always be a family endeavor. And when my father had stepped away a few years ago, stating he had wanted to see the world, and also see if his sons could actually take up the mantle, I had stepped in— not that the man believed we could.

My brothers were in various roles within the company, at least those who had wanted to be part of it. But I was the face of Cage Enterprises.

So no, I hadn't smiled often. There wasn't time. We weren't billionaires with mega yachts. We worked seventy-hour weeks to make sure *all* our employees had a livable wage while wining and dining with those who looked down at us for not being on their level. And others thought we were the high and mighty anyway since they didn't understand us. So, I didn't smile.

But I had smiled that night.

It had been a gala for some charity, one I couldn't even remember off the top of my head. We had donated between the company and my own finances—we always did. But I couldn't even remember anything about why we were there.

Yet I could remember her smile. The heat in her eyes

when she had looked up at me, the feel of her body pressed against mine as we had danced along the dance floor, and then when we ended up in the hallway, bodies pressed against one another, needing each other, wanting each other.

And I had put aside all my usual concepts of business and life to have this woman in my arms.

And then my mother had called and had shattered that illusion.

"Your father is dead."

She hadn't even braced me for the blow. A heart attack on a vacation on a beach in Majorca, and he was dead. She hadn't cried, hadn't said anything, just told me that I had to be the one to tell my brothers.

And so, I had, all six of them. Because of course Loren Cage would have seven sons. He couldn't do things just once, he had to make sure he left his legacy, his destiny.

And that was why we were here today, in a high-rise in Centennial, waiting on my father's lawyer to show up with the reading of the will.

"Hey, when is Winstone going to get here?" Dorian asked, his typical high energy playing on his face, and how he tapped his fingers along the hand-carved wooden table.

I stared at my brother, at those piercing blue eyes that matched my own, and frowned. He should be here soon. He did call us all here after all."

"I still don't know why we all had to be here for the reading of the will," Hudson whispered as he stared off into the distance. Neither Dorian nor Hudson worked for Cage Enterprises. They had stock with the company, and a few other connections because that's what family did, but they didn't work on the same floors as some of us and hadn't been elbow to elbow with our father before he had retired. Though dear old dad had worked in our small town more often than not in the end. In fact, Hudson didn't even live in Denver anymore. He had moved to the town we owned in the mountains.

Because of course we Cages owned a damned town. Part of me wasn't sure if the concept of having our name on everything within the town had been on purpose or had occurred organically. Though knowing my grandfather, perhaps it had been exactly what he'd wanted. He had bought up a few buildings, built a few more, and now we owned three-quarters of the town, including the major resort which brought in tourists and income.

And that was why we were here.

"You have to be here because you're evidently in the will," I said softly, trying not to get annoyed that we were waiting for our father's lawyer. Again.

"You would think he would be able to just send us a memo. I mean, it should be clear right? We all know what stakes we have in, we should just be able to do things evenly," Theo said, his gaze off into the distance. My younger brother also didn't work for the company, instead he had decided to go to culinary school, something my father had hated. But you couldn't control a Cage, that was sort of our deal.

"Why would you be cut out of the will?" I asked, honestly curious.

"Because I married a man and a woman," he drawled out. "You know he hasn't spoken to me since before the wedding," Ford said, and I saw the hurt in his gaze even though I knew he was probably trying to hide it.

"Well, he was an asshole, what do you expect?" James asked.

I looked behind Ford to see my brother and co-chair of Cage Enterprises standing with his hands in his pockets, staring out the window.

With Flynn, our vice president, standing beside him, they looked like the heads of businesses they were. While they wore suits and so did I, we were the only ones.

Dorian and Hudson were both in jeans, Hudson's having a hole at the knee. And probably not as a fashion statement, most likely because it had torn at some point, and he hadn't bothered to buy another pair. Theo was in slacks, but a Henley with his sleeves pushed up, tapping his finger just like Hudson, clearly wanting to get out of here as well. Ford had on cargo pants, and a tight black T-shirt, and looked like he had just gotten off his shift. He owned a security company with his husband and a few other friends, and did security for the Cages when he could, though I knew he didn't like to work with family often. And I knew it wasn't because of us. No, it was Father—even if he had officially *retired*. It was always Father.

And he was gone.

"Can't believe the asshole's gone," I whispered.

Ford's brows rose. "Look at that, you calling him an asshole. I'm proud."

"You should show him respect," Mother said as she came inside the room, her high heels tapping against the marble floors. I didn't bother standing up like I normally would have, because Melanie Cage looked to be in a *mood*.

She didn't look sad that Dad was gone, more like angry that he would dare go against their plans. What plans? I didn't know, but that was my mother.

She came right up to Dorian and leaned down to kiss his cheek. She didn't even bother to look at the rest of us. Dorian was Mother's favorite. Which I knew Dorian resented, but I didn't have to deal with mommy issues at this moment.

No, we had to deal with father issues at this point.

"I'm going to go get him," Flynn replied, turning toward the door. "I'm really not in the mood to wait any longer, especially since he's being so secretive about this meeting."

As I had been thinking just the same, I nodded at Flynn though he didn't need my permission. However, just then, the door opened, and I frowned when it wasn't just Mr. Winstone walking into the conference room.

I stared as an older woman walked through the door following Mr. Winstone, and four women and another man with messy hair and tattered cut-up jeans that matched Hudson's walked behind them.

The guy looked familiar, as if I'd seen him somewhere, or maybe it was just his eyes.

Where had I seen those eyes before?

"Phoebe? What are you doing here?" Ford asked as he moved forward and gripped the hands of one of the women.

"I was going to ask the same question," Phoebe asked as she looked at Ford, then around the room.

Those of us sitting stood up, confused about why this other family—because they were clearly a family—had decided to enter the room.

"We're here to meet the lawyer about my father's death, Ford. Why would you and the Cages be here?" she asked, and I wondered how the hell Mr. Winstone had fucked up so badly? Why the hell was he letting another family that clearly seemed to be in shock come into our room? This wasn't how he normally handled things.

Ford was the one who answered though—thankfully—because I had no idea what the hell was going on.

"Phoebe, we're here for my dad's will reading. What the hell is going on?" he asked. Phoebe looked around, as well as the others.

I stared at them, at the tall willowy one with wide eyes, at the smaller one with tears still in her eyes as if she was the only one truly mourning, and at the woman who seemed to be in charge, not the mother. Instead she had shrewd eyes and was glaring at all of us. The man stood back, hands in pockets, and looked just as shell-shocked as Ford.

But before Mr. Winstone or anyone else could say anything, my mother spoke in such a crisp, icy tone that I froze.

"I don't know why you're acting so dramatic. You

knew your father was an asshole. He just liked creating drama," she snapped.

As I tried to catch up with her words, the older woman answered. "Melanie, stop."

This couldn't be happening. Because things started to click into place. The fact that the man at the other end of this table had our eyes, and that everybody looked so fucking shocked. I didn't know how Ford knew this Phoebe, and I would be getting answers.

"We had a deal," my mother continued, as it seemed that the rest of us were just now catching on. "You would keep your family away from mine. We would share Loren, but I got the name, I got the family. You got whatever else. But now it looks like Loren decided to be an asshole again."

"What are you talking about?" the shrewd sister asked as she came forward, her hands fisted at her side.

"Excuse me," I said, clearing my throat. I was going to be damned if I let anyone else handle this meeting. I was The Cage now. "Will someone please explain?"

"Well, I wasn't quite sure how this was going to work out," Mr. Winstone began, and we all quieted, while I wanted to strangle the man. What did he mean how *the hell this would work out*? What was this?

This seemed like a big fucking mistake.

"Loren Cage had certain provisions in his will for both of his families. And one of the many requirements that I will go over today is that this meeting must take place." He paused and I hoped it wasn't for effect, because I was going to throttle him if it was. "Loren

Cage had two families. Seven sons with his wife Melanie, and four daughters and a son with his mistress, Constance."

"We went by partner," the other mother corrected.

I blinked, counting the adults in the room. "Twelve?" I asked, my voice slightly high-pitched.

"Busy fucking man," Dorian whispered.

Hudson snorted, while we just stood and stared at each other.

This could not be happening. A secret family? No, we were not that cliché.

"I can't do this," Phoebe blurted, her eyes wide.

"Oh, stop overreacting," my mother scorned.

"Do not talk to my daughter that way." The other mother glared.

"It was always going to be an issue," Mother continued. "All the secrets and the lies. And now the kids will have to deal with it. Because God forbid Loren ever deal with anything other than his own dick."

"That's enough," I snapped.

"Don't you dare talk to us like that," the shrewd sister snapped right back.

"I will talk however I damn well please. I am going to need to know exactly how this happened," I shouted over everyone else's words.

Out of the corner of my eye I saw Phoebe run through the door. Ford followed and then the tall willowy one joined.

"Shit," I snapped.

"Language," Mother bit out.

I laughed. "Really? You are going to talk to me about language."

I looked over at James, who shrugged, before he put two fingers in his mouth and whistled that high-pitched whistle that only he could do.

Everyone froze as Theo rubbed his ear and glared at me.

"Winstone," I said through gritted teeth. "I take it we all have to be here in order for this to happen?"

He cleared his throat. "At least a majority. But you all had to at least step into the room."

"Excuse me then," I said.

"You're just going to leave? Just like that?" my mother asked.

I whirled on her. "I'm going to go see if my apparent *family* is okay. Then I'm going to come back and we're going to get answers. Because there is no way that I'm going to leave here without them."

I stormed out the door, and thankfully nobody followed me.

Of course, though, I shouldn't have been too swift with that, as the woman who had to be the eldest sister practically ran to my side, her heels tapping against the marble.

"I'm coming with you."

"That's just fine." I paused, knowing that I wasn't angry at these people. No, my father and apparently our mothers were the ones that had to deal with this. I looked over at the woman who Mr. Winstone and the mothers had claimed was my sister and cleared my throat.

"I'm Aston."

"Is this really the time for introductions?" she asked.

"I'm about to go see your sister and my brother to make sure that they're fine, so sure. I would like to know the name of the woman that is running next to me right now."

"I'm running, you're walking quickly because you have such long legs."

I snorted, surprised I could even do that.

"I'm Isabella," she replied after a moment.

"I would say nice to meet you Isabella..." I let my voice trail off.

She let out a sharp laugh before shaking her head. "I'm going to need a moment to wrap my head around this, but not now."

"Same."

We stormed out of the building, and I lagged behind since Ford was standing in front of Phoebe who was in the arms of another man with dark hair and everybody seemed to be talking all at once.

"I just. I can't deal with this right now," Phoebe said, and I realized that something else must have been going on with her right then. She looked tired, and far more emotional than the rest of us.

I looked over at the man holding her and blinked. "Kane?" I asked.

Kane stared at me and let out a breath. "Wow," he said with a laugh.

"We'll handle it," Isabella put in, completely ignoring us. "And if we need to meet again later, we will." Then she looked over at Ford and I, with such menace in her gaze, I nearly took a step back. "Is that a problem?"

I raised my chin, glaring right back at her. "Not at all. However I want answers, so I'd rather not have the meeting canceled right now. But I'm also not going to force any of my," I paused, realization hitting far too hard, *"family* to stay if they don't want to."

And with that, I turned on my heel and went back into the building, with Isabella and Ford following me. Everyone was still yelling in the interim, and I cleared my throat. As Isabella had done it at the same time, everyone paused to look at me.

"Read the damn will. Because we need answers," I ordered Winstone, and he shook like a leaf before nodding.

"Okay. We can do that." He cleared his throat, then he began going over trusts and incomes and buildings and things that I would care about soon, but what I wanted to know was what the hell our father had been thinking about.

"Here's the tricky part," Winstone began, as we all leaned forward, eager to hear what the hell he had to say.

"The family money, not of the business, not of each of your inheritance from other family members, but the bulk of Loren Cage's assets will be split between all twelve kids."

"Are you kidding me?" Isabella asked. "What money? We weren't exactly poor, but we were solidly middle class."

"We did just fine," the other mother pleaded.

My mother snorted, clearly not believing the words.

I glared at the woman who raised me, willing her to say *anything*. She would probably be pushed out of the window at that point. Not by me, by someone else, but she probably would've earned it.

The lawyer continued. "However to retain the majority of current assets and to keep Cage Lake and all of its subsidiaries you will have to meet as a family once a month for three years. If this does not happen, Cage Enterprises will be broken into multiple parts and sold." He went on into the legalese that I ignored as I tried to hear over the blood pounding in my ears.

"You own a town?" the other man asked.

I looked over at the one man in the room I didn't know the name of. "Not exactly."

"Kyler," Isabella whispered.

In that moment, I realized that I had a brother named Kyler — if this was all to be believed.

"This can't be legal right?" the tall willowy person said.

"Yes Sophia, it can," their mother put in.

Oh good, another sister named Sophia.

Only one name to go. What the hell was wrong with me?

I forced my jaw to relax. "Are you telling us that we need to have all twelve of us at dinner once a month for three years in order to keep what is rightly inherited to us? To keep people in business and keep their jobs?"

"We don't need the money, but everyone else in our employ does," James snapped. "As do those we work with."

"Damn straight," Dorian growled.

"How are we supposed to believe this?" I asked, asking the obvious question.

"First, only five must attend, and two must be of a different family." The lawyer continued as if I hadn't spoken. "Of course you are *all* family…"

"Again, how are we supposed to believe this?" I asked.

"Here are the DNA tests already done."

"Are you fucking kidding me?" Isabella asked.

I looked at her, as she had literally taken the words out of my mouth.

"Isn't that sort of like a violation?" Kyler asked, his face pale.

"We need to get our own lawyers on this," James whispered.

I nodded tightly, knowing we had much more to say on this.

"There's no way this is legal," the youngest said, and I looked over at her.

"What's your name?" I asked.

"Emily. Emily Cage Dixon," she said softly, and we all froze.

"Your middle name is Cage?" I asked, biting out the words.

"All of our middle names are Cage," Sophia said, shaking her head. "I hated it but Dad wanted to be cute because our father's name was Cage Dixon, or maybe it wasn't. Is he also a bigamist?" she asked.

Her mother lifted her chin. "We never married. And

no, your father's name was not Dixon, that was my maiden name."

"What?" Sophia asked. "All this time…are our grandparents even dead?"

"Yes, my parents are dead. The same with Loren's." The other mother's eyes filled with tears. "I'm sorry we lied."

"We'll get to that later," Isabella put in, and I was grateful.

I let out a breath. "In order to keep our assets, in order to keep the family name intact, we need to have *dinner*. For three years."

The small lawyer nodded, his glasses falling down his nose. "At least five of you. And it can start three months after the funeral, which we can plan after this."

"This is ridiculous," Hudson murmured under his breath, before he got up and walked out.

I watched him go, knowing he had his own demons, and tried to understand what the hell was going on. "Why did he do this?" I asked, more to myself than anyone else.

"I never really knew the man, but apparently none of us did," Isabella said, staring off into the distance.

"Leave the paperwork and go," I ordered Winstone, and he didn't even mutter a peep. Instead, he practically ran out of the room. James and Flynn immediately went to the paperwork, and I knew they were scouring it. But from the way that their jaws tightened, I had a feeling that my father had found a way to make this legal. Because we would always have a choice to lose everything. That was the man.

"It's true," my mother put in. "You all share the same father. That was the deal when we got married, and when he decided to bring this other woman into our lives."

"I'm pretty sure you were the other woman," the other mom said.

I pinched the bridge of my nose.

"Stop. All of you." I stared at the group and realized that I was probably the eldest Cage here, other than the moms. I would deal with this. We didn't have a choice. "Whatever happens, we'll deal with it."

"You're in charge now?" Isabella asked, but Sophia shushed her.

I was grateful for that, because I had a feeling Isabella and I were going to butt heads more often than not.

I shrugged, trying to act as if my world hadn't been rocked. "I would say welcome to the Cages, because DNA evidence seems to point that way, however perhaps you were already one of us all along."

Kyler muttered something under his breath I couldn't hear before speaking up. "You have my eyes," he said.

I nodded. "Noticed that too."

The other man tilted his head. "So what, we do dinners and we make nice?"

I sighed. "We don't have to be adversaries."

"You say that as if you're the one in charge," Isabella said again.

"Because he is," Theo said, and they all stared at him.

I tried to tamp down the pride swelling at those words —along with the overwhelming pressure.

Theo continued. "He's the eldest. He's the one that

takes care of us. And he's the CEO of Cage Enterprises. He's going to be the one that deals with the paperwork fallout."

"Because family is just paperwork?" Emily asked, her voice lost.

I shook my head. "No, family is insane, and apparently, it's been secret all along. And it looks like we have a few introductions to make, and a few tests to redo. But if it turns out it's true, we're Cages, and we don't back down."

"And what does that mean?" Isabella asked, her tone far too careful.

Theo was the one who finally answered. "It means we're going to have to figure shit out."

And for just an instant, the thought of that beautiful woman with that gorgeous smile came to mind, and I pushed those thoughts away. My family was breaking, or perhaps breaking open. And I didn't have time to worry about things like a woman who had made me smile.

The Cages needed me and after today's meeting there would be no going back to sanity.

Ever.

Chapter Two
BLAKELY

Dear Diary,
Love at first sight can't exist. Because if it did, he'd have called.

THREE MONTHS LATER

BY THE TIME THE SEVENTH DOOR HAD BEEN metaphorically slammed in my face, I probably should have taken the hint. Only I didn't know exactly what hint that should be at this point in my desperation.

ME:
They said no, and this time didn't even bother to put on a fake smile as they pushed me out of their lovely high-rise.

ISABELLA:
Seriously? Not even a real "excuse?"

ME:
Nope. I'm out of options.

ISABELLA:
As much as I hate to say it, you know there's one more option.

ME:
I know. I have an interview with them at 3:00.

ISABELLA:
You didn't tell me?

I winced knowing that it probably sounded as if I had been hiding things from her, but I had. But there were reasons. Tricky, complicated reasons on more than one level.

ME:
I really hoped not to have to use this last straw.

ISABELLA:
I see. You're meeting with them.

ISABELLA:

I know why you didn't tell me. And it's not just because of the obvious reasons. But good luck. Okay? And I'm pretty sure I can kick somebody in the shins if it doesn't work out.

My lips twitched, a smile nearly covering my face after staring at her words for far too long.

ME:

It'll be fine. I'm going to make this work.

ISABELLA:

And if it doesn't?

ISABELLA:

Forget that. It's going to work. I'll stop being Debbie Downer over here.

ME:

First, you aren't the only one, as that's pretty much the only feeling I have right now. My own Debbie Down-ness. Is that a word?

ISABELLA:

We can make that happen.

ME:

Okay, I have to get ready. I love you. Have fun at work.

ISABELLA:

You know I won't. But you've got this. I believe in you.

I set my phone aside and went back to my bedroom to

see exactly what suit I should put on. I'd already worn a suit for my first interview, and since I hadn't even been able to finish the awkward meeting, I figured wearing the same one for this second interview of the day was probably not a good idea.

It had been three months since I lost my job. Three months because my former boss was an arrogant asshole. And in that time, I'd worn more suits than I could count, all of my wardrobe at this point, just to see if I could make a living in what I was good at.

I sighed, searching through the various colored blouses that I had hanging up, wondering what color would show that I was smart, good at my job, and innovative.

"Not red, I wore red yesterday for that terrible interview. Not green, because that's what I'm currently wearing."

I looked at the pale pink top that would go great with dove gray pants. I hated the fact that this color reminded me of everything that had gone wrong. However, maybe that's exactly what I needed. I pulled out the silk top, and set it aside, knowing that this had to work.

I still couldn't quite believe that I was nearing thirty, unemployed, and running out of resources and plans to figure out my next step. I had rent due, and while I had a decent savings account, thanks to my previous job and the fact I didn't like spending money, it was going to dwindle fast if I kept having to pull out money just to survive.

The problem, however, I was a business manager of

sorts, but one that specialized in strengthening business assets. Meaning I needed to work for somebody else to help them work better. And while it made sense in action, on paper, it looked like I had many skills, but I wasn't brilliant at any of them. The term jack-of-all-trades had been bantered a few times to me, but I knew it wasn't because of who I was. Okay, maybe it was exactly because of who I was.

I had worked for Howard Enterprises since graduating from college. I had been top of the class in business at Boulder, which wasn't an easy thing to do. Especially since most of the people surrounding me had been legacy students, guys who had known exactly what they wanted to do for the rest of their lives because they could work for their families' empires. At least in a smaller sense. We weren't an Ivy League college, so I wasn't rubbing elbows with those who would one day rule the world, but I wanted to at least help those ruling our part of the world. And I had been good at it.

Howard Enterprises had taken me on as a college grad and not even through internship. I'd had a full paycheck, a retirement fund, medical insurance, and my own desk. Yes, the desk had been a little wobbly, and there hadn't been a single window in the office I shared with four other people, but eventually I had worked up to my place. I had worked right under Mr. Howard and had dealt with his inability to save a PDF and his blowups at every single little thing. And while he had been a jerk, and prone to temper tantrums, he had never treated me with anything but respect. At least in the sense of his respect toward anyone else. I didn't have to fight in the boys' club that so many of my other friends—including Isabella—had to do every day.

I had been an equal, and I had been damn good at my job.

Even though Mr. Howard didn't always listen to my advice, which would inevitably end up with some form of downward spiral, I had still done good work. And yet, it hadn't been my whole purpose. I'd wanted to do more, do better. I hadn't always agreed with the business practices that man had chosen, but I had done my best.

And then I had lost it all.

Lost it all because Mr. Howard hadn't liked a single dance.

I shook my head, pushing that thought out of my mind.

No, he would've found another way to fire me, like any other egotistical asshole who didn't want somebody telling him what to do. Because while I had been good at my job, I had been expensive, and did voice my opinion. Maybe that had been wrong, but it hadn't been why I lost my job.

Nor was it why I couldn't get a job now.

The Howards had power. Maybe not as much power as their rivals, but enough. And now, every time I tried to get a job in this city, doors were slammed in my face because they did not want to get involved in the rivalry between the Howards and the Cages.

A rivalry that I wasn't even sure that the Cages were aware of.

I quickly put my hair up, and then let it fall down again, not knowing what to do with it, and feeling itchy beyond all reason.

The problem was that I was an idiot. I had shared a single dance and a single cup of coffee with Aston Cage. The sexy and chiseled president of Cage Enterprises. And because I had dared to dance with him in front of Mr. Howard, he had seen it as disloyalty.

One pink slip later, I had found myself booted out of the comfort of a job that I was damn good at but didn't love.

And here I was, unemployed, and really fucking annoyed.

Aston Cage was not my enemy, and yet it sure felt like it.

He probably didn't even remember my name or my face. It had been a kiss, a dance, a touch, and then nothing.

No call, no text, nothing.

He had walked away after promising to speak to me again and left me behind in shambles. Then again, I wasn't even sure Aston Cage was aware. Because why would he be aware of anything that was beneath him. Just like Howard Enterprises and Mr. Howard himself was.

Just like I was.

But now, I needed him to give me a job.

I pinched the bridge of my nose and quickly took a deep breath, trying to remember the meditation that Isabella had taught me. Which was ironic considering

Isabella was way more high-strung than I was. But I wasn't going to dive too deeply into that.

There was a knock on my door, and I frowned, going to answer it, wondering who could be here around lunchtime.

And as if I had conjured her up, my best friend stood at the door, hair a little frazzled, with stress all over her face.

"What are you doing here?" I asked, pulling Isabella into a hug.

My best friend hugged me tightly. "I figured you needed your person."

We rested our heads on each other's shoulders and stood there, both women in business attire, and with the weight of the world on our shoulders. Even if it didn't always feel like that.

"I love you."

"I love you too." She pulled back and looked me up and down. "That's a good look. You're going to do great."

"Are you sure it's not weird?" I asked, speaking of the giant elephant in the room. Or was it a gorilla?

She cringed but shook her head. "No, it won't be weird. However, it *has* been three months."

I frowned, until everything clicked. Because Isabella wasn't only my best friend, she happened to be the secret sister of the Cages.

It seemed that Daddy Cage had been busy in his all too short life and had fathered twelve children—over two sets of families. And while apparently Isabella's mother knew of it, and actually knew Aston's mother, they hadn't told their kids until the reading of the will.

That evening my best friend had shown up to my house and raged for a good hour before breaking down into tears. Tears I knew she wouldn't have shown anyone else in the family.

And that was when I blurted that I had made out with her brother.

Things weren't awkward at all.

"So you have to have the big family dinner soon then?" I asked, knowing the three-month reprieve was now over.

"I don't understand how this will is legal, but it is. And I have to have dinner with that side of the family. Once a month. For three years."

She said each word with such fierceness, that I worried that she was going to have an aneurysm or something.

"But it doesn't have to be you each time, does it?"

"I'm not going to force my family to do it if I can't."

"Are they all that bad though?" I asked, hating myself for even asking.

Isabella scowled at me. "Ford seems fine. He knows Phoebe at least," she said, speaking of her sister, and apparent brother. It was very confusing.

"I still can't believe that the Cage I went on a coffee date with happens to be your Cage."

"I don't like the fact that our Venn diagram has become a circle. It's very annoying."

My lips twitched at that.

Isabella just rolled her eyes. "The Cages, I hear, are decent with business. They're not going to push you out of the office just because you worked with Howard. In fact, I'm pretty sure they owe you."

I cringe. "I probably shouldn't put that on my resume, right?"

"You damn well should. It's all Aston Cage's fault."

My heart did that little twisting motion that I hated so much whenever I heard his name. It wasn't as if I really knew him. There had just been heat and chemistry and then nothing. Not a single communication. Not even a pigeon to send over a note. I would've preferred an owl, or something. But no, there was nothing.

And while I realized he had enough on his plate with his business, the funeral, and apparently this new family, I still felt slighted.

"He should have texted you back. I'm sorry, we all have things to do even though we're dealing with our father, the evil mess. He should have texted."

I cringed. "I really shouldn't have told you about that. It's going to cast him in a bad light for you." I didn't want Isabella to start off on an even worse foot with the people she could now call family. My twinge of regret shouldn't have a bearing on the family she now had—best friends or not.

"Of course it's a bad light. He's egotistical, and growly, and wanted to take over the whole meeting."

I raised a single brow at her, and just stared, before she rolled her eyes again. "Stop it. It sounded like you were describing yourself. I mean, I love you, but you are bossy when it comes to your siblings."

"I am not." We both burst out into laughter, and I felt lighter than I had in days.

She shook her head. "Fine, I'm a mess. Maybe not as messy as dear old Daddy was."

I blanched. "I don't know how he had the time. I mean, *two* families?"

"Dad was rarely around in the end. He was too busy playing with his *real* family."

I reached out and grabbed her hand. "I'm sorry about your father. And I am annoyed that I have to go ask the Cages for a job, and yes, disgruntled that he didn't text."

"I wish I could kick him," she mumbled.

I waved her off. "I have complicated feelings when it comes to Aston and the family, which I shouldn't. Because it didn't mean anything."

"Clearly."

"That doesn't mean you should cast a bad light on them. You don't know how he was to the others, do you?"

She shook her head, her gaze going distant. "No. I don't know them. Phoebe knows Ford, and he seems like a good guy. But he doesn't really hang out or work with his brothers as much. At least that's what I've been able to gather."

"So maybe you should get to know the family? I mean it's not going to be easy. They could all be horrible people for all I know. But you won't know until you try. And you don't have to put all of it on you. You do have a few sisters and a brother who can take your place for a dinner or two."

Isabella crossed her eyes at me and sighed. "That is true. However, I'm going to be the one that stands in from my side of the family. At least at first. Until I get to know these Cages."

"Aren't you a Cage too?" I asked, knowing that while I needed to get out and get ready for my last-ditch effort at getting a job, this was just as important. If not more so.

"I don't know who I am anymore. Which isn't the greatest feeling in the world. However, this isn't about me. I took a lunch break, which I never do, so I need to head back to the office. And you need to go get this job. And if they don't give it to you, I'm going to hate them even more than I probably will."

"Don't hate them. They're family. Family you don't know yet."

"You have amazing parents, and I'm happy that you do, but apparently I didn't have the parents I thought I did."

And with that, we hugged it out, she helped me pick up my jewelry, and we each headed out in different directions. I had no idea how that family was going to handle what they needed, and I was grateful that I didn't have to deal with it. However, I needed a job.

And thankfully, my interview was not with Aston. I knew he had more important things on his mind than a single dance and promise that he failed to keep. So I would push that out of my mind and focus on the desperation of my bank account.

Cage Enterprises was in one of the familiar high rises of Denver, and gorgeous. Everything was high-end, and yet didn't look cold and stuffy. There was a warmth in every aspect of ambiance. I had to wonder where that came from. I had only met three of the brothers, including the man I'd be interviewing with, so perhaps they just hired a decent decorator.

I went up to the front desk and the man there smiled up at me. "Hello, how can I help you?"

My stomach tightened but I reminded myself I didn't have another choice...and the Cages would be honored to hire me. And if I kept telling myself that, I'd believe it. "Hi. I am Blakely Graves. I'm here to meet James Cage for an interview."

He nodded, that pleasant smile on his face. "Of course. You can go up to the elevator and up to level eighteen. Someone will be at the top and will be able to help you. I'll let them know that you're on your way."

"Thank you." Again, tension slid into me, wrapping it's spindly fingers around my chest.

"No problem. And good luck." He winked as he said it, and I warmed a bit, liking the friendly atmosphere.

Everybody seemed as if they weren't on the edge, stress pounding into them, like they had at Howard Enterprises. They all had work to do, but they weren't growling in every corner. Or maybe that was just what the first floor felt like.

I made my way up to the eighteenth floor and rolled my shoulders back as I walked out into the upper lobby. The person who met me there smiled softly and gestured for me to go to one of the offices in the corner. I really wanted this to work. I *needed* it to work. But I tried not to look around too much soaking in my surroundings. I didn't want to like this place too much and have to walk away. I kept having to do that every time.

I sat down in the chair opposite a large desk and sat my bag next to me. "Thank you so much," I said to the woman who had taken me to the office, and she smiled softly.

"No problem. Can I get you some water? Some tea? Coffee?"

"I'm fine, thank you so much."

"No problem, Mr. Cage will be here soon."

"Do you call them all Mr. Cage?" I asked, and then could have kicked myself. "I'm sorry. Forget I asked that."

The woman laughed and shook her head. "Sometimes. Usually we go by first names here, but I was trying to sound a little more professional since it's an interview."

I held back a laugh, feeling as though I might not have stepped in it after all. "I'm so glad I could put my foot in my mouth for that."

"You didn't even come close to that. Don't worry. He'll be here soon."

She winked and walked away, and I had to hope no one else overheard. While that was a friendly exchange, it probably wasn't the greatest way to start an interview.

I looked around the office, at the usual fare of dark furniture, the full glass wall behind it, and knickknacks and awards all over the bookshelves. It seemed like a typical office, and I was wondering why I was trying to figure out if I could sense something about the Cages from knickknacks. Honestly, this probably wasn't even a main office. It could just be a meeting space that they had for interviews and small meetings. Yet I couldn't help but be curious. The Cages had always interested me, even though I hadn't really focused on them too much until that fateful date.

And now, they were Isabella's family. Like it or not, the connections remained.

A familiar man in a dark gray suit and bright blue tie walked in, and I stood up quickly, holding up my hand. "Hello there," the man said as he shook my hand and tilted his head as he looked at me. "Good to see you again."

I held back a cringe, letting my hand fall. "Hello, James. Mr. Cage."

The last time I had seen him had been when he had walked in on me and his brother making out in a hallway. Oh good. Maybe I could just hide somewhere underneath this chair and the interview could end quickly.

"Call me James. There are way too many Cages here."

"I'm sorry to hear about your father," I said, and when his eyes tightened ever so slightly, I realized I had stepped in it again.

I was oh for three so far.

"Thank you. He's missed."

I cleared my throat, going full into my insanity of this situation. "Before this starts, I should probably also add that Isabella's my best friend," I blurted, realizing that if I was going to strike out completely, I should put all things on the table.

His eyes widened for a moment, before he swallowed hard. "Interesting. The world's pretty small, isn't it?" he asked, his voice soft.

"It seems so. I mean, I think the first time we *met* is when you added me to a group chat?"

His eyes filled with laughter then, and he shook his head. "I'm not the one who added you."

"Didn't they blame you?" I asked.

"No, that might've been Theo." He waved it off. "Theo is a chef. He owns The Teal Door."

My eyes widened at his comment. "I've never been able to get into that restaurant. And I've tried."

"It's hard for me to get in and I'm family." A pause. "So... I'm going to be honest."

I braced myself.

James leaned forward. "I don't know why you haven't been snapped up. Or why you're still looking for a job after three months since leaving Howard Enterprises."

That made me blink. "That's not what I thought you were going to say."

"I figured we should lay everything on the table since you did the same."

"The truth?"

"That would be nice."

I cleared my throat. "Mr. Howard didn't like the fact that I danced with Aston. That's it. He found a way to get me out and has used everything in his power to make sure

I can't get a job in this city. I don't understand why exactly, because I never did anything to that man other than try to help his business, which I did. But if you talk to him as you probably should since he's my former employer, he fired me. He found a way to do it so it was legal, but the real reason is because I danced with your brother."

"Do you want me to kill him?" he asked, his voice low.

I was a little worried he was serious.

"Mr. Howard? Or your brother?"

He burst out laughing, and I relaxed marginally. "We can fight that, you know. You shouldn't have been fired for a single dance. And it's not like we're in a rivalry with the Howards."

A smile covered my face, and he gave me a quizzical look, raising his brow. "I thought to myself earlier that I wasn't sure you guys were aware you were in a rivalry. And it seems that I was right."

He rolled his eyes. "I'll never understand some business practices, but here we are. Blakely? We need you here. You're good at what you do, and we wanted to snap you up before, but you were a constant at Howard Enterprises. Now you're not, and we want you. Are you going to be okay working here?"

It felt as if everything skidded to a halt, and it took me far too long to catch up. We had sat down as we had begun talking but I stood up then, confused.

"Just like that? I'm hired?"

He shrugged as if he hadn't just changed my life. "We

can go over salary and benefits and hours and everything, but we want you. And I know you need the job. And to be fair, I was a little worried that you weren't going to want to take it because of well..."

And the other elephant in the room raised its trunk. "You don't have to worry about that. I haven't spoken to him since that evening."

Confusion covered his face. "He didn't call you?"

I winced. "I don't know if that's any of your business in an interview, but no."

He flinched. "I think we are past the point of not allowing any personal things into this interview. I apologize."

I shook my head, wondering why I'd snapped back as I had. "No. You're right. I'm the one that blurted that Isabella was my best friend."

"And that's the second thing. Is she going to be okay with you working here?"

This time I smiled. "I think she promised to come and kick shins if I didn't get hired. So thanks for that."

He grinned then. "I think I'm going to like this sister of mine."

"She's my *best* friend. And one of the most amazing people I know. So I hope you do. And I'm really sorry all of this happened and it's such a mess. But we do not need to talk about that. And I'm sorry that I know so much about it."

"It's actually kind of nice that someone else knows outside of the family. I mean the media pretends they know, but they don't."

I shook my head. "I can't even imagine."

He waved it off as if it was nothing, though I knew it couldn't be. "So, are you okay then working here? We're complicated, we're demanding, but we're not going to fire you because you dared to even breathe next to our supposed rival."

I press my lips together, wondering what the catch was. Who were these Cages? And why was I inevitably connected to them?

But in the end, it didn't matter.

"Yes. I'm in."

He held out his hand again, and I shook it, as a wide smile covered his face. "Good. Now we can let the world know we poached you from our new rivals."

This time I rolled my eyes. "Oh, he would love that."

"Oh, we'll make *sure* he knows."

"As long as it doesn't blow up in our faces."

"We can handle the embers." He looked over my shoulder and from the way that he stiffened ever so slightly, I froze.

I knew exactly who was behind me in that moment, and who I knew I would inevitably see here.

However, James was my boss. My *new* boss. And as I turned to see Aston Cage there, I was afraid of what I was going to see.

And afraid of what I wasn't.

Chapter Three

ASTON

In case you're trying to catch up, the Cages are "now" as follows:

Aston, Flynn, Hudson, Dorian, Isabella, James, Theo, Sophia, Kyler, Ford, Emily, and Phoebe.

SHE WAS EVEN MORE BEAUTIFUL THAN I HAD remembered. And considering the memory of her still haunted my waking dreams, that was saying something.

She wore a pale pink top with some kind of silk bow thing, as well as gray pants, and I couldn't help but think of how that top looked exactly the same color as the dress I had last seen her in. The dress that I nearly crumpled in my hands in my haste to have her.

It had been three months since I had seen her, three months since I had ignored her text, and had never called her back. I wasn't always a complete asshole, but when it came to Blakely, apparently, I could not help it.

"Blakely?" I asked, surprised my voice had come out as coherent at all. Considering it was only one word though, I should not put the cart before the horse.

I should not give myself too much praise.

I looked past her, realizing that she was in my brother's office, and James just gave me a knowing look. Although what he could know confounded me.

"Hello Mr. Cage," she said.

Mr. Cage. Well I probably deserved that. "I didn't realize you would be here today." Why did it sound like I had a stick up my ass? Probably because just the sight of her felt as if I'd been hit with an anvil.

Weeks of texting, just light conversations with two people who didn't even know each other, a single coffee date, a single dance, a single kiss that could have turned into more.

Ours was a tryst of promise, a hope that had led to nothing. Because I had made it that way.

And now she was here. In my brother's office. On my floor.

"I want to introduce you to our newest employee," James said, and my gaze pulled back to my brother, as I hadn't even realized I had been staring at Blakely again.

"Excuse me?" James gave me a pointed look, and I cleared my throat before looking back at Blakely. "Welcome to the team. I assume you'll be working under James since I don't know what job you applied for."

I had never sounded so stilted and idiotic in my life.

Her face paled, and I hated myself.

"She's going to take Johnson's place. And hopefully do a better job."

I nodded, remembering the man who had a promising start, and then hadn't been able to follow through on any of his lofty ideas and lies.

And now it all clicked, remembering what Blakely had done at Howard Enterprises.

"So you're no longer working with Howard?" I asked, so confused as to why she would be here.

James cleared his throat and gestured me into the office. I closed the door behind him and couldn't help but notice the way that Blakely stiffened, staring between us.

Because of the way that the company was structured, Blakely would not be working for me. She would only work for James. And yet that thought didn't make this situation any easier to swallow in this moment.

"Is there a reason that you closed the door?" Blakely asked, her voice smooth, as she stared at both of us.

James sighed. "I assumed you didn't want your personal business blasted all over the office," James said rationally, and I felt anything but rational.

"What business?" I asked, feeling as if I were three steps behind. I had purposely not looked into anything that Blakely could be attached to, including Howard Enterprises. Because if I had, I would've wanted to reply back. I would've wanted to reach out.

And my family was in a state of shambles, and I couldn't focus on anything else but keeping them sane and healthy. By keeping us connected. We had that blasted dinner later tonight, where I had to somehow break bread with my new family members, and I had no idea how it was going to go.

So that was what I was focusing on, and not Blakely.

"I was fired," Blakely said simply.

I blinked at her, realizing that statement was anything but simple. "What?" I asked, my voice a growl.

"Aston," James warned.

I was grateful for the chaperone in this conversation.

"It's fine. I have a new job now, and I'm happy. There's no need for anything to be awkward." She smiled, though I wasn't sure if it was real or not.

"What happened?" I asked.

Blakely gave me a confused look before turning to James. "You knew that I was searching for a job, and he didn't?"

"No, your position would be under my purview, not his section. We separate our companies underneath the umbrella of Cage Enterprises so we don't fight anymore. Brothers and all."

She blinked, and I had no idea what she was thinking. It was easier to know her when we were just texting, when she was a stranger on the other line. And I desperately wanted to know what she was thinking.

"I was fired because Howard didn't like our dance," she said pointedly.

My hands fisted at my sides. "Are you fucking kidding me?"

"I'm not kidding you. He put it in different words and

found another reason for me to lose my job. And for the past three months—"

"Three months?" I cut her off. "You've been out of work for three months?"

She winced, her cheeks turning a rosy shade.

"Aston. Seriously?" James grumbled.

"Yes. Because Howard didn't want me to have a job. And I figured coming here of all places probably wouldn't be the best bet."

"I'm going to kill him," I growled.

"You are not," Blakely said, her voice strong, that same strength that I had liked three months ago.

"Excuse me?"

"This is my business. Yes, he's a terrible man, and if I had the time and the wherewithal, I could have found a way to sue him or get vengeance, but it doesn't matter. I have a new job. Your brother hired me. And I'm going to be the best at it. So we don't need to make things awkward."

"Oh this isn't awkward at all," James said.

I shot him a vicious glare. "Quiet."

"No I think I'm not going to be quiet. Because this is my office. And Blakely is my new employee. I don't want you to screw it up with your alpha man tendencies."

Blakely's lips twitched.

I shook my head. "He had no right to fire you."

"He didn't. And it's going to be fine. I am amazing at my job, and I'm going to help Cage Enterprises be even more elite than you already are."

"See, I like the sound of that. We were going to try to

poach her anyway," James said with a shrug, and Blakely looked over at him.

"You keep saying that, and yet I had no job offer," she said, her eyes dancing.

Why the hell was I jealous of my brother? It wasn't like Blakely was mine. However James was her boss, and that meant nothing could happen.

Not like anything could happen with us. There was no *us*. I had put the nail in that coffin quite nicely.

"I'm only going to say this once," James continued, "Blakely, I'm so glad that you're here, and we will get your paperwork done as soon as you're out of this office. However, as I hate awkward situations, why don't the two of you talk for just a moment before you do that?"

"There's really no need."

"And you love awkward situations," I put in.

A laugh escaped Blakely, and I smiled. And when our gazes met, she immediately turned away, and I sighed. I deserved that.

"I will be in the office across the hall," James said after a moment, hands in pockets. "When you're ready, Blakely. You can go over your paperwork and everything with my admin and myself. And you can start on Monday."

"Thank you, Mr. Cage."

"Call me James." He moved forward and held out his hand. Blakely shook it, and for some reason I wanted to rip my brother's arm off.

Okay, maybe I was acting like an alpha male. I really needed to get control over myself.

James opened the door, and left it open, giving both of us pointed looks, before walking out. That meant I wasn't about to close the door again.

"You don't have to worry, I'm not going to make this any more awkward," she said after a moment.

"There's not going to be an issue. I am just sorry that you were forced out of your job to begin with."

"Honestly, I was going to try to find a new place anyway. He wasn't a good man to work for."

I sighed. "My brother's the best."

"So I won't be working with you at all?" she asked and winced. "Mostly because I don't want it to be awkward. Not because of anything else."

I sighed, and really wished James had closed that door. "I'm sorry."

She stared at me then and let out a hollow laugh. "I was a little resentful of you for these past three months, which is like no time at all. But we're both adults, and I realize that you have a life of your own, one that has changed so abruptly, I can't even imagine."

I swallowed hard, knowing I didn't deserve her niceties. "I'm sorry I didn't call," I repeated.

"And I'm sorry about your father."

Ice slid over me, a reminder of exactly why we were in this situation. "I'm the head of the family now. And though we aren't in regency England where I have to protect the estate and livelihood of my siblings, it's exactly like that," I said with a laugh.

"And now you have more siblings," she said softly.

"So I see you're watching the news?" I asked dryly.

Blakely sighed and picked up her bag, clearly ready to go speak with James. "Sometimes, but not about you. You should know that I've already told James this."

"What?" I asked, uneasy.

"My best friend in the world is Isabella."

And with a snap, the door finally clicked closed on anything that would've happened with Blakely. There was no way it would ever have worked out to begin with.

"I see," I said icily, and Blakely just laughed. Laughed in my face.

"You and Isabella are so alike it's a little scary."

I wasn't sure what to make of that. "I don't know her, so I guess you are going to be the expert in that."

"You're going to like the other Cages. I promise."

"How can you be so sure?" I asked, my voice softer this time. I didn't hate them. I didn't know them. I hated my father and my mother for that matter. I hated the situation we were in. But no, I didn't hate these new siblings of ours.

"I know because of that group chat. You guys were joking with each other and laughing and being just brothers. And that's how they are. Sisters and one brother, but they're close. And you guys are clearly close. I don't know how it's all going to work, but you'll find a way. And I understand why you didn't call."

"I need to make sure my family doesn't crumble even more than it already has."

Her eyes softened for the barest moment before becoming unreadable once again. "That's all that you can ask for, honestly. I know it's hard and will continue to be, but I suppose you never calling ended up being the outcome we both needed."

"And why is that?" I asked, dread in my stomach.

"Because I'm working here. And we're already awkward enough. So it was lovely to see you, Aston. And I'll see you around the office. But no resentment here. Promise."

I wasn't quite sure that I believed her, but I stepped out of the way when she passed me, without another word.

As I ran my hand over my face, a familiar voice echoed behind me.

"Well, this is going to be fun."

I whirled on Flynn and narrowed my gaze.

"Don't worry, you guys were discreet," Flynn said, and I moved past him, annoyed as hell. My office was on the other corner of the building, and Flynn followed me along, nobody really paying attention to us. If they needed us, they would call out. Because we weren't the domineering bosses that didn't want to hear from anyone beneath us. But everybody had a job to do, and they were working cohesively. That didn't always happen.

I walked into my office, really wanting a drink, but realizing that it was far too early in the day. I would have a drink at dinner. Probably many drinks at dinner.

Flynn closed the door behind him and raised a brow at me.

"So. You never did text her, did you?"

"Of course I didn't. When would I have had time for a

personal life? Between the endless media calls, lawyer visits, or secondary DNA testing, when?"

"You didn't have to do it all yourself you know. You could have asked for help."

"You all did what you could, but you have lives. We did the funeral as best as we could, and that was a farce."

Flynn rolled his eyes as we both remembered the immense funeral held for a man of power, and a man of lies.

We had invited our father's friends and acquaintances, and they had told stories that I hadn't listened to, and grieved with us, even though everything felt empty.

The problem was people from both sides of his life had come. People who knew him as Phoebe and Isabella's father, and people who knew him as our father. There were countless connections in the state alone, and it wasn't as if he could hide so many lies from every single person around him.

"Denver isn't that big of a city, more people must have known," I mumbled under my breath.

"Probably. But you know boys will be boys," Flynn said as he flopped into the office chair.

"That's my chair. Get up."

"No I don't think I will. Are you going to be okay working with Blakely?"

"Of course I am. It wasn't like we were anything."

"But you could have been. I liked her."

"You saw her for all of five minutes," I said dryly.

"Yes, but I liked the way that you smiled every time you secretly texted her."

I narrowed my gaze at my younger brother. "How the hell did you know we were texting?"

"Because you practically giggled like a schoolgirl when you thought of her."

"I did not," I said, aghast.

"Yes, you did. But that's fine. If nothing's going to happen, make sure that you don't go pining around her. From what I heard of her skills, she's going to be great for our business."

"We need someone who can organize ten things at once without breaking down," I said dryly.

"Well, you're usually the man for that."

"Right now I'm doing a hundred things at once."

"And that's just fine. She's going to help James, and you don't even have to see her."

"She's going to be working on the same damn floor, Flynn."

"So it shouldn't be a problem. You know what's going to be a problem though," he said, his voice trailing off.

I pinched the bridge of my nose, really needing a drink. "Dinner."

"So, do we have our special flow chart yet of who's going when?" he asked with a laugh.

"No, I'm sure Isabella will have a pie chart of some sort with a color-coded wheel for us," I said with a laugh.

"That does sound like our sister, doesn't it?"

Sister.

"Is she older or younger than you?" I asked, a frown on my face.

"Younger."

"So she's a little sister."

Flynn shrugged. "Yes, which I don't really think matters in the end. We're all so close together that I'm pretty sure our moms were probably pregnant at the same time with a couple of us," he said before giving a full body shudder.

"I really don't want to think about that."

"Same. But there's not much we can do about it."

I raised a brow. "I think the point of these dinners is we do have to do something about it."

"Then we make nice. They aren't the enemy you know?"

"You sound like Blakely."

His brows rose. "Oh?"

I shook my head. "It seems that fate and the world have collided to hate me. Isabella and her seem to be best friends."

"No shit?"

"Not in the slightest."

"Well this dinner is going to be interesting. I wonder if we can get any background on them from Blakely," he said, a curious glint in his eyes.

"Don't. Don't put her in between. We are going to figure this out. It's not like we're going to battle."

"And yet it feels like that, doesn't it?" Flynn asked. "And look at you being all protective."

"First off, fuck you."

"No thanks," he said, giving me a wink.

"Second, she's just starting off here, and after having

to deal with that asshole boss of hers, she doesn't need us to be assholes trying to use her for information."

"What happened with Howard?"

As I explained it, Flynn's gaze went steely, and he stood up.

"Do you want me to do something about it?" he asked, that blade in his voice that most people didn't hear. Because he was the happy one, the sweet one. The funny twin to Hudson's growl.

They didn't get the blade.

"No. She doesn't want that handled."

"I can still look something up."

"Discreetly," I said after a moment. "But we're not going to put her in the middle of anything."

"Meaning stay away from her?" Flynn asked.

"I know you're joking with me, but let's not," I snapped.

"You're going to need to get a rein on that temper of yours. Especially if you're going to work next to her."

"It'll be fine. It's not like we were anything."

"And isn't a loss of something that could have been just the worst then?"

"Stop being philosophical and go back to work. And don't forget to be at my house by five-thirty."

"I thought dinner was at six-thirty?" he asked.

"And you're going to help me cook."

"You're cooking?"

"I can cook."

"I know you can cook. I just assumed you'd have this catered."

"They don't need to think of us as the assholes who get things catered on our first dinner. Next time we can order pizza."

Flynn sighed but nodded. "You're right. We want to make a good impression. Because Dad really messed us up, didn't he?"

"Understatement of our lifetime."

And with that, Flynn went back to work, and I tried to ignore the fact that Blakely walked by my office, smiling as she talked to James.

This was going to work. Everything was going to be fine. And as I looked down at the broken pen in my hand, ink spilling everywhere, I realized that no, I wasn't fine.

Chapter Four
ASTON

Rule #2: Never lie to your family.

"So you're really going all out here, aren't you?" Dorian asked as he popped a grape into his mouth. I glared over my shoulder at my younger brother and looked at the three grapes left in his hand.

"Did you get that out of my fridge?"

"Of course I did. I'm hungry."

"You're here early to help me cook along with the others. You're not supposed to be eating the random things in my fridge that aren't for dinner."

"You're supposed to feed me. *Feed me.*" He drew out the words, and I rolled my eyes.

"How old are you again?" I asked, and Dorian just beamed.

"I'm you know, thirty. But that is not childlike."

"I swear you act younger around me just to piss me off, don't you?"

"Of course. It's what I do." His face went serious then, becoming the Dorian that people in the business world saw. "Are you okay?"

Since I was pretty sure that Dorian didn't know about Blakely, he had to mean about tonight's dinner. At least I hoped so.

"I'm fine. We're having roast chicken, mashed potatoes, three kinds of vegetables, a cheese plate appetizer, and Isabella and the others said they would bring dessert."

"Is it the roast chicken that has a lemon stuffed up its ass?"

"You're so elegant. But yes. There's rosemary in there as well."

"Wasn't that Grandma's recipe?"

"Or our neighbor's. It's not like Mom and Dad really cooked," I said dryly.

"It's not like Dad was around to cook for us anyway." A pause. "Well, it seems he was a little busy."

"What the hell are we going to do?" I asked, finishing the mashed potatoes.

"We're going to do what we always do, muddle through it and pretend that we're masters of our domain."

I grunted. "I really hate the fact that it seems that could be our true tagline."

"We try. So there needs to be five of us, right? Two from our family, three from theirs?" Dorian paused. "I need to find another way to say that."

"Because we're supposed to all be family apparently?" The fact that we wanted labels or were unsure what to even call each other just told me how much of a farce this whole situation was.

"You looked at the group chat, Ford and Aston are coming."

"So that's four of us, we still need two of them then. Not quite five." I shook my head. "I don't know who else is coming, as it's not like we have a spreadsheet."

"I'm honestly surprised. It's been three weeks. Shouldn't there be a color-coded spreadsheet in the works from either Flynn or you?"

My lips nearly formed a smile and I shook my head. "We're all treading the same water, trying not to drown. We'll figure out exactly what dear old Father wanted."

Dorian smiled, though it didn't quite reach his eyes. "Mass chaos and disarray? Because that seems like his style."

"At least he bought his own tombstone. I don't have to deal with the marble or whatever the fuck he wanted. His estate will handle it all, and I don't have to even go to his grave site, and kick at him." I still couldn't quite believe the venom in my voice at that, but what else was I supposed to say?

"I didn't always hate him you know," Dorian said softly.

"I know. Sometimes he was great. I wouldn't be where I am in this job without him." And didn't that gall?

"I don't know, I feel like you came out of the womb in a little baby-sized suit."

This time I let the smile come. "Yes, complete with tie and briefcase. Diapers were a bitch."

"What are we talking about with diapers?" Flynn asked as he came into the kitchen, eyes wide at everything I was doing at once. Ford was behind him, and without a word, immediately went to check the chicken.

I waved him off. "It's just resting."

Ford leaned forward. "I'm just making sure we don't give any of us food poisoning. Wouldn't that be a great way to start this."

"I really want us to actually get along to spite that man. Is that weird?" Flynn said, and I turned to him, realizing that my brother might be on the right path.

"Meaning we all get along and become one big happy family, and we can look down at Father and kick him?" I asked.

Ford burst out laughing, Dorian joining him, as Flynn just rolled his eyes.

"You really believe he's down in Hell?" Flynn asked.

"I don't even know if I believe in Hell, but if there is, he's burning down there. There's got to be a few carnal sins that he broke."

"More than a few," Dorian said with a laugh.

The doorbell rang at that moment, and my spine tensed once more.

"They aren't the enemy," Ford whispered.

I met my brother's gaze and nodded. As the only one of us settled down and married, sometimes I felt that Ford knew exactly what he was doing with his life. The fact that he was the youngest of us all probably should have worried me. But it didn't. He had found his path right away and hadn't taken a no from fate for an answer.

"I'll go get the door," Flynn said as he hurried off, Dorian on his tail.

I sighed. "I know they aren't the enemy. We keep reminding ourselves that."

Ford squeezed my shoulder. "At this point Dad's the enemy. But I've felt that way for a long while."

I looked over at my youngest brother. "I'm just glad that you know Phoebe at least. That's at least a touchstone."

"And I know she's not going to be here tonight. She's out with Kane," he said, speaking of Phoebe's boyfriend.

I groaned, sad that someone I actually knew wouldn't be there. "Well, at least we can get the introductions over with."

"I don't know them either and I want to. Because Flynn's right. I want to spite Father. So fuck him."

"Damn straight." I made sure all the burners were off, things settled in their serving dishes and still warming, and made my way into the living room.

Isabella stood there, wearing a soft blue dress, and wide eyes—a surprise. Sophia stood next to her, her chestnut hair in curls down her back. She had straight hair when I had seen her before, and I didn't know which one was natural. I didn't know anything about our family it seemed.

"Welcome," I said, not bothering to hold out my hand. I didn't want it to seem too formal. Of course, my house was a little more formal than most.

"Your home is lovely," Sophia said, as she held out a covered dish. I immediately took it from her and looked down at it, feeling awkward as hell. "It's a Boston cream cake pie thing." She winced. "It's like a Boston cream pie, but has cake in it? I'm not quite sure how to describe it."

That made me smile. "I don't know exactly what you're talking about, but if it has chocolate and Bavarian cream? I'm happy."

"Then you'll be happy," she said with a bright smile.

"Sophia is actually a really great baker." Isabella frowned. "I have no idea why I said *actually* like that. Sorry. I'm just going to let my words tumble over one another."

"Then we can all be twins," Flynn said. "Of course, my twin isn't here right now," he said with a grin.

"Oh yes, so are you Flynn or Hudson?" Sophia asked.

Flynn winced. "I'm sorry for not actually introducing myself. I am Flynn. Hudson isn't here."

"He's the one who lives in the small town that you apparently own?" Isabella asked, her brow raised.

"Let me go put this in the refrigerator, and we can explain to you about the small town that we accidentally own," I said, my voice only slightly gruff.

"I've always wanted to live in a small town," Sophia said softly.

"And then you wouldn't have been able to dance for the Denver Ballet if you did," Isabella said with a small smile. "We are city girls. Even though sometimes we live in suburbs, we also like to live in downtown. You know, with takeout, noise, and the ability to walk places."

"I don't know, I'm sure you could walk in a small town."

Intrigued, I put the pie cake thing in the fridge, and walked out into the seating area that was connected to the open kitchen.

"You were in the ballet?" I asked, honestly surprised. She did have a dancer's build, but the Denver Ballet was hard as hell to get into.

Sophia smiled softly and nodded. "I was principal for two years, before I decided that breaking my body every day to fight for the same role as twenty-year-olds really wasn't ideal."

"You were principal?" Ford asked, awe in his voice.

"She's a brilliant dancer," Isabella said, pride beaming on her face. "While I had academic clubs in the evening and would play field hockey for school in some club, she was the one doing full-time school, and at least three different dance classes at once. I still don't know how Mom was able to drive us to all our events and practices."

As we handed out drinks and took our seats in the front sitting room, I felt like we could relax ever so slightly. The women were leading the conversation, and I didn't mind. I wanted to know them. Since we had to spend the next three years with them, if not more. Plus, Isabella was Blakely's best friend.

No that wasn't a good reason. I shouldn't know that.

"What other sports did they play?" Dorian asked, leaning forward.

Isabella's eyes tightened for a minute, but I didn't

know exactly what that was about. "Phoebe did soccer and academic clubs mostly."

"I think I've seen pictures of her in soccer," Ford said, smiling. "They were comparing soccer teams with her and Kane," he said, speaking of Phoebe's boyfriend.

"She was really good," Isabella said.

Sophia laughed. "Phoebe tripped over her feet more than often not, but she tried." She winced. "I didn't mean to disparage her. But she would be the first to say it."

"Oh, she *was* the first to say it," Ford said with a laugh.

Isabella continued. "Emily, the second youngest, did swim team, soccer, and volleyball. But she always had friends to drive her around, thankfully."

"Very thankfully considering I don't know how Mom did it all. Especially since Dad wasn't around often." Sophia winced.

I held up my glass. "Well at least we have a common theme here. Dad didn't drive us to sports or after-school clubs either."

"I don't know if I should feel good about that, meaning he didn't value one over the other, or sad that he didn't value any of us at all," Isabella said with a shrug. "Of course, that's plainly evident in what we're doing here, isn't it?"

There was silence for a moment, before Dorian cleared his throat.

"And what about Kyler? I mean, we might as well round out the siblings."

"Kyler did football and was the quarterback of his high school team," Isabella said, pride in every word.

"Really?" I said, looking over at Dorian.

"Well, that's interesting. We're going to have to compare notes. What high school?"

She named a school on the other side of town that we wouldn't have played, and then again, Kyler and Dorian, our other QB in the family, were enough years apart in age that they would never have been in high school simultaneously.

"Kyler also started a band in high school, much to Father's chagrin," Sophia added. "He didn't mind the sports, didn't mind the academics, but dancing and football? Not his favorite."

"Well Kyler's doing a damn good job for a guy who wasn't allowed to practice too often then," Flynn said, and I realized that I hadn't looked up Kyler's band. I should have. But I'd been so focused on the estate, and work, and trying to keep everyone else afloat, I hadn't.

"Caged and Reckless is on tour right now, that's why Kyler isn't here," Sophia said softly.

I blinked and leaned forward. "Wait, Kyler is the lead singer of Caged and Reckless? I love that band. How did I not put that together?"

"Well, looks like our brother is on all of our top ten rotations," Flynn said as he whistled through his teeth.

We all froze for an instant, with Flynn calling Kyler his brother, before we took an awkward drink. We'd been calling the women our sisters out of a forced habit, but for a family that grew up as only brothers, adding another one felt different.

"I don't know how the time stamp of who's going to be at dinner next month or where it's going to be, but most of us live in Denver, so I guess it makes sense it would be us who meet more often," Isabella said.

I nodded. "And my house is big enough for all of us, but we don't always have to be here. I don't want you to feel like I'm taking over."

"That's what I was going to say," Isabella put in. "I was talking to Blakely earlier, and she warned me not to take over like I usually do. But I've always done it with my siblings. I can't help it."

Sophia squeezed her sister's hand. "And we love you for it."

Isabella had so casually dropped Blakely's name, that I swallowed hard, trying not to think too much about the woman that wasn't part of my dreams.

Isabella continued as if she hadn't dropped a rock in the pond that was my mind. "We can make a schedule for dinners in the future because that's what dear old Dad wanted, and we're trying, but this is awkward. And I don't know what else we're supposed to say. We can go over childhood trauma, what we did in high school, what majors we had in college, but I don't know what he wanted."

I stood up, gesturing toward the kitchen. "Dinner is ready to be served, and we can talk over dinner exactly what we want out of this." I looked around at the people who were all my siblings, in one way or another, and nodded tightly. "That man does not own us. We will not allow him to change everything about us. So let's figure out a way to make this work."

"I would love that," Sophia said with a smile. "I don't want the resentment over what that man did to hurt us. I'm sure you are all very lovely, and Phoebe speaks highly of you," Sophia said, gesturing toward Ford. "So let's make this work. Whatever this is."

And as we made our way to the dining room, each bringing something from the kitchen, the awkwardness settled in more.

Here we were, breaking bread with people who we shared DNA with, and nothing felt right.

And maybe we just needed to get over ourselves.

"I forgot to ask if you have any allergies?" I asked, frowning. "I didn't even think to ask, I'm sorry about that."

"It's okay, none of us have food allergies," Sophia said.

Isabella rubbed her arms. "I suppose we should make notes of who has allergies, and who will be in town when. You know, little things that we should know. I don't even know if any of you guys are married. Or have children. Are we aunts?" she asked, her brows raised.

Ford cleared his throat. "I'm married. But you both know that."

"We do, but anyone else?" she asked.

I shook my head. "No. None of us have been fortunate as of yet."

She nodded, her expression unreadable for a moment before she blinked it away. "Same here."

"I wouldn't say all of us are single," Dorian said.

I scowled at him. "Really?"

"I'm just saying, I feel like I need to ask everyone's middle name from now on to make sure that I'm not accidentally dating a sibling." He visibly shuddered.

I choked on my drink. "Are you kidding me?"

Dorian raised a brow. "Don't think it hasn't crossed your mind. We were very lucky. I mean, there are horror stories out there about children who were donation-conceived, finding out that they're married to their sibling. That's just one less thing I'm going to hate Dad for."

"Thank you for that lovely image that is never going to leave my brain." Isabella said it so matter of fact, that we burst out laughing, trying not to, and I did my best not to throw a roll in Dorian's direction.

"Should I ask for Cale's family tree?" Sophia asked, blinking. "I mean, I feel like this is pertinent information."

"His name wouldn't be Cale Cage," Isabella said, her eyes dancing.

I leaned forward. "I take it your boyfriend's name is Cale?"

"Yes, and I should probably ask him…you know, if he knows exactly who his parents are."

"Great, we're going to need a questionnaire from now on for anyone we sleep with," Flynn muttered, and while Sophia laughed, Isabella just shook her head.

"Hopefully it's just the twelve of us." Sophia paused, shuddering again. "*Twelve*."

I held up my drink, knowing that this was probably as

good as it was going to get, at least for the first dinner. "To the twelve of us. And spiting that man."

Everybody held up their glasses, and toasted, and I figured that was at least one way to get the ball rolling.

By the time everybody left and we had a plan in place for the next month, I was tired, grumpy, and felt off.

I just wanted to go to bed and pretend this hadn't happened. But we couldn't.

I had rules, and a life put before me. At this point in my life I honestly thought I'd already be married, maybe a father, starting the next generation of Cages. Instead, I was single, looking at a vast family tree that exploded in front of me, and thinking about a woman that I couldn't have.

The doorbell rang and I frowned, a small part of me hoping it was Blakely.

Which would be idiotic because she didn't know where I lived. Of course, Isabella could have told her. Yes, Isabella could have told Blakely where I lived, and Blakely was here to make everything far more complicated.

No, that would break the rules. Not that I knew what this rule would be.

I opened the door, and cursed at myself for not checking who it was at first.

A blonde woman stood there, in a white suit, and red lips. The suit was form-fitting, a soft blouse that billowed in the wind. I knew she had a six-thousand-dollar purse on her arm, because I had bought it for her, and bright green eyes that shined under the moonlight.

"Meredith."

She leaned forward and pressed a kiss to my cheek, and I did my best not to push her away. That scent of Chanel Chance slid over me, and I knew the only reason I had an inkling of what it was called was because yet again, I had bought it for her.

I took a step back and realized that was a mistake because it looked as if I was letting her inside. She took one step forward, and I blocked her entry.

She raised a perfectly manicured brow and pouted those bright red lips. "Aston. It's so lovely to see you."

"What are you doing here, Meredith?"

"I just wanted to say once again I'm so sorry for your loss. I know you were close to your father."

I thought I had been. But clearly, I hadn't.

"So you said at the funeral," I said through gritted teeth.

"And I wish I could have said more that day, to reach out to you like we once had been. You did so much for me when we were together, you were so caring, and I regret to this day that I broke off our engagement."

I held back a snort at that, because she might have been telling the truth. We had been engaged for nearly a year when she had broken it off, suddenly for no reason. I didn't know if it was for another man, or that she just didn't love me. It had been a blow like no other, and I hadn't wanted to see anyone else until that dance with Blakely.

"Thank you for your condolences, but it's getting late."

She stared into my face, those bright green eyes filled with something I couldn't understand. "Just know if you need a shoulder to lean on, I'm here. I was on my way home from another event, and I couldn't help but drive down your lane like I used to. Muscle memory I suppose. But I miss you, Aston. I hope we can still be friends. And I hope you know I can be that shoulder. Especially with so many changes in your life. What with secret siblings? I couldn't even believe it when I heard."

Oh yes, her gossip circles had run wild with it, but I just shook my head. "Thanks for your condolences," I repeated. "But it's late," I repeated again. "Goodbye, Meredith."

"Well goodbye. And I'll talk to you soon."

I didn't say anything in answer, instead closing the door in her face.

I didn't love Meredith anymore. I didn't want her. I wanted the one woman I couldn't have.

And yet, nothing it seemed went my way.

Chapter Five
BLAKELY

Dear Diary,
  Sometimes plans change. And sometimes they change you.

Stepping into the Cage offices felt as if I were stepping into a new phase of life. I didn't want to speak in metaphors, didn't want to speak in flowery language that confused me, but I couldn't help it. Everything felt different. As if maybe I wasn't making a terrible mistake. Oh, I probably was. Totally. But I didn't have to make that terrible mistake.

And it wasn't as if I had any other choice or anywhere to go.

I waved at the admin, who smiled at me and pointed

toward the elevators. Everybody seemed so happy to be here, something I had noticed the first time, but still couldn't quite believe. I hadn't realized how toxic my previous job had been until I had been able to step out of it and realize that maybe I needed something a little more positive.

This was going to be a change. Something different.

I could do good work here. I had of course heard of the Cages before I had even met Aston and his family through that text message chat. And not just because my previous boss hated them. No, they did great work in our side of business. Not only did they build new businesses and find ways to make them more approachable and ethical, they worked toward environmentally friendly avenues. They were in real estate development, environmental research, and were small business backers. They even had a microloan program that made me smile just thinking about. My previous employer was more into gaining momentum with increasing financing, than anything. And now I'd be able to get my hands into many of the projects the Cages worked on. At least, that's what James had told me. For all I knew they were all liars, and I was going to get right back into the situation I had been in before, except for now I'd be working near a man I had made out with in public. Of course, everything was going to be fine. And I wasn't going to panic.

As I stepped foot onto the floor, I looked up, surprised. James Cage held out a cup of coffee, his perfectly sculpted hair shifting slightly as he tilted his head.

"Good morning. And welcome to your first day with the Cages."

I took the offered mug from him and blinked. "Am I going to expect this kind of service from the bosses every day?"

He snorted and shook his head. "No. You can bring your own coffee or get it from the staffroom. You don't have to pay here, and if you're a person who needs lids because you spill everywhere, let me know."

I looked down at my bag in one hand, and the coffee mug in the other. "I think I can make it to my desk. I really hope so."

He laughed and took the mug gently back from me. "Come on over, and I will show you to your office."

I blinked. "An office? Not a cubical with a desk."

"We treat our employees well here, and you're about to do tons of work, so you're going to need the space for everything. Plus, you'll have a small seating area, and by small, I mean two tiny chairs that could break at any moment. That would be for your meetings. Because you're going to have lots of meetings."

I tried to hold back the excitement because *an office*. "You're really upselling it for me here."

"I try. Come on, let me show you around, and then you're going to meet your team."

"I get a team?" I ask, my stomach twisting into knots. We'd gone over some of my responsibilities but not the details. Apparently, there were *many* details.

"You do. And an administrative assistant, who is currently working with my administrative assistant to get all the paperwork done. Don't worry, we're not throwing you to the wolves right away."

"Maybe tomorrow."

He let out a snort but nerves still hit me. "Your office is three down from mine, and you have this small window. I know it's not perfect, but who knows, you can rise in the ranks. We have to make sure you have something to work up to after all."

I set my bag down and reached for the once again offered coffee cup. "I'm still confused as to why you are the one showing me around. Do you do this for all employees?" I asked, a little uneasy.

James studied my face, before nodding. "I do. Anyone in my department. Same with Flynn, and Aston. It's not just because we accidentally scared you with our group chat one time. And I do apologize."

I bit my lip. "It honestly wasn't too bad. Though I still don't know who was who."

"Eventually you might be able to figure out some of it once you get to know us, but we'll keep it a mystery for now. So we went over some of the responsibilities and duties that we'd want you to have, and our schedule for meetings, but I'm going to go over it again as we introduce you to the staff. Sound good?"

"It sounds great." I took a sip of the coffee, and smiled because it was light and sweet and exactly as it'd tasted that first day after James had shown her around. "Perfect."

"I should be honest to say that I did not remember. My admin did. Sorry."

That made me smile. "Then I'll have to thank them."

"Well you're going to get to know them well, as well as your admin as soon as you start working with them fully. So let's get going."

Out of the corner of my eye I saw Aston at the other end of the hall, speaking to a woman in a gorgeous red pantsuit, as they went over paperwork, and then moved the other way. His back had been to me, so he wouldn't have even noticed me, but I noticed him.

This was going to be a problem if I let it. So I wasn't going to let it. I was going to pretend that everything was fine as always.

"Blakely?" James asked, and I pulled myself out of my reverie, and smiled. "I'm ready."

Thankfully he didn't question it.

It turned out that I loved this place. I had only been working for a few hours, and I already felt as if I belonged.

Garcia, my admin, grinned at me over paperwork. Actually grinned. "It's going to take a while for you to get used to all the ins and outs and acronyms, but I've got you. I'm really excited to see how you can manage this next project of ours."

I nodded, a little nervous because I was being thrown into the deep end, even though this was exactly what I had wanted.

We were going to try to maximize our output for this small business that the Cages had invested in, without losing any staff, or creating panic. It was my job to make that work. Meaning I would work with the Cages themselves, and this small business. On top of that I'd be working on the microloans program.

I had four other people on my team in addition to Garcia. Jeanette, Ruby, JR, and Max all worked with me on projects, but also bounced around with other team leaders so that way they could gain the experience and make sure that we weren't missing key elements in our connectiveness. I liked the fact that the Cages seemed to think about the whole, and not just their small part in isolation.

It was weird to think that after so many years of trying to find ways to improve, and not cheat my way through business like the Howards wanted, I might have found something that seemed far too good to be true.

By the time I finished my first meeting, truly feeling that I had been thrown into the deep end with a small life vest, James stood in my door.

"Doing okay?" he asked, that brow raised.

I swallowed hard. "Sure?"

"Was that a question or a statement?"

"Definitely a question. I can't believe you're throwing me into this huge project on my first day to be honest."

"You're not alone on it. Garcia was working with the previous person in your position and knows what they're doing."

"That's good, because I feel like I'm going to let you guys down."

"If you do, then you'll figure out a way to fix it. And it's not like you're making major decisions on your first day without a safety net. I'm going to have to be the one that approves everything, and you're going to have to really wow me in order for that to happen."

"That's the tough talk I'm used to."

"And I didn't yell or throw anything."

I winced. "I think he only threw a pen once. It wasn't in my direction."

James's face darkened. "Mr. Howard never had much to do with me, other than the fact that he hated my last name. He really had it in for Aston though. Probably because of the whole president thing."

Just hearing Aston's name once again made my stomach tighten, and I ignored it.

"So he's the president of Cage Enterprises."

"That's his title, and I'm the co-chair. Flynn is the vice-president. In the end, we all do the same thing in different departments, so that way we can oversee each other, and not have to be each other's bosses. We get along as siblings, but not always. And our fights don't need to bleed over into work."

"Well that's a novelty."

"I know, right?"

My phone dinged, and I looked down at it, smiling at a familiar name.

> ISABELLA:
> Doing okay? Do I need to save you?

"It's almost lunchtime, so I'll leave you be, but I'm not going to lie and say I didn't see whose name was on your phone screen."

I blushed and shook my head. "I'm sorry. It's not what

THE FOREVER RULE

you think." I paused. "Not that I know what you're thinking right now."

He just laughed, shaking his head. "She's family. Apparently. It's not like it's espionage. You're not spying on us for another company. She's your best friend."

"And I don't usually take personal texts during the day. And frankly, I got fired for espionage before. So I'm not going to do it again. Even though I didn't do it the first time," I blurted.

His face went dark again. "We can fight back you know."

"And you want me to, what…get my old job back? No. I'm sure that he would find other ways to get me out. And I needed to leave. I can't go back to that now that I see how you guys work."

"Well, that makes me happy to hear. But we Cages hate liars. Funny right? Considering what my dad did." He paused and frowned. "I can't believe I just said that out loud."

"I'm not even going to question that, because I know it's not my business."

Even though technically it could have been. Considering his father, the liar, having died had clearly affected my life. But in the end, I wasn't the one hurt by it. No, that was the man in front of me, and the woman currently texting me.

"As for Isabella?" He continued. "You know her more than I do."

Was that a question? No, I wasn't sure where he was going with that. "You're going to figure out who she is soon. That's the whole point of your dinners, right?"

He shrugged. "I guess. But this isn't something you can really prepare for."

"Well she's my best friend. And it is a small world."

"And we're all part of it. Welcome to Cage Enterprises, Blakely. We're really happy you're here. Even though things are a little messy."

I shook my head at that and went back to work after I texted a quick check-in with Isabella. I was fine, and she didn't have to worry about me. At least not here.

When lunch rolled around, I went to the company cafeteria, grateful that the company served food. I hadn't known exactly how I was supposed to deal with my breaks or anything for the day, considering it was day one and I was already working hard on true projects, but Garcia had mentioned that people eat at the cafeteria, they bring their own food, or they go out. The Cages tried to make it a family affair, where you didn't feel like you were forced to eat with your coworker, or work through lunch. Although Garcia had mentioned the bosses usually worked through lunch.

I picked up a salad and sparkling water, and went to go sit in the corner, by the windows of the high-rise, and look at the mountains. They always calmed me, even though they were so vast and immense that it seemed as if it was a little too much.

You felt small and insignificant, at least in the grand scheme of things. And I supposed that only made sense considering where I stood now.

"Is this seat available?" a deep voice asked.

I froze, trying to keep my breath under control. I looked up to see Aston standing there, that dark suit of his molded to his body in just such a perfect way that it worried my senses.

"Yes, I don't really know anyone yet."

He raised a brow much like his brother and took the seat in front of me. He had some form of wrap and diet soda, and I shook my head.

"This is all surreal."

"Pretty much. But I don't always work through lunch like Garcia said."

I blushed. "You heard that?"

"I hear everything," he said with a laugh. "I'm not a growly boss." He paused. "I'm not *your* boss actually," he said softly.

I couldn't feel any eyes on me, as people were talking among themselves, moving in and out of the room. When Flynn came in to sit with another group, I realized that though the Cage brothers sometimes worked through lunch, they also sat with their teams. So maybe this wasn't unusual. And yet I couldn't help but wonder if it was.

"So how's your first day?" he asked, as he unwrapped his sandwich.

"Busy. You guys are sure throwing a lot of trust at me."

After he swallowed and took a drink, he cleared his throat. "James must like what you do. We didn't hire you because of who you are, who you know. We hired you because you're damn good at your job. And James wanted to hire you before. I didn't know that, but then again, things were interesting at that time, weren't they?"

I did my best to hold back my blush, but I knew I had failed.

"I guess things are a little weird. I mean, I don't even know how exactly everything works here, but gossip always runs through businesses, and floors, it doesn't matter where you work. They're going to talk."

"And they do that. They all want to know exactly what's going on with the Cages, but they don't outright ask."

Surprised he'd even said the words, I frowned at him. "And do you want to talk about it with me?" I asked, only being slightly sarcastic.

"Yes. I do."

I blinked, confused. "Why?"

"I have no idea. But that's probably a mistake after all."

"Probably," I said, playing with my salad, no longer hungry.

"If you want to talk about it, about everything that happened, I'd love to hear."

"And I won't burden you with it?" he asked, seemingly taking a step back.

"That's what friends are for," I said, trying to put some lightness in my tone. "It won't be a burden."

He tilted his head and studied my face. "Friends."

"Aston, I can't ruin this," I whispered.

"I know. I know."

"But I'll listen? Because you're not my boss. And maybe *The* Cage needs somebody to vent to that isn't his brothers."

After all, we couldn't be anything more, not when we each had so much going on in our lives. Right?

"Okay then. And I take it your number hasn't changed?" he asked, and I smiled.

"It hasn't. I'm surprised you haven't deleted it from your phone." I winced. "Sorry about that."

"No no. It was rude of me. And maybe that's why we should talk."

Suddenly uneasy, I nodded, as we finished our lunch. Thankfully we only talked about the job, and when his admin came to take him back to the office, an emergency call on the line, I cleaned up my mess and went back to my work. Because this is what I was good at, what I needed to be good at.

I couldn't let anything else get in the way.

When I finished my first day, slightly elated, slightly worried, I made my way back home, texted Isabella that I survived, and immediately called my mom.

"Hello there, baby. How was your first day at work?"

"Great. They're a good company."

"I love that you sound surprised at that. But then again, it's a company that makes millions and billions or whatever however many dollars that is. So of course they're probably corrupt."

I laughed. I couldn't help it. "Or maybe they're okay."

"Maybe. As long as you're safe, my baby."

"I love you, Mom."

"I love you too. Your dad's outside playing with the lawnmower. Do you want me to get him?"

"No, I'll call you both tomorrow. But I have a job. They don't treat me like crap yet. And I think I'm going to like the projects I'm on so far."

"Good. And if you want your dad to beat up that man, you let me know."

For a moment I thought she meant Aston, then I realized she meant my old boss.

"It's okay. He's my past. That whole company is. Let's work toward the future."

"Of course. Now, are you and Isabella going to come over for dinner this weekend?"

"Maybe. It depends on her schedule."

"I know she's so busy with that job of hers. She works far too many hours for being on salary."

"I keep telling her that, but she's stubborn."

"Now that's an understatement. I hope she's doing okay, I know she's going through so much with her family. And isn't that a coincidence that it happens to be the Cages?"

"I'm trying not to think too hard about that. But Isabella's fine with it, and they seem to be fine with it. I'm going to pretend that I'm not in the middle of it."

"That's my girl. You live in your own sense of reality. That will totally be safe."

"I sense the sarcasm."

"I love you, baby. Make sure you eat a real dinner, and not some microwavable thing over the sink. You need your protein and fiber."

"I will, Mom. I love you."

We said our goodbyes, and I stood there, phone in hand, knowing that I was loved. I had two parents who adored me, who would've taken me in if I needed help after not having a job for three months. They would've done anything for me. Same as Isabella.

I wasn't alone.

And yet, I couldn't help but feel a little disconnected.

I sighed, and changed into joggers and a tank top, and made a healthy dinner thanks to my mom because I had been thinking about ordering pizza, and then went to look at my folders that I had taken home, trying to study up on this new job I did not want to ruin.

An hour after dinner my phone buzzed, and I looked down, my stomach once again tightening.

I let it ring one more time before finally answering.

"Aston."

"You answered. I was afraid you wouldn't."

"I was afraid you wouldn't call." I hadn't meant to blurt that, and when he was silent for a long moment, I was afraid I had messed up.

"I wasn't sure I would. I should have called before. But I thought that pushing you away, and everything that wasn't my family, would be safer. And yet nothing feels very safe right now."

"I don't know what that means, Aston," I said honestly.

"I don't think I do either. Let's do coffee."

I froze. "Is that a good idea?"

"No. Not in the slightest. But let's start over. Before everything."

"I don't think it's a good idea."

"It's not."

"Then I guess we should do it?" I asked with a laugh.

"Yes. Because I'm not your boss."

"You keep repeating that as if you're trying to remind yourself that."

"I'm trying to remind the both of us."

Tingles went up my spine, and I knew this was a mistake.

But instead of saying no, instead of hanging up, I let out a breath. "Tomorrow?" I asked.

"Tomorrow. After work?"

"Coffee after work?"

"Well, I'm addicted to caffeine so we should."

I let out a breath. "Okay."

"Good, Blakely. I missed you on my phone."

"Then you should have called," I whispered.

"I should have."

And with that, I hung up, but knew I would see him tomorrow. At work, and then after.

This was totally a mistake.

And yet I was going to make it anyway.

Chapter Six

BLAKELY

Dear Diary,
 What if he's not a mistake? Or what if I'm his?

"I'M SO GLAD THAT YOU HAVE THE TIME TO TAKE THIS walk with me." I reached out and gripped my mom's hand and pulled her out of the way of a passing biker who was not using the bike lane.

"I'm glad you're here too, but let's not get run over."

My mom looked over her shoulder, and I could sense the glare on her face even though I couldn't see it.

"I love riding my bike, I love people who are riding to save the environment, and to help their bodies, and just for fun. But I hate actual bicyclists."

"Same. But if I say that, I feel like a jerk."

"I will be the jerk for both of us. It's like they didn't see the huge sign that bicyclists were supposed to be on the bike path, not the walking path."

She elevated her voice for that last part, and I held back a smile, since another bicyclist nearly ran into us. That guy just flipped us off, and my mother grinned, and flipped him off in return.

"Such a relaxing walk, isn't it?" Mom said with a laugh.

I took her hand, and once again pulled her out of the way of another bicyclist. "Okay next time I'm just going to walk out in the middle of the road. I'm less likely to get hit by a car than one of these idiots in a helmet," I grumbled.

My mom let go of my hand to wrap her arm around my shoulder. "I love you so much. I'm really glad you got my temperament instead of your father's."

I rolled my eyes. "Really? Dad's the calm one. I thought you would want me to be the one who can actually sit through stress-inducing moments, and not want to wring their necks."

"While that's true, it's really good for you to know your worth, and to hit back. Plus, you see your father at CU games. He's a menace."

"Sko Buffs," I said with a laugh, as someone else cheered the same thing back. "It's like a cult."

"No, Denver Broncos fans are a cult. Even though it's been a while since the Elway days."

"I'd much rather be an Avalanche cult member. Have you seen the thighs of hockey players?"

Mom rolled her eyes. "That is true. And they're constantly moving. But the whole skating around on death blades and trying not to lose their teeth? I don't know if that's sexy."

"Not all hockey players lose their teeth."

"Enough of them that there are actual articles about how many teeth they have lost and there are leaderboards. It's a little scary."

"Well I promise I'm never going to date a hockey player. How's that?"

"You know you shouldn't make promises like that. Who knows, the next man you could see could be a hot forward for the Colorado Avalanche, and then you're married and happy and a WAG."

"Yes, because I really want to be a WAG of a hockey player."

"It would be cute though. Because you could always wear cute little coats and scarves and mittens when you're in the ice rink. It would really help with my hot flashes to visit you at the ice rink."

"First of all, most hockey players are going to be far younger than me, because as soon as they hit my age, they're ancient in the sports world."

"Honey, you're twenty-nine. Please stop calling yourself ancient."

"Only in the sports world. I'm barely able to call myself an adult at this point. Don't worry."

"I'm not quite sure about that. You started a new job

with a company that I actually admire. That sounds like an adult move to me."

I held back my wince, but I didn't blame her for the little jab. "I'm sorry it took me so long to get out of that situation."

My mother, a high-powered attorney who had broken through glass ceilings for most of her career, pulling others in her wake, just squeezed my hand. "I adore you with everything that I am. And you are allowed to work for horrible bosses and try to do good things. And you do. I love the microloan programs that you are working with now. And the small businesses that you were trying to nurture before. And while your old boss didn't let that happen completely, I know you tried your best. I'm just really pissed off that you wouldn't let me go at him legally."

I hadn't told my mother everything that had happened behind the scenes, because while they hadn't had to falsify any documents in order to get me fired, the ethics code and propriety statements that I had had to sign when I had been hired meant that there was enough leeway for them to get me out. Because of that dance with Aston. It didn't make any sense, but in the end, I was in a better place. I just hated the fact that they had pushed me down to this point in the first place.

"It's all in the past. I'm working with people that you like, and people that I admire, and we're going to kick Howard's ass in business whenever we can."

"Now that's my competitive daughter."

"I try."

"So, we've talked about work, we've talked about the maintenance issues you've had at your place that your father will go work on."

"I can handle them on my own."

"Let us help. You're our baby girl. It's what we do."

"If he wants to, but I *can* do things on my own."

"I've always known you could, but asking for help is okay."

"I really think you should look in the mirror when you say that."

"Ouch," Mom said with a laugh.

"That's all I'm saying."

"So, anything else we should know about? Anyone in your life that's new?"

I narrowed my gaze at her, wondering if Isabella had mentioned anything. Of course my best friend wouldn't. Just because my mom happens to adore Isabella, it didn't mean that my best friend would break my confidence. However, my pause seemed to have done it all on its own.

"There is somebody. Tell me about him."

We made our way to a food truck, and I bought us both breakfast tacos and coffee. "Eat this and stop prying."

"You're lucky I love you, and that I love egg and potato and bean tacos."

"I went with barbacoa, because eggs are disgusting."

"You love deviled eggs."

"That doesn't count."

"Now tell me," Mom said, and I did my best not to get grease everywhere, knowing that the barbacoa taco was probably going to settle in my stomach later and I was going to regret it, but it was fine.

"It's nothing."

"It's something if you're hiding it. Who is he?"

"It's not really a thing. It's just coffee."

"Coffee. Tell me more."

"There's nothing to tell. It's just coffee and an introduction."

"So a blind date?" she asked, curiosity in her gaze.

I shook my head. "Not exactly."

"You know the more mysterious you act, the more I want to know."

"You know it was so much easier when I was a teenager. I could tell you everything. And Dad of course. You guys have loved me and taken care of me my entire life, and I've always been able to come to you. But it's weird now. Isn't it?"

"Life is never easy. But it can be fulfilling and loving. And you don't have to tell me if you don't want to. I pry because I love you."

"I feel like I should embroider that on a pillow for you," I said dryly.

"You can get it for me for Christmas."

"I just might," I said, before finishing my taco, grateful for the wet wipe that I had picked up from the truck.

"It's a coffee date, and not our first date."

"Oh?"

"Though I'm not sure the first time we had coffee counted."

"You've lost me," Mom said as she rolled up her leftover foil.

I took it from her, and threw everything in the trash, as we continued our walk to the parking lot.

"It's with Aston," I said softly, and my mom froze.

"Aston Cage. The man you danced with?" she asked, and I was grateful that her voice was low. It wasn't like the Cages were famous and people would know their names just by saying it out loud. But it felt a little too public. The Cages weren't in the news anymore. There were countless other things going on in the world, but they had been for a time thanks to the whole secret family thing.

And I didn't want things to get weirder than they already were.

"Yes. Just coffee. I don't know what's going to happen, maybe we're just going to start over so things aren't weird. But I don't know if they're weird at all now. Because it could be fine for him, and I could be the one freaking out."

"So you are freaking out," Mom said softly.

"Maybe? I don't know. I really liked him, Mom." I hadn't meant to say that out loud, and frankly I hadn't even been sure it was true until the words were out. My mom squeezed my hand, her face softening.

"I know, baby girl. But the timing wasn't right. And I still am a little angry that he never called you."

"He had reasons. I mean sort of big scandal reasons," I said, my voice low.

"There are always going to be reasons, but there

should be other ones to remind you that you have a life worth living."

"It's probably a horrible mistake."

"Is he your direct supervisor? Or has any input on your hiring, firing, or paychecks?"

I shook my head. "No. The company is separated enough that Aston has nothing to do with me. Other than the fact that he may be in a meeting or two. James is the only one that is in charge of my career for now."

"So there's that thing. But it would still be dating a coworker. Is that allowed?"

"Yes. And the fact that I looked it up kind of worries me," I said with a groan.

"No, you're being careful. And I adore you for it. Now, it's just coffee, right?"

"Just coffee. Today in fact."

My mom's eyes widened. "What? That's not enough time."

"Excuse me?" I asked, and looked down at my leggings and workout jacket. "You don't think my sweaty self is good enough for a coffee date?"

"I meant enough time for me."

Alarmed, I took a step back. "What? You're not coming."

"No, no. I meant emotionally. I'm going to need to go and vet him again. You know, get my team on the whole background check."

"Mom," I warned.

"I'm kidding. Kidding. Sort of. Your dad would want to do the background check."

"Yes, because he has friends that could actually do that." My father was a retired firefighter who still worked with the stations and crew, just not active—which my mother and I were honestly thankful for. Growing up and being so afraid of what would happen to my father when he was out on call had always been a worry. But between his long shifts, and my mom's equally long hours, they had somehow found a way to raise me, and be the best parents in the history of ever. I never felt any lack of time with them because they were always there when they could be.

"Just be careful, okay? I don't want your future, your career, or your heart to be hindered by anything that the Cages could do."

"They're not evil."

"I would hope not, since they're Isabella's family as well. Now, that's another thing. Would Isabella be okay with you dating her half-brother?"

I grimaced.

My mom continued before I had a chance to answer. "You should tell her. Before the coffee date. No matter what has happened in your life, Isabella has always been there for you."

"I know that. I just also know that things are awkward between them now. There's no hate involved... I think. But things are weird."

"That seems like a very large understatement."

I nodded just before my alarm went off, and I sighed.

"I have to head back and get ready for more coffee."

"Call Isabella. And have fun, okay? If you're willing to give it another chance, he seems like a wonderful man."

"I don't know if he is or not. But I want to find out. And that's what worries me."

"Just breathe. And know that your father and I know people just in case," she said, so seriously, I had really hoped that I saw humor in her gaze.

We made it to our cars, said our goodbyes, and I called up Isabella on my way to my house to get ready.

"This is Isabella," she said on the other line, and I frowned.

"Why are you working today?"

"Yes, I understand, I can give you a call back."

"Is he in the office with you?" I asked, because there was only one *he* here. Her boss. It seemed that Isabella and I were great at finding shitty bosses. At least I had resolved that issue. I just hoped Isabella could.

"You're right, I'll give you a call right back."

I sighed as I got onto the highway, my knuckles a little white because I hated traffic, and it seemed that I was constantly in between eighteen-wheelers.

It only took a few moments for my phone to ring again. I answered quickly, still nervous.

"Hello," I said, and Isabella let out a dramatic sigh.

"Sorry about that, my office door is closed. I'm fine. I just have to fix a couple of mistakes at work."

"Your mistakes?" I asked, though I knew the answer.

"Of course not. And while I would say that I never make mistakes, I can. Not often, but I do."

"I'm sorry, babe. You shouldn't be at work right now."

"I shouldn't, but it's life. I need a paycheck. Now, are you okay?"

"I'm fine," I said, taking my exit. "I just wanted to let you know that I, um, am getting ready to go to coffee with Aston."

Isabella was silent for so long, I had a feeling that I had made a terrible decision. Everything was far too complicated, and I should probably just text Aston back and say no. And walk away.

Only part of me really didn't want that.

"Good," Isabella said after a moment, and I nearly jerked the wheel.

"What?"

"Good. I don't know him. He seems like a nice guy. And it's all weird and awkward when it comes to dinners and the fact that he's my brother and I don't even know him. But you kept thinking about him, and while part of me wanted to hate him for not calling you back, we both know why he didn't."

I sighed and pulled into my neighborhood.

"I know. Maybe it's just going to be coffee. I don't know. But if there was something, I'm afraid that if I let this go, I'm going to regret it. And I already have so many regrets."

"Well don't be me and live in those regrets, okay? And just know that if he hurts you, I am his sister now, so it means I will have more access to him to kill him."

"Don't tell me things like that," I said, laughing.

"It's true though. And if things don't work out with you two, it won't be too awkward, because I don't even know him. That just means I won't have to get to know him."

"See, that means I shouldn't do this. I want you to know your family."

"Well I'll figure it out. You should get to know him too. It's not all about me, you know."

"I'm okay if it was," I said honestly. I pulled into my garage but kept talking on Bluetooth while I sat in the car, not wanting to end the call accidentally. My Bluetooth hated my phone.

"Enjoy yourself. People say he's a good man. And apparently, I'm surrounded by brothers now, and we're outnumbered. I could use someone on the inside. You know, one on my side."

"Now I'm a mole?"

"No maybe a double agent. I like that."

"I really don't want to get into the middle of your family drama, but I feel like I'm already there."

"It's why I love you. Just go have coffee. It's just a stimulant. You're fine."

"I love you."

"I love you too. But, when details come out about your coffee and anything else, we may have to work with some code names or something," she said dryly.

"Deal."

We said our goodbyes, and I quickly got out of the car, and got ready. I only had twenty minutes to shower, sort of do my hair, and put on makeup.

It was just coffee after all, but I still wore linen pants and a cute top. I had chopped off a few inches of my hair recently, so now it went right past my shoulders, and took less time to blow dry, thankfully. I didn't curl it or spend any excess time on it, because I didn't want it to look like I was truly trying too hard. Just maybe trying a little bit.

I slid my feet into sandals, grabbed my bag, and made my way to another coffee shop that was in another suburb of Denver. We weren't going back to Taboo, not near our office. No, this was going to be different. It had to be different.

I pulled into the parking lot, and saw Aston already there, standing outside the coffee place in worn jeans and a Henley. Women passed him and couldn't help but glance at him. But he wasn't looking at any of them. Instead he just stared off into the distance, toward the Rocky Mountains, and I wanted to know what he was thinking.

There was just something about him. And yes, I was making a mistake.

There were so many reasons not to do this. Not to get out of this car, and not to have coffee.

And yet, I wanted to.

So I got out of the car, took a few steps toward him, and when he turned in my direction, his eyes darkening, something twisted inside, something soft, and I let out a breath and smiled, and made my mistake willingly.

Chapter Seven
ASTON

Rule #3: Only lie to your family if #2 is unavoidable.

My breath caught as Blakey walked toward me. I had to wonder why that continued to happen to me whenever I saw her. I should have been used to it by now, but clearly, I wasn't.

The fact that I was there at all after blurting out an invitation meant I was going down a path that wasn't a smart decision for either of us. Yet I wasn't sure if I could have made any other choice.

I knew what I needed to do—focus on family and try to figure out how the hell we were supposed to function in the wake of my father's lies.

And yet I couldn't stay away.

Blakely Graves was a distraction of the highest order.

She was all wrong for me and the complications of this single coffee were insurmountable—work, Isabelle, family, and our one dance. And yet I couldn't pull my gaze away from her.

I was in trouble.

"You came."

I hadn't realized I was going to speak until the words were out, but here we were.

"I was thinking about canceling, so I guess I shouldn't be surprised that you're surprised that I'm here."

"Well then I'm glad that you came." I reached out for her hand and brought it to my lips like I had that first time. We both froze, and I shook my head, letting her hand fall after I gently brushed my lips against her skin. "I still don't know why I do that."

"And I still don't know why my heart flutters every single time. It's very noble of you. And very weird."

My lips twitched. "Noble and weird. I suppose I should put that on my business cards."

"It would probably work," she said with a laugh.

"So, late afternoon coffee?" I asked, wondering what the hell I was doing.

"That sounds delicious to be honest. And then, do you want to go for a walk? I mean, I already went for a walk today, but I could use another one."

I tilted my head. "You did?"

"With my mom. Not with another man." She paused. "I don't know why I said that."

"I suppose that it's good that you didn't have another

date this morning," I said, that odd sense of jealousy dissipating.

"So this is a date," she said softly.

I nodded. "A coffee date. I'm not good with labels, nor am I acting very smooth. But sure, let's go for that walk."

We made our way inside, and I pressed my hand to the small of her back, letting her walk in first. Once again, the action felt normal, as if it was something that I did often. I wasn't sure why the feeling continued as if we'd done this countless times before. Somehow it was as if it were a mix of anticipation and comfort at the same time.

We ordered our iced coffees and made our way to the other side of the café to wait for our order.

"So you're an iced coffee guy?" she asked, a smile on her face.

"It's warm outside, and I felt like it. What, is iced coffee not real coffee?"

"There was this guy that I dated who said black coffee was the only way to drink it. Maybe espresso if you are in Italy. But adding cream or sugar would just desecrate it, and iced coffee? That was just something that was so millennial-coded that it was a disgrace to all coffee."

I snorted. "That sounds like he's compensating for a few more things if he's that adamant about coffee."

"I wouldn't know. By dated, I really meant I went on two dates with him, and then walked away very quickly."

"Where did you meet him?"

"At the gym." She grimaced.

My lips twitched. "Really? The gym? What line did he use on you?"

"What? I met you through a text message. I suppose one should be cliché, the other should be really random."

"I guess so. But for the record, drink your coffee however you damn well please."

"Thanks for the permission." She rolled her eyes and my smile widened.

"So, you met this guy at the gym. What did he say to lure you out to a condescending date?"

"Um, I think he mentioned something about the TV show that happened to be on in the background, and we laughed. I don't really remember much. The only thing that wasn't forgettable about him was his disdain for coffee orders."

I already didn't like the guy and decided to change the subject to something better than her dating past.

When our names were called, we went to pick up our drinks, and made our way outside of the suddenly very busy café. We bumped into a few people, and I noticed the way men's gazes went straight to Blakely. There was just something about her, and it was with immense pride that I stared every single one of those men down.

She was with me. If only for the moment.

Yes, I was in trouble.

"There's a park around here I think, we just have to walk a block."

"No problem, I'll follow you."

"I live a few streets down, but it's not walkable. I used

to come here to do some work on my laptop when I was able to find a seat."

"You worked from home sometimes?" I asked, curious.

She snorted and gave me a look. "Do you really think that he was that enlightened about working from home? No. But I always had to bring work home, and sometimes I didn't want to sit in my house and work until way too late. So I spent Saturday mornings at my laptop in the café. It was like a retreat."

"That sounds like he's an asshole." I sipped my iced coffee with some form of milk and sweetener. I hadn't been too descriptive when I ordered, but it tasted just fine.

"Is working from home something that you're interested in?" I asked, oddly curious.

"Maybe? I really like the office." She paused. "Should we be talking about work?"

"I'm not your boss, Blakely. And we do tend to spend a lot of hours on work."

"It's your name on the side of the building, at least metaphorically."

I laughed. "No we don't have our names plastered on the side of that building."

"That building?"

I winced. "We may have a few buildings in that small town that I mentioned."

"Cage Lake. Well, if you're not going to be plastered on the side of the building, you might as well be in the town name," she said with a laugh.

"I didn't name it. If that helps."

"I don't know if it really does." A smirk played on her lips.

I shook my head and took another sip as we finally made our way to the small park. People were walking around with strollers, little kids on bikes, but it wasn't too busy. It was that time in between lunch and dinner where people were already at their afternoon activities, so it made sense.

"I tend to bring work home because I can't help it, and I know a few of my employees like working from home. Others do this hybrid sort of thing. I don't care as long as the work gets done. Although there are a few things that do work better when you're in the building."

"I get it. I really want to get to know everybody so I can figure out what path will work for me. So I like coming into the office. But I have to say, being able to work in my pajamas? That would be amazing."

And now I was trying not to imagine what Blakely wore to sleep. Well, that wasn't helping.

I cleared my throat so I wouldn't have to adjust myself in public and gestured toward her coffee. "So how's the coffee?"

"Light and sweet, just like I like it. I can barely taste the coffee."

I grinned. "Sounds like a plan. Anything to annoy that man."

"Exactly. Spite is a great motivator."

I nodded. "Tell me about it."

"So, how's your family doing?" she asked.

I raised a brow.

"What? We talked about work, and the other part of you that I know is your family, at least the periphery. And I'm running out of topics without putting my foot in my mouth. Except for the fact that I think I just did that."

I sighed and put my hand on the small of her back again to gently push her out of the way of an oncoming bicyclist. "We're fine. Just working often."

"Isabella said that your first monthly dinner didn't blow up. So that's a good thing."

I tilted my head in acknowledgement. "I'm glad she thought that."

"Your second one's coming up in a couple of weeks."

"It is. Which feels like far away, and yet not far enough."

"Because you're forced into it? Or because it's them."

"The forced scheduling. I don't like what my father did. I don't even know how he did it. The logistics of it alone confuses me. But he hurt my brothers, and my half-siblings. The fact that I had them for nearly my entire life, and I never knew them? Pisses me off to no end."

"I can't even imagine."

"I love my brothers. I love the fact that some of us like working in this business, while I have a chef, a bartender, and business owner as a brother. I have an artist, and now it seems that I have more."

"Like a rockstar," she said with a grin.

I shook my head. "I can't believe that Kyler Dixon is my brother."

"So you know his music?"

THE FOREVER RULE

"Caged and Reckless — I always liked the name. Ironic now." I cleared my throat. "I'm starting to listen to it more. And look at Emily's designs."

"She's really wonderful with graphic and digital art."

"So I can see on her social media." I'd looked up each of my new siblings, wanting to know more, even though I wasn't sure if it felt like a form of stalking or not.

"You haven't asked her?"

"No, I've only met her the once."

Blakely met my gaze, but I couldn't read the question in them. I wanted to learn, though. "You'll figure it out."

"I hope so. Even though it doesn't always feel like I will."

"If we're talking too much about your family, we can stop. I just really don't know what I'm supposed to say."

"It's a big part of my life right now. So I get that." I paused, trying to come up with what I wanted to say. When it came to business, I was the man of words. The man of action behind those words. But these days with family…and now Blakley, I couldn't seem to find them. "What are you looking for, Blakely?"

She paused, and we moved to the side so other walkers could pass us. "What do you mean?"

"This. Us."

She gave me a weird look and I didn't blame her as I didn't know why I was asking the question in the first place. "I just wanted coffee, Aston. I'm starting a new chapter of my life, and for some reason I couldn't say no when you asked."

"I'm glad you didn't say no. I didn't want you to."

We stood there for a moment, as I told myself to stop looking at her. To walk away.

Because my family had rules. Rules set in stone by the father who had lied to us this whole time. But these rules protected my family. And I had to make sure that I wasn't the one who stirred us up anymore. I had a feeling that Blakely would be the one rule I could break.

And that scared me more than anything.

"What is it that you want?" she asked, pulling me out of my thoughts.

"I don't know. And that scares me because I'm not usually the person in the unknown."

"So we finish our walk. And we stop putting so much pressure on ourselves."

"I want to see you again," I blurted.

Her eyes widened. "So maybe that's not pressure."

I leaned down and brushed my lips against hers, needing her taste, needing to breathe. This wasn't our first kiss, but it felt like a first.

Because even in the short time that had passed between when this had occurred the first time and now, we were completely different people. An eon had passed in a moment of time, and it was all I could do not to need her.

I pulled away, and she smiled up at me, her pupils wide.

"Oh."

"Oh."

"So just a walk."

"Just a walk. And maybe one time I can take you out for dinner, and not just coffee."

"I do like coffee."

And so, knowing that this was far too complicated, and against the rules, I slid my hand over hers, and we continued our walk. And I did the one thing that I never did.

I just lived in the moment.

AFTER OUR WALK, I DIDN'T HAVE TIME TO DWELL ON IF and when I would see Blakely again outside of work.

No, because tonight was the Cage family dinner. And not the one interested in the will, but one for an equally obsessive and emotionally manipulating reason.

Thankfully it wasn't at my house tonight, but rather my mother's.

As I walked up the path, my steps faltered. *Mother's.* Not mother and father's. Not my dad's at all. Because he wasn't there anymore.

Had I really given myself time to grieve? No, the answer would always be no. But who was there left to grieve? The man that I had put on a precipice, even though sometimes I hated him, hadn't been that man at all. He had been a liar, a cheat, a manipulator.

No wonder he had been in and out of our lives for so long. Not because he was hardworking or wanted to spend more time in Cage Lake than not. It wasn't that he was doing overseas trips—trips that hadn't happened at all.

It was because he was living a second life, one under the radar that none of us knew about.

And I didn't know the man who had raised me or had claimed to raise me at all.

I had watched them lower his casket in the earth, and I hadn't felt a damn thing. Ice over flesh, and nothing but determination to fix his wrongs.

But how was one supposed to fix the wrongs he was unaware of?

And how was one to fix the wrongs that they made in his stead?

"Is there a reason you're standing out here and looking broody?" Dorian asked as he threw his arm around my shoulder and pulled me in for a hug.

Dorian was slightly taller than me, and wider. Mostly muscle, and all bruteness. Of course, he used that in his business to win over the high-class clientele at his bar.

He owned The Gilded Cage, because of course our family needed to put our name in everything, every fucking thing around us.

"Just thinking about how Mom lives here all alone now, and probably will never visit Cage Lake."

Dorian snorted. "Of course she won't. She is not about that small town life. Dad only ever played at it because Grandpa liked it."

I nodded, wondering if Dorian felt the same about me.

"Is it weird that we spent summers away in the mountains, and living a completely different life?"

"I wouldn't necessarily call it completely different. It was just our life."

"I don't know, running barefoot in the woods, cutting open our feet, and letting our dad put Band-Aids on our wounds felt a little more idyllic than anything."

"You must remember a different summer than I did," Dorian said dryly. "Because Dad wasn't the one that bandaged our wounds. You were."

I frowned. "How is that even possible? I'm only four years older than you."

"Yes, and in those four years you got to be the big brother."

"And I'm only two years older than the twins," I corrected, speaking of Flynn and Hudson.

"Yes, and five years older than James, and seven years older than Theo." Dorian frowned. "You know, I can rattle off those ages quite quickly, but I'm going to have to figure out the family tree with the others."

"Did I hear childhood age math?" Theo asked as he came forward and wrapped his arm around my other side. I was trapped between my two outlandish brothers.

"Is there a reason that you're sandwiching me?"

"Because we're going to march you into that house for dinner. If we have to go, you have to," Theo explained. "Now, are we going over ages again? I don't like the fact that I'm continually being pushed down the ladder of ages."

"Ford is still the baby of the main siblings." Dorian

paused. "Okay, that sounds kind of asshole-ish to the others."

"Yes, because calling them half-sibs probably isn't the best thing to do," Theo answered.

"Let's not say that in front of them, because I'm pretty sure that it's going to be Phoebe that kicks our asses," I said dryly.

"Or Phoebe's boyfriend. Who happens to work with Ford. Oh, my God, why did Dad have to try to repopulate the Earth?" Dorian pinched the bridge of his nose. "He makes everything so complicated."

"Of course he did—he's Dad," Theo said, not bothering to explain that comment. And then they did indeed march me into the house, not bothering to let me finish my conversation. Or my downward spiral of thoughts.

Flynn and James were already inside, whiskey in hand as Mother stood between them, glaring at them as she spoke. She was probably dressing them down for something, but who knew what it was going to be.

I looked around, frowning when I realized that we were missing two people. "Where's Hudson and Ford?" I asked, my voice barely above a whisper. But of course, my mother had ears like a bat.

"Hudson is stuck in that God-forsaken town with a rockslide of some sort. So he couldn't even make it to see his own mother," Melanie Cage complained.

Considering my mother's favorite phrase was "I don't mean to complain," it was a little ironic.

Then her words hit me, and I moved forward. "Is he okay? Did anyone in town get hurt?"

We had a responsibility for the town because we owned so many of the businesses and the land. We weren't mayors or responsible for any of the actual political aspects of the town, though I had a feeling Hudson might be part of the town council. Mostly because the town wouldn't have it any other way. While it wasn't in the bylaws, the town still required us join in on the planning and upkeep of the town. We never wanted to mess with the small-town politics that came with our responsibilities, so we always acquiesced.

Mother cleared her throat. "He said he was fine, no one got hurt. But I didn't ask much. I'm just disappointed he's not here."

"It's not like he can fend off a natural disaster," Dorian said, and my mother's face brightened.

That was Mom. Every time she saw her baby, she couldn't help but love him. And I had no idea why it was Dorian. He wasn't the oldest, wasn't the youngest. It was like once she got to him, she decided he would be her favorite, and the rest of us would all wait for the scraps. Not that I minded. I didn't need much from Mom these days.

"And what about Ford?" Theo asked. Flynn tried to do a cutoff motion with his hand, wincing, as James turned his back.

Mother lifted her chin. "Ford is with the other family. Because apparently, his priorities have shifted."

I let out a sigh, annoyed at the familiar refrain. "He's *married*. Of course he has responsibilities with his family."

"Hmm." She gestured toward the bar. "Make your

drinks, and then we'll have dinner. Chef says it should be soon. We're having roast beef, but no extra starches."

She moved away, and left us behind to stand there, wondering why the hell we were even here.

"So, dinner's going to be fun," Dorian said dryly.

"At least Mom likes you," Flynn muttered into his drink, and James choked.

"We're not supposed to say that out loud," James said with a mock whisper.

Theo just shook his head and poured the rest of us drinks. I ended up with two fingers of whiskey and lifted it to my lips.

"Cheers," I muttered, and downed half of it.

"That's a sipping whiskey, dumbass," James muttered, but I didn't care. I was going to need a lot more alcohol to get through the evening.

"So, how was your date?" James asked, and I nearly dropped my glass.

"What?"

"A date? You mean he got out of the house?" Dorian asked, hand on his chest.

"I for one, am shocked," Theo teased, and I flipped them both off.

"I have no idea what you're talking about," I lied.

"You're going to have to lie a lot better than that," Flynn put in, shaking his head. "Especially when you go on a date with someone that we know."

I scowled, glaring at the two brothers I worked with. "Are you serious? Are you having me stalked?"

James scowled right back. "I overheard you. Nobody

else did, thankfully. So of course I want to know how it went."

"And then he told me, of course," Flynn put in, and gestured toward our other brothers. "And we needed to bring you into this. I'll text Hudson and Ford later so that they know."

"Thank you, I appreciate it," Dorian said with a wink.

I sighed. "Why did I have so many brothers?"

"I should really text Kyler too then," Flynn added.

I snorted. "You should. In fact, we should really make a whole group chat with the twelve of us. It'll be unhinged."

"I'd have to turn off notifications at that point," Theo said, shaking his head. "So, who are we dating?" he asked.

I shook my head, not wanting to answer. At their stares, I gave in. "We're not dating. It was coffee."

And a kiss I couldn't stop thinking about.

"Blakely, my new hire," James said, although there was a bit of ice to his words.

I looked up at him, confused. "What is with the tone? She doesn't work for me. It was just coffee."

"*For now.* I see the way that you two are around each other. And while it's not ethically wrong, it is a shit storm. You know what Dad always said, remember the rules, and don't mix business with pleasure."

"First, fuck off. Second, are we really going to worry about that certain rule," Dorian said, surprising me.

"You know I can answer for myself," I said dryly.

But Dorian continued anyway. "You shouldn't have

to. Fuck Dad's rules. He didn't live by them. As is evidenced by twelve kids."

The others started bickering, and I just stood between them, wondering if any of us were grieving.

We could just walk away, let everything go to a trust, and not deal with any of the mess that he had left behind, but part of me didn't want to do that. I wanted to get to know the people who had been fucked over just as much as we had. I just didn't like the fact that there were strings that came with it.

"You're not going to say anything?" Theo asked, his voice soft.

"You guys are saying enough for me. And no, I don't know if I'm going to date Blakely. It was just coffee." And yet I had been the one to say I wanted more. Only the moment I'd stepped away, I'd heard my father's voice in my head and getting away from his words had always been a problem for me—even when I lied to myself it wasn't.

"Just don't mess it up, okay?" James asked, his voice serious. "I'm not saying you will, or would do it purposely, but I like her. And she's a good employee, and she's Isabella's friend. It's just a catastrophe waiting to happen."

"Because I'm just like Dad, The Cage. Because I'm going to fuck it up just like he did?" I asked, the malevolence in my tone surprising me.

James didn't react, but the others stared at me as if I'd lost my damn mind.

"No one is saying that."

"The world is saying that. Every one of our business contacts think I'm going to be the one that steps into Dad's shoes. And they don't even know half of the shit he's done. So you're right, maybe I will be the one to fuck things over like he did."

"That's not what I'm saying," James said.

I shrugged, setting my drink down. "You know what, give Mom my regards. I'm not in the mood to deal with her attitude anyway. I have enough for all of us."

"Aston," Flynn said as he came forward, and I took a step back.

"No, I'm just not in the mood."

"I wasn't meaning to start a fight," James put in.

"No, you were just warning me off Blakely."

"Because I don't want either one of you to get hurt."

I snorted, and then grabbed my things. "I'm out. I have shit to do."

"Running away from the problem? Maybe that is a Dad thing," James whispered.

Dorian whistled through his teeth, as Flynn scolded him. But I let the remark slide. Because it was true.

Instead, I pulled up my phone as I walked outside, leaving them behind. If I was going to be reckless, I might as well go all in.

ME:
What are you doing?

BLAKELY:
Reading. Paperwork mostly.

> **ME:**
> Can I come over?

> **BLAKELY:**
> ...

> **BLAKELY:**
> Yes.

And then I looked at her address, nodded, and figured I'd make another mistake. Following in my dad's footsteps just like James thought I would. I might as well enjoy my time on the way to Hell. All on the path to breaking every rule along the way.

Chapter Eight
BLAKELY

Dear Diary,
I have no idea what I'm doing.

I WAS DONE SAYING THIS WAS A MISTAKE AS THAT would just be repeating myself. And maybe it wasn't one after all. The moment that I texted my address, it felt as if I had had an out-of-body experience. So now here I was, frantically cleaning my house, and wondering why I had invited Aston over.

No, that wasn't exactly how that had happened. He had asked to come over, and I was freely giving in.

This didn't mean anything other than he would be in my house, but it meant more than that. It had to.

I swallowed hard and tossed my throw pillows on the couch and tried to make my blanket look casual on the corner, but I wasn't a decorator. I had no idea what I was doing. I ran to the bathroom and pulled my hair out of the bun I had put it in when I had gotten home, and fluffed out my hair, and tried to look somewhat normal. I hadn't bothered to take off my makeup from earlier in the day, so there was at least that. I slid on some lip balm, put my bra back on, and decided he was just going to have to deal with the real me.

The same linen pants, but I'd put on a double tank top with a cardigan. And every mess that I made. Including this evening.

When my doorbell rang, I nearly jumped out of my skin, grabbed my phone so I could turn off the alert that someone was at my door, and did my best not to run to the front door. It still felt as if I was doing this whole adult thing wrong.

When I opened the door, he stood there, in all of his six-foot-something broad-shouldered, thick thighs glory.

The fact that I was even thinking about his thighs told me that I needed to get a grip.

And not a grip on Aston himself.

He stood there in dress pants and a button-down shirt, looking so poised and professional, and a far cry from what I currently looked like.

His gaze swept mine.

"I feel like one of us might not be dressed for the occasion." And then I blushed, wondering exactly what this occasion could be. He raised a brow, and I swallowed hard, trying not to let him see more.

"I just left a horrendously annoying dinner with my family, and Mother always makes us look slightly presentable."

"So you're saying I don't look presentable?" I teased, before taking a step back.

"You're just letting me walk into that one, aren't you?" he asked dryly.

"I try. But why did you leave your dinner? Was it terrible?"

He shrugged, his gaze going around my place, and I tried not to feel slightly awkward about it. I had made a decent living and had only gone through some of my savings after losing my job. But it wasn't like a house a Cage would have. We clearly had grown up in different tax brackets.

I had grown up in a normal household, at least as normal as anyone could be this day and age. I had gotten student loans, had made my way through college, and now was here, trying to earn a living. It wasn't grand, but it was home. And I wanted it to stay that way at least for a little bit longer.

"I think I might've overreacted with my brothers. And I just needed to get out of there."

"That doesn't sound like you," I said softly.

"And you can tell exactly how I would react already?" he asked, and he didn't sound condescending, he sounded honestly curious. Of course, he was right. I had no idea who he truly was. In essence, I had no idea who I was to this man, nor did I truly know him at all. He had been a figment in my mind, something that began with conversations in which we've been strangers, into something far bigger in my mind than it was in reality. And that was something that I needed to understand, to cling to.

I wanted to know who he truly was, beyond who I thought he was. I wanted to know why every time I thought about what we could have had, my heart ached. Or why I couldn't stop thinking about him—even when I knew it would be better to walk away.

"I didn't mean to overreact. We were just talking about nothing and everything, and then as usual, someone said something stupid, and somebody else overreacted. It's just the fact that I'm usually not the overreacting one."

"Maybe it was your turn?"

"Maybe. Or maybe I just feel a little off kilter."

His gaze met mine, and I swallowed hard. Why was he here?

"So you didn't eat then," I blurted. "I can make you a sandwich."

He smiled. "You don't need to make me a sandwich, Blakely."

"You didn't eat, let me feed you. Please?" I asked, wondering why I was begging him to let me feed him. I had no idea what my brain was doing, but I was just going with the motions. Whatever motions those may be.

"Okay, I could eat. Honestly, I don't know why I left before dinner was served. Mother usually has a decent roast beef."

"So your mother cooks?" I asked, wondering about the tone in his voice. Of course, I really only knew about the other woman from Isabelle's single meeting. And it hadn't been pleasant.

"My mother doesn't cook," he said, that deep chuckle from his chest oddly attractive.

"Oh. But I thought you said..." I trailed off, and he shook his head.

"My mother has a great chef. Or she has had a few great chefs in her lifetime. She gets tired of them after a while and fires them."

I scrunched up my nose as I pulled out ingredients for a sandwich. "Well, I do have deli meat roast beef. How about that?"

"That sounds perfect. You really don't need to make me one."

"No, I'm doing it. Just going to have to get over it."

"Okay, if that's what you want."

"That's what I want," I said after a moment.

"So, what was it like growing up with a chef?" I asked, feeling only slightly awkward.

"Not as fancy as it might sound," he said with a chuckle.

"I'm sorry, but the fact that you call your mom Mother in that upper crust tone, and you have a private chef? Sorry. You're a little higher class than you're trying to have me believe."

He rolled his eyes. "Okay true. But it wasn't always like that. The family only started making the money that they're making now recently. At least in the last twelve years or so."

"So you didn't grow up with that silver spoon?"

"Not really. I mean, we had the town, but that wasn't exactly how it sounds."

"Yes, because having a town named after you isn't unique at all."

I thankfully still had a baguette, and cut it in half, and pointed to the condiments. He tapped the mayonnaise and mustard, and I was surprised because it was what I liked too. Most people in my life happened to hate mayonnaise, so this felt like a perfect match. Or maybe I was thinking too much about condiments.

I quickly finished setting up the sandwich and pushed it toward him, and he just shook his head.

"What?" I asked, slightly crestfallen.

"I can't believe I just made you make me a sandwich."

"You didn't make me. In fact, I'm making you eat one. Can I get you something to drink?"

"Water's fine." His stomach growled, and I swore he blushed. "Okay, thank you. I'm really in need of this sandwich."

I poured two glasses of water, because I was suddenly parched with him at my kitchen island, and stood across the granite with him, as he ate.

"So, town?" I asked.

He wiped his mouth with his napkin and shrugged. "The story goes that my great-grandfather helped found the town. Although, that story doesn't really make sense in terms of actual time and history."

I laughed. "Okay, so someone rewrote history."

"I'm pretty sure what is now Cage Lake was called something else. My brother Hudson would know more since he lives there full time."

I wanted to ask more about that, but I held back, wanting to hear about Aston himself.

"But the town was fully incorporated, rather than what it had been before with my great-grandfather."

"And he put his name on it?"

"Of course he did. The lake itself was manmade. And it actually helped some of the irrigation and ice flow. When the highway was put through the mountains, it changed the way that the natural formations worked, and the lake was a good idea. Again, you should ask Hudson, I'm not quite sure exactly how all that works."

"Says a man who helps build environmentally clean architecture."

"I help fund it, and I help with the paperwork. I also help with the overall designs, not so much the structural engineering. That is why I hire others."

"Well that's good to know at least."

"Are you going to tell me you know all about the structural engineering?"

I shook my head. "Not even the slightest. Although I'm doing my best to learn a little bit of everything with these microloans program."

"That's James's baby, and I'm proud of him for it. He's kicking ass. And you are going to help make that even better."

"That's the goal. Now, go back to that town. I'm intrigued."

"There's not much to it. We spent our summers there. I'm now realizing that we might've spent our summers there so that way Dad could say that he was working in town, but really he was spending time with his other family."

I nearly choked on my water and shook my head. "I hate the logistics of that."

"I have no idea how he did it. Other than the fact that he wasn't around as much as I really thought he was. He was just so big in my mind, that I didn't realize that many of his business trips weren't actually business trips."

"And Isabella had always said that he was absent often. I guess nobody realized how absent." I didn't want to divulge into Isabella's truth any more than that, so I just gave him a sad smile and he nodded, seeming to understand.

"We didn't live in a mansion, in fact, I had to share my room with two brothers."

"Of course you did. But there are many of you."

"Seven of us. At least in the house. The fact that my mother, a woman who perpetually didn't like children, and was ice cold to most, had seven children still astounds me."

I winced. "Oh, that's not nice."

"Not even a little. We didn't have nannies, we had Mother. And yes, she makes us call her Mother. Dorian gets away with calling her Mom, and I bet the others do as well. I just got in the habit of it, and frankly, I do sometimes add that little accent to it just to annoy the fuck out of her."

The curse surprised me, and I beamed. "Oh, look at that. See you don't always follow the rules."

Something slid over his face, but I didn't know what exactly that meant.

"I try to follow those rules," he whispered. Then he cleared his throat. "The town is far west of Denver, up in the mountains, but not the high hot elevations where the side of the mountain will make part of the area perpetually dark."

"I've driven by those places, where there's always snow no matter what."

"Except during fire season," he said with a shudder, and I joined in, remembering the fires that had crested over the mountains throughout the years.

"Well, considering that Isabella and her family grew up east of the Colorado Springs suburbs, and moved up north later, it sort of makes sense that you guys didn't cross paths."

"I guess so. Still though, the miles that man must have put on his car." He rolled his eyes as he said it, but there was still an anger there.

"Well, I'm glad that you didn't have that silver spoon, even though you do have a town named after you."

"Not after me. After my great-grandpa, the land baron."

I laughed at that. "You should look more into that history."

"I should. I was too busy looking toward the future, trying to make sure that I could bring the company to this new age along with my brothers. Not everyone wanted to follow in my dad's footsteps, at least in terms of work."

He scowled a bit, and I had to wonder exactly what footsteps he was thinking about in that moment.

"We were pretty normal. I don't know if we're too normal right now," he said dryly.

"No, I don't think secret families are too normal. I, however, was blessedly boring and normal," I put in, wanting to steer the topic away from the hard parts, at least for now.

"I would love to hear about boring and normal."

I shook my head. "My mom's a lawyer, Dad's a firefighter."

He raised a brow. "Really?"

"Really. They worked a lot, but between all of my after-school programs and sports and everything, it really worked out that I could see my family often, and yet they were out of the house more often than not."

"And you're still in touch with them?"

I nodded. "I had that walk with my mom this morning. And I have dinner with them often. I'm very blessed with my parents. I'm an only kid, which sounds a little shocking with your eleven siblings."

He shook his head. "I could barely keep up with the seven before," he said dryly.

"Totally. I can't even imagine."

"So, blessed and boring. Any ex-boyfriends I should worry about?" he said, surprising me with the straightforwardness.

I swallowed hard. "No. I had two serious relationships in my early twenties, but they didn't go anywhere." I shrugged as I said it, and honestly, I didn't feel anything. They had both been nice guys, but nothing had happened. I didn't feel that heat. Nothing like I felt right now. And that should worry me.

"That's oddly surprising," he said, as he stood up and took the plate to the sink. He just raised that brow at me, as he washed his dishes and set them in the drying rack. I stared at him, wondering why this felt so domestic. And normal.

"One ended after college because he wanted to go to grad school on the east coast, and I wanted to stay here. And the other was right out of college, and we just didn't suit."

"Did he want you barefoot in the kitchen making him a sandwich?" he asked, that smirk on his face.

This time I rolled my eyes. "Pretty much actually. He wanted marriage and babies, and he didn't want marriage and babies with me. And honestly, I didn't want that with him so I wasn't too heartbroken when we broke up."

"So no current boyfriends."

I scowled at him. "I've kissed you how many times now? No, no serious boyfriends at all. But what about you?" I asked, softly. "Is there someone I should worry about?

Other than him of course.

He shook his head. "I don't share. And I don't cheat. I was in a serious relationship for most of my twenties, and I was engaged."

I choked on my own spit and blinked at him.

"What?"

"Yes, I was engaged. Meredith was a wonderful woman, and in the end we didn't suit."

"Oh." I wasn't sure what I was supposed to say. I hadn't known he had been engaged. Although, when was I supposed to have figured that out. "Can I ask what happened?"

He shrugged again, and yet I wasn't quite sure if he was as nonchalant as he was trying to seem.

"She broke it off." He said it so succinctly, that it took me a moment to catch up.

And something inside of me twisted, just ever so slightly. As in the other woman had walked away. And was he still thinking of her? No, I couldn't let that get in my head, and yet, there it was.

"But I would've done it soon anyway."

I felt like my emotions were all over the place in this moment. "Oh?"

"She was nice. Good at her job. Pretty," he said, that humor in his gaze again, and I narrowed my gaze at him.

"Oh really?"

"Really?"

"I don't know if I should be hearing about other pretty women while you're in my kitchen."

He leaned forward and brushed a strand of hair from my face. "But she didn't make me lose my mind."

I swallowed hard at the low growl of his voice.

"She didn't make me forget that I'm in a fucking meeting and all I wanted to do was text you."

"Oh," I whispered.

He smiled then, the heat in his gaze intoxicating. "Yeah. Oh."

And then he lowered his mouth to mine, and everything went blank. His hands were gentle on my face, but his kiss was anything but. I couldn't breathe, couldn't think—and I didn't want to.

Instead, I kissed him back with the same ferocity, all doubts about what could be firmly pushed out of the window.

And then he was gone—standing two feet away from me, chest heaving.

"That's why I can't think," he growled.

"I know the feeling." I wasn't sure what else to say.

"I'm going to go. Not because I don't want more. But because I don't want to fuck this up. And I tend to fuck these things up."

Frowning, I moved forward. "Aston…"

"I already screwed things up with us once, so I'm going to go. Not forever, but just so I don't fuck you against that counter and lose my damn mind."

I pressed my thighs together, my eyes wide. "That's… that's a picture."

"Yes it is. One that I want. Sometime. But first? First we take the time so I don't screw it up." And before I could say anything to that and dig deeper into the whys of it, he left me with one more bruising kiss…and then he was gone.

Out of my kitchen. Out of my home.

But definitely not out of my memories.

And I hoped…not out of my life.

Chapter Nine
ASTON

Rule #1: There is no such thing as forever.

As the eldest of the family, it was time for me to take charge. At least in the essence of trying to move forward. Speaking with Blakely as I had, knowing that I was making moves that I normally wouldn't, reminded me that I at least needed to try.

That was how I found myself on the other side of the table with Isabella.

I had opted for a small diner that served comfort food, and a place that I liked to relax. It wasn't a fancy overbearing place, and it wasn't a loud place with children running up and down the aisles. I figured Isabella wouldn't mind it, but the problem was I didn't know her. I didn't want to alienate my new sister, and I had been afraid to even ask Blakely where I should take Isabella for lunch, because that felt as if I were getting insider

THE FOREVER RULE

information. Then again, I needed that insider information. So I had texted her.

> **ME:**
> Where should I take Isabella for lunch?

> **BLAKELY:**
> That's an odd way to say hello.

I had grimaced, and quickly typed.

> **ME:**
> Good morning. It was great seeing you last night. Now, where should I take your best friend for lunch where she's not going to hate me.

> **BLAKELY:**
> I was just kidding with you. And lunch with Isabella? That's so sweet. And she doesn't mind anywhere. Honestly, food that she doesn't have to cook herself is always a win.

> **Me:**
> So nothing pretentious.

> **BLAKELY:**
> LOL. Probably not for your first sibling date.

> **Me:**
> Don't make it weird.

> BLAKELY:
> Oh, I'm going to make it weird. I'll see you on Monday?

I had swallowed hard, wondering what the hell I was going to do with myself and her.

> ME:
> Yes. Monday it is.

And that was how I found myself in front of Isabella, both of us seated across from each other in a booth, feeling awkward as hell.

"Thank you for joining me for lunch," I said, tapping my fingers on the table. Isabelle's gaze went straight to the motion, and I stopped.

Now I was developing a nervous tick about this family. It seemed about right.

"I was honestly surprised that you asked me for lunch. And since it's just the two of us, I guess it doesn't count toward our monthly meal."

I grimaced. "Do any meals you eat with the siblings you knew about your entire life this month count?"

"Touché."

"Here's the deal..." I began.

Isabella just grinned. "I was waiting for that."

I continued as if I hadn't heard her. I liked her biting tone. Honestly, it reminded me of Flynn's when he was in a mood, and myself for that matter.

"I'm seeing your best friend, and we're newly found siblings. I think we should just deal."

Isabella spluttered in front of me and shook her head. "You're *seeing* Blakely? That's the label you're using?"

I shrugged, knowing that label might not have been correct, but it was something. I wasn't completely jumping off the deep end. Or maybe I was. "I want to see her, and we have gone out. I'm not quite sure what other label I should be using. And frankly, that's a discussion Blakely and I need to have."

Isabella smiled so sweetly, I had a feeling I said the right thing. "You're right. I am usually very bad at those conversations, so more power to you."

"So you're not seeing anyone?"

"No. There's really not time for boyfriends and dating with my current job."

And that seemed like a decent segue. "From what you've said, and what Blakely has mentioned—"

She cut me off. "So you and Blakely talk about me?"

"There really is no good way to say this. Because if we never mentioned you, it would feel like the elephant in the room of not doing so because it is a very large part of our lives. And if we did talk about you, it would feel like talking about you behind your back, wouldn't it?"

"I don't like the fact that you have answers for everything. And yes, I'm being obstinate because I'm annoyed about this situation. I'm not always annoyed with you. I promise."

That made me smile. "Well that's always a good way to start." The waitress came over, and we ordered two different types of closed sandwiches with fries and handed over the menus.

"Before we get into the other awkwardness, I was surprised you chose this place. I've driven by it a few times, but I've never been."

I shrugged. "I used to sit in that booth over there with my homework after school and do as much as I could before I had to go home."

"I'm almost afraid to ask what your childhood was like."

"It wasn't terrible. I can only complain about the way Dad treated us, and my mother for that matter. But it wasn't terrible. Everything was always loud at the house, because there were so many of us, and I just wanted to pretend I was an only child for a minute."

She nodded, understanding in her gaze. "As the eldest I get that. And honestly, I thought my house was loud with the number of siblings."

"Yes, the numbers are a little worrying."

Her lips twitched.

And it felt as if we'd been speaking for hours, though it hadn't been that long. We were jumping from topic to topic, speaking of numerous things as if we'd known each other for years. The comfort in the interaction should have been unsettling but it wasn't. And perhaps that was the unsettling part of the entire situation.

"Seriously though, do you like your job?" I pressed.

She sighed. "I don't know if it's any of your business, but no. I hate it. I work too many hours, I deal with too many people who have no idea what they're doing, so I have to do their work for them as well. And if I'm not perfect, I get yelled at, and I'm just not in the mood to deal with it anymore."

"Have you been looking for another place of employment?" I asked, honestly curious. From what I could tell, Isabella was competent, and was steadfast in protecting her family. I would have assumed she'd have found a job that she liked. But then again, not everybody liked their jobs. I was lucky in the fact that I was born into mine, and I knew I was privileged.

"I've tried before, but starting over is hard. First I tried to have an interview, and then my sister was attacked."

I froze, trying to remember if I had actually known that.

"What?"

Isabella grimaced. "I thought you knew because of Ford. Phoebe? She was attacked. Twice actually." She shuddered. "I'm just glad that Kane was around both times to help her."

I rubbed my temple, annoyed with myself. "I knew that. At least in the periphery. I try not to think about Ford's job too much because it scares the shit out of me. I just hadn't put two and two together that Phoebe was your Phoebe." I paused. "Our Phoebe."

Her eyes warmed at that, and she looked far less tired when she did. "Our Phoebe. This is going to take a long time to get used to."

"And we're going to fuck up a lot," I muttered.

"Oh yes, we are. I fight with my siblings all the time, because it's what we do. And I love them."

"Same with my brothers. We don't have the deep fractures in our relationships that some large families have. I think it's because we bound together against my mom's attitude and our father's ineptitude."

"My problem is I really liked my mom. She was wonderful to us. And the way we grew up, Dad was in and out of our lives, not just for work, but because we thought they separated. It's how they had put it."

I shook my head, astonished. "Seriously?"

"Seriously. So in my mind, my mother was a strong single mom who was working to keep us all afloat. And I don't even know if that's true."

"So Dad wasn't supporting you guys at all?"

"I don't know. I can't talk to my mom about it, because she's mourning a man that I apparently didn't know. It's not like I haven't met our father. He ate dinner with us, he was there on Christmas morning."

"Busy day since he was also there at our Christmas mornings," I said dryly.

"Because he always had to work and would leave early. So I don't know the man that you know. And I didn't know my mother this whole time."

"Sadly my mother knowing about a secret family and being icy cold about it doesn't really change my view about her."

Isabella grimaced as the waitress set down our food. We said our thanks, and we each picked up a fry, playing with the edge of it. I didn't even think Isabella realized that we were doing the same movement, and I had to wonder exactly how genetics worked.

"I'm sorry that you had to deal with that woman. Because I had an amazing mom."

"I'm sorry that this broke your view of her."

"And I think that's what I hate the most. I never liked Dad. And that's a horrible thing to say about a dead man who happens to be your father."

"Dad was an asshole. I don't like him very much either."

"But we all had our certain relationships with him. I went into accounting with large corporations because my dad helped me with numbers when I was little, and everything just clicked. And it was all a lie."

"Not all of it. We have to believe that. If it's all of it, then nothing makes sense."

"And that's the problem. Nothing does make sense. But then again, this is a very weird situation."

"I can't believe that I didn't really know it was Phoebe that was hurt that whole time," I said, bringing me back to the beginning of our conversation.

"And the fact that Ford, a man that I met, happens to be my brother as well? I always thought he looked familiar, but I didn't realize that it was because all of you guys have Kyler's eyes."

I sighed, and bit into the fry. "You know what's weird, I really like his music."

Isabella beamed. "He's brilliant. I can't believe that he's going on tour and has albums. He's really making something of himself, and it's so strange because he's my baby brother."

"Has the scandal broken in his circles yet?" I asked, honestly worried.

She shook her head. "Not really. I think there were a couple of articles, but now they've moved on to a new thing. Kyler doesn't share most things. He puts on a smile, pretends he's a lazy musician, but I don't know everything. I wish I did."

"Well, maybe he'll confide in a brother."

She scowled at me, and I just laughed.

"I was kidding, but you never know. I grew up in a house of just boys. So I feel like Kyler's situation is probably completely different than the rest of ours."

"Oh no I didn't even think about that. He was stuck with all of us girls, and now you guys outnumber us."

"Pretty much," I said with a laugh, and we continued to eat, discussing each of our siblings in turn. It felt like something had changed, as if maybe we weren't adversaries, but allies in this war against history and family.

"Back to your job. So Phoebe getting hurt made you not look?" I asked, trying to get the image of Phoebe hurt out of my mind.

"I missed a big interview, and then it set me back for a bit. And even before that, I was ready to start the process, and then Sophia retired from ballet, and wanted to open a dance studio. And I ended up having to stay on so that way I could help her co-sign."

My eyes widened. "That was selfless."

"It is what family does. And in the end, I didn't even have to truly co-sign because Sophia did really well for herself, but it's what family does. And then Kyler got a little bit bigger, and I wanted to be able to have the time off to travel, and starting over would've been hard, and then Emily was looking for jobs, and happened to get an interview at the same place that I was, and I knew that they weren't going to be able to hire both of us, so I stepped back."

"And you still work in a job you hate," I said softly.

"Pretty much."

"You'll work with us," I said, finally blurting what I had been trying to put into words this entire time.

She froze, her fry halfway to her mouth. "I don't need charity."

I shook my head. "It's not charity. It's work."

"I'm a forensic accountant, Aston."

"And are you really performing the job that you want right now?"

Isabella stared at me for long enough I was afraid I'd overstepped once again, bug eventually she shook her head. "No. I'm doing other types of accounting because that's what they put on my table, but I'm trained as a forensic accountant. Do you really need one?"

"Of course we do. We buy other businesses and buy into other businesses. Blakely's job is to help organize those businesses, underneath James's purview. But we need another forensic accountant on the team."

"So I would work for you or James or Flynn?"

I shook my head. "With us."

"I'm not quite sure that is how it works."

"It's how we'll make it work. I don't work for my

brothers. Yes, Blakely works for James, but she's not family." I cringe. "I'm not doing this right."

"No you're right. I'm just surprised."

"You shouldn't be. One day the will's going to be split twelve ways evenly. Beyond the holdings we already have. My brothers and I, at least everyone but Kyler all made our own income outside of what Dad left us. And Kyler is doing damn well. We aren't billionaires, we're not even truly multimillionaires."

She raised a brow.

"We're not. The company does well, but we don't take huge salaries. We aren't the megalomaniacs with the monocle laughing over our heaps of money."

"And here I thought you were Scrooge McDuck, diving into his vault of money."

"Diving into coins does not seem sanitary, and honestly it's just asking for a broken bone."

She laughed at that, and I finished my sandwich, knowing I wouldn't have much time to eat later.

"Take the job. Do something you want to do. Or hell, work with us for a little bit, get something else on your CV, and then find another place. If it doesn't work out, it doesn't work out. But we have the space, the needs, and why do something you hate?"

She sighed and shook her head. "You really are the eldest, aren't you?"

"So says the other eldest."

She grimaced. "I'm no longer even close to being the oldest sibling anymore. Most of you guys are older than me by a couple of years."

"You know, I think you and James are the same age. Like a couple of days apart."

Isabella grimaced. "Don't remind me of that. Because that means well, Dad was, well, I don't want to think about it."

I shudder. "No, we're not going to think about that."

As we finished our lunch, she raised a brow at me. "Okay, let's say I take this job. Who would I be working with?"

"All three of us. And if you need to worry about the hierarchy, it would be a vote with all three of us."

"I'm okay with that. I don't need to come in and be the CEO of the company or anything. I'm not that insane."

"There's a lot of places to work, and you don't even have to work in the same building."

"Because you guys own so many buildings. And a town?"

I sighed. "Yes, I mean I only personally own a house that I rent out most of the time. Hudson lives there."

"That's why it's so hard for him to get on the schedule for the monthly dinners."

"Same with Kyler."

"I don't mind though, them having to travel so far to us seems a little ridiculous for dinner."

"That's what I was thinking. Also, because the town was founded by our great-grandfather, at least in his mind, things were passed down. And then my brothers and I bought some more of the land from a company that Dad sold to."

She frowned. "What do you mean?"

I ground my teeth, before forcing myself to relax. "Dad was on his way to selling it to a company who wanted to build a strip mall in the small town."

Her eyes widened. "Are you serious?"

"Yep. So we outbid him, had to get loans because again, we aren't multimillionaires. But we were able to give the land back to the town. We've never lived in town full time. We were there for summers as kids, but I try not to think of it as us owning a town."

"Dad really was an asshole."

"He was." We were both silent for a moment, memories of my time with Dad filling my mind and I had a feeling Isabella's was doing the same.

"So do you go to the lake often? Or is it really just Hudson's place?"

"I used to go more. But I don't really take time off."

"I don't know what time off is."

"You do get vacations with us."

"Well, that's good. A little scary though."

"We are scary, but I promise we don't bite."

She rolled her eyes. "You should go to the lake though. If you are this stressed that you're having a peace talk lunch with me, you should go relax."

"And should I take Blakely then?" I ask, only teasing.

Her eyes narrowed, and I realized I might have stepped in it, before she shrugged. "Just don't fuck with her. But maybe? She hated her last job so much, even more than I hate mine. And then she spent three months dealing with the fallout. So maybe having a weekend at a

THE FOREVER RULE

lake would be good for her. But I don't want the details. It was already awkward enough."

I blinked, a little confused. "Oh. Maybe." I had only been kidding, but now the idea held merit. Of course, that meant I would have to break my own rules.

But I was getting good at that.

As we'd settled the bill, splitting it evenly because of course we did, we headed out of the small diner. Isabella frowned and I looked down at her.

"What is it?"

"I just realized that Sophia's studio is down the block."

"Really?" I asked, looking where she pointed. "I didn't know that. I must have walked by it a thousand times."

"It really is a small world. I don't like it," she said with a laugh.

"Noted."

As if we had conjured her, Sophia came around the block, hand in hand with a tall man with broad shoulders and blonde hair.

"Who's that," I whispered.

"Her boyfriend. His name is Cale." I raised a brow. "Spelled with a C. Don't worry, Kyler already made all the vegetable jokes."

"I don't know if he's made *all* of them," I muttered.

Isabella laughed, her shoulders shaking.

Sophia's eyes widened as she spotted us. "Hi. This is nice."

"Hello Sophia," I said, an unfamiliar awkwardness settling in again.

Isabella moved forward to hug her sister. "We were just having lunch."

"And no blood was shed?" Sophia said, and I tilted my head.

"Not yet anyway." I looked over at Cale and realized that this man was touching my baby sister. Well then, that was a new feeling of protectiveness that I hadn't been expecting.

Isabella looked at me, and her eyes filled with laughter.

"This is Cale."

"It's nice to meet you," the other man said as he held out his hand, and I shook it firmly. I didn't squeeze too hard, because I didn't think it was my place to really protect Sophia. But maybe it should be.

"It's nice to meet you."

"We were just heading to a place that I know a couple blocks from here for a drink. Do you want to join?" he asked, and I tilted my head, and looked around the block to figure out exactly where we were.

"Are you going to The Gilded Cage?" I asked, curious.

Cale's eyes widened. "Yes. I love that place."

Sophia and Isabella both burst out laughing, and then Cale blinked before he shook his head.

"I didn't even think about the name. Do you own it?"

"No, though our brother Dorian owns the building."

"The whole building?" Sophia asked. "I still rent my small section."

"It's what he wanted to do. And then he runs the

bar of course. We should go see him. I know he's working today." I looked at Isabella. "Are you okay with that?"

"Well, it seems that we have to celebrate things, and I need to put in my two weeks' notice."

Sophia's eyes widen. "Are you serious?"

Isabella rolled her shoulders back and I wasn't sure if she was trying to protect herself from the oncoming questions or the job itself. "Yes. It seems that I'll be working with the big brothers."

Sophia clapped her hands. "Oh this is amazing. I hate your job."

"It sounds like we do have a lot to celebrate," Cale said, as he gestured down the block. "Lead the way."

"And I get to see another brother. This sounds like a plan." Sophia laughed, and wrapped her arms around Cale's waist, and we all walked our way toward The Gilded Cage.

It was a high-class bar that had a VIP section for high clientele, and other stations for people who walked in off the street. Of course, we were family, so we could go wherever we wanted.

Dorian met us at the door, and looked between us, confusion settling on his face for just an instant, before he put on his lazy smile.

"Well, this is an interesting family reunion." He looked over at Cale, and narrowed his eyes in the same way that I had a feeling I had earlier.

"But you're new."

"Hi, I'm Cale. I'm with Sophia."

Dorian gave him a once over, and nodded tightly, before holding out his hand.

"Nice to meet you. I'm the pretty brother."

Cale just laughed, a camaraderie in his gaze.

Sophia and Isabella looked between them. "I don't know if I'm going to like this many brothers."

"And I thought Kyler was bad," Isabella snickered, and something settled into place.

No, we weren't truly family, not yet. But we were getting there.

And maybe, maybe this could work. Despite my mother, despite my father, it could work.

I just had to hope to hell I didn't ruin things with Blakely in the process.

Chapter Ten
BLAKLEY

Dear Diary,
I really hope I wore the right panties for this evening.

As I walked out of my latest meeting, feeling oddly high on success, I tried my best not to skip down the hallway to my office. Working here was completely different than working at my previous place. I hadn't realized how suffocating my last job had been. I hadn't been able to do what I was good at. I had somehow been shuffled into doing paperwork for others, and focusing on what they wanted, rather than what I'd been hired for. It had been constant walking on eggshells, making sure I didn't rock the boat. Everything that I had done had been so I could keep my job, a job I hadn't even liked.

Now I had a team that wanted to do good things, and I was learning along the way.

There was a knock at my door, and I looked up to see James standing there, tablet in hand as he continued to work.

"Yes?" I asked, not feeling nervous at all about the fact that my boss was standing in front of me. What a novelty.

"I'm looking over that proposal you sent, and it's great. I have a couple of suggestions for it, that you don't need to take into an account, but I think could help."

I smiled and stood up, going toward him so I could look at his tablet. It was just easier when I knew he had that manic energy and sometimes he just couldn't sit down.

"No problem. It's just a proposal. There's what, twenty more steps before we can put anything into action."

"Exactly. Flynn always rolls his eyes at me when I say that we need those twenty steps. He likes ten."

My lips twitched. "I don't have any siblings, just my folks. I love my parents, but I don't know if I could actually work with them."

"Oh, this is why I'd never work with my parents. I can work with my brothers, because we call each other out for things, and we listen to each other. But if all seven…" He paused and then cleared his throat. "If all twelve of us had worked in this building, it would be too much."

"Well there's going to be four of you now," I said, smiling at that new information.

Isabella had sounded worried and yet excited at the same time when she had put in her two weeks' notice. Her first day was on Monday, and I couldn't wait to see what happened. I was nervous for her, and the rest of the Cages, but it was going to be nice to have my best friend working nearby.

"It was Aston's idea, but honestly, Flynn and I should have come up with it too," James said with a shrug. "Hell, I realized I just said that working with everybody would be too much, but if people have the skills to make this work? Why not. Anything to make the company even better than what Dad thought it could be."

I heard the bitterness in there, but he smiled so brightly, so much like Flynn in that moment, I couldn't say anything.

"Do you know if she's going to work in this office, or another."

"She has the option of working at either one of our buildings. I don't actually know where she lives, and Aston is handling all of that. We have more than one accountant on our team, and since she's going into forensic accounting, she'll be working more with Aston than me."

"It's going to be nice though, right? You'll be able to know her."

"Yeah. More than just at dinners where things are awkward and we're doing speed dating for siblings." He paused and cringed. "In a not really weird incest way that I just said."

"I sort of understood," I said with a laugh.

"Anyway, I like the proposal, and I'll send over these notes."

"No problem."

"And you don't have to stay for the whole day you know. You already did the work that we wanted. You can just head home and do more work there, but we're not going to force you to work late tonight."

My teeth bit into my lip slightly, and I let out a breath. "That would be nice. Because I sort of have to get ready for a date tonight."

James tilted his head, before he sighed. "I really hope it's with my brother because I do not want to deal with his grumpy ass if it's not."

"And that's not awkward at all," I teased.

"What? He was a complete grump for more than one reason when the thing with you guys didn't work out the first time."

"For obvious reasons that had nothing to do with me," I said, a little shocked about his words, considering his father had died as well.

"We Cages are doing our best about not actually leaning into our grief and pretending it's not real. So you don't have to worry about that. I'm pretty sure he was grumpy about the other thing."

I shook my head, not knowing if he was telling the truth or not.

"But anyway, yes. It's with him. And I don't really want to talk about it at work."

"No problem. I don't want to have to deal with HR."

"Anyway, I will go home and finish work. Thanks for the option."

"It's what we do. We want you to stay here, and not find a new job after we help you train up all of your skills."

"Is that a problem often?" I asked, honestly curious.

"More than you would think," he said, as Flynn called him over. "See you in the morning."

And then he left me standing at my office door, wondering what the hell had just happened.

I probably shouldn't be dating the boss's brother, but here we were.

We had been on two more dates since that first one, and we had kissed, laughed, but hadn't done anything else. It was like he was taking his time with me and stressing me out all at the same time. I just wanted to know what he wanted. Of course that meant I had to figure out what I wanted.

With a sigh, I pushed that from my mind for now, and packed up my things to go. I hadn't seen Aston that day since he was working with a team on another floor. And for the past week to be honest, he had been in different buildings, meeting with potential investors, and doing things on his side of the business. Which meant that we had the space that we needed, and it didn't feel overwhelming.

At least in that sense.

I made it home quickly, and while I put on a face mask to hydrate, I looked over the rest of my files and continued to work for a couple of more hours. All the while getting ready for this date.

I didn't know why I was so nervous, but I really couldn't help it.

At half past six, the doorbell rang, and I looked down at my wrap dress and heels and hoped that it was good enough. Or that I wasn't overdressed. All he had said was that he was taking me to dinner.

And the fact that I had put on my laciest panties and bra set, notwithstanding. Because I had to decide tonight if I wanted Aston Cage to see my underwear or not. And frankly, with the way that I had to press my thighs together when I thought about him, I really wanted him to see my underwear.

And with that thought in mind, I opened the door, and nearly swallowed my tongue. He stood there, his hair brushed back from his face, and that chiseled jawline relaxing as soon as he saw me. He was always so tense, but it was nice to see him slightly softened. He had on a dark blue buttoned-up shirt, but he had rolled the sleeves up, and dark pants.

He looked edible.

And that was going to be a problem.

"You look amazing." Then he shook his head, and I frowned. "Amazing isn't a good word. Delectable? Edible? Fucking sexy as hell? How about that."

I grinned and shook my head. "You can keep adding words, I don't mind. Let me grab my bag."

"Seriously though, I love that dress on you."

I blushed, and grabbed my bag before walking out and locking the door behind me.

"Thank you. I'm not going to lie and say that it was the first thing that I picked out. Please don't look at my closet because it might appear as though a tornado went through there."

His lips twitched, but he reached around to press his hand to the small of my back, leading me to his car. He was so warm, so big. And I needed to rein in on whatever the hell was going on with me.

"I didn't ask where we were going. Which in retrospect I probably should have considering you know, clothing."

"You look beautiful. And appropriately attired for Le Petit Pearl."

My eyes widened. "Fancy French food? Look at you go."

"Not too fancy. I didn't have to wear a suit jacket, and gasp, I'm showing forearms."

I wiggled my brows as we got in the car. "I mean, forearm porn is a thing."

He paused in the act of starting his car. "What?"

"I didn't say anything," I blurted, my voice slightly high-pitched.

"No, you're going to have to explain what that means." He'd started the car, and pulled out of the driveway, and we made our way toward the restaurant.

I gave in, knowing he'd persist. "It's just that when a man pulls up his sleeves to show off his forearms and we can see the muscles there, and sometimes the veins, it just does things. I can't explain it."

He looked at his arms, and then at me, before looking back to the road. "Forearms. I guess you learn a new thing every day."

Our conversation moved on to easier topics, and thankfully not just his forearms, by the time we made it to the restaurant. There was an actual valet in front, and I just shook my head, a smile playing on my face.

"What?" Aston asked as he helped me out of the car.

"You said it wasn't fancy, and now there's a valet."

"Because this parking lot is terrible, so they need sixteen to eighteen-year-old kids to park our cars for us."

"I don't know if that actually helps my nerves or not."

"Tell me about it."

We walked up to the maître d', and as he leaned forward to speak, I looked around the gorgeous room, and was grateful I had picked this dress.

"Cage, party of two."

"Yes Mr. Cage, we have you down."

As we followed her toward a table against the windows so we could see the mountains before sunset, I looked up at Aston.

"What happens if there's more than one of you at dinner? I mean, what if you guys picked the same place?"

"That's never happened to me, although I think Dorian and Flynn have had that issue before."

"It probably doesn't help that there's so many of you."

I shook my head. "No, or that Hudson and Flynn are twins."

"And identical."

"Yes. We all look alike, including Kyler for that matter, but they're the identical ones. Hudson has his hair different now, so at least it's easier for Mother to tell them apart."

We sat down, as I took the menu, my attention only on Aston. "What does that mean?"

"My mother's not the most observant when it comes to her children. She refused to get a nanny when we were kids, even though there were seven of us, so we pretty much raised ourselves like the terrors we were. I could always tell the difference between the twins, so could all of my brothers. But Mom never could."

"That's..." I let my voice trail off, shaking my head. "I don't know what to say to that."

"There's nothing to say. That's just my mother."

Thankfully we changed the subject, as I had never been to this restaurant, and wanted to know what I should have.

I ended up with a chicken dish that was so decadent I knew I wanted leftovers.

Of course, the portions were tiny, and there probably wouldn't be any.

"I need to go wash my hands, I will be right back," I said after dinner.

Aston just smiled at me. "No problem. Did you want dessert?"

"Yes, but I don't know if I could really do a flourless chocolate cake again."

"You're right, I think they need a better pastry chef,"

he whispered, his voice low, and I just smiled, before making my way to the restroom.

I washed my hands, and then checked my makeup, my heart fluttering a bit. Tonight was good. I felt like I was getting to know him more, and things just felt easy. And it always scared me when things were easy.

I turned to go back to the table, when a hand gripped my upper arm, and stopped me. I froze, confused, and looked over to see a blonde woman with bright red lips, and gorgeous eyes smiling down at me. But there was nothing nice in that smile.

"Excuse me?" I asked, looking down at her hand on my skin. "Is there something I can do for you?"

"You know this is just temporary right?" she whispered, and I paused.

"I think you have the wrong person. Please let me go."

"He was mine. Aston Cage was mine and we're just taking a break. So don't get comfortable in that seat."

I blinked at this other woman, and had to wonder if this was his ex-fiancée? Or one of the countless women that I had seen on his arm before. It shouldn't matter to me, even though it did a little, but I just stared at her, and then at her hand on my skin.

"Don't be like this. You aren't that person."

"What do you mean by that?" the other woman asked, her hand falling.

"Are you his ex-fiancée?" I asked, knowing that I just needed to get the facts right before I left. My heart raced, but she just stared at me, eyes widening.

"So he told you about me."

I swallowed hard, realizing that yes, this beautiful woman was the ex-fiancée. And even though he had said she had broken it off, she didn't seem over it. But I wasn't that person. I wasn't going to just stand here and take that. "I don't know why you're here, or why you're talking to me, but Aston loved you." Her eyes widened at my words, but I was going to tell the truth. "Meaning there has to be good in you. Don't pit yourself against me. Don't lower yourself to fighting me in a bathroom. We're both above that."

The other woman's eyes widened again, before they narrowed into slits. "Then just don't get in my way."

I sighed, knowing I wasn't going to get through to her in that moment. What I had said was true. And Aston had loved her, so there was some good about her. Because those were Aston's choices. And I didn't know what this woman wanted now.

"Just go. You're not going to scare me out of whatever's happening between us."

The other woman just glared at me, before she walked out as if she didn't have a care in the world, and I finally let my heartbeat slow down just a bit, the bile on my tongue fading away.

"Are you okay?" another woman asked, and I hadn't even realized we had had an audience.

I smiled and nodded and was grateful that his ex-fiancée hadn't squeezed too hard. I wouldn't have a mark on my arm. "I'm fine. I just don't exactly know what she wanted."

"I have a feeling you know exactly what she wanted,"

the other woman said dryly, before shaking her head. "But you handled that well. Good on you."

I wasn't quite sure that was true, but nonetheless I smiled at her, before going back to the table. I didn't tell Aston. Everything felt good. Right. And I didn't want to ruin the night. So when he finished signing the check, and we headed out to his car, I pushed all thoughts of that altercation out of my mind, and only focused on tonight.

"So, where am I taking you?" he asked, and there was so much promise in that question, that I swallowed hard and looked directly at him.

"Let's go to your place."

A smile slowly crawled over his face, and he nodded. "My place sounds pretty good."

And as we drove there, I focused on the now. Because that was the only thing that mattered in this moment.

Nerves settled over my skin as soon as we were inside his house, and he handed over a gin and tonic. "I only have diet tonic for some reason. I hope that's okay."

"Oh that's fine with me. I usually can't tell the difference." I sipped the crisp drink and noticed that Aston had added the perfect amount of lime. "It's wonderful."

"Well, it's an easier drink than mine," he said.

I looked at his Manhattan. "I don't know if I could drink cherry and bourbon."

"Well they are a match made in heaven," he said, as he brought the tumbler to his lips. I did the same with my glass, and then licked my lips as a drop of my drink slid out.

His gaze latched onto my mouth, and I swallowed hard.

"I think I'm done with the drink," he said, his voice low, and I set my drink down with a nod. And then he was on me, and I couldn't think. He cupped my face, his mouth pressing against mine with such ferocity, I could barely breathe. He tasted of liquor and sweetness, and I wrapped my arms around his neck, needing him closer. When he reached around me and gripped my thighs, I let out a shocked gasp. And then he lifted me up off the floor, and I wrapped my legs around his waist.

"I want you on a bed first. I'll take you on a couch, against the table, anywhere later. But I want to see you sprawled out over my bed."

I nodded, my pussy pulsating. "Yes. That's what I want too."

"Good." He kissed me again and led me to his bedroom. I didn't know which direction he was going, if we went upstairs or anything. I was so focused on him and his taste, it was like I was out of reality.

Aston set me on the bed, and I let out a moan as he gently tugged on the tie to my dress.

"I've been wanting to unwrap you since I first saw this damn dress."

I swallowed hard, knees going weak. "Oh."

"Damn straight."

"It's all I've been thinking about since I first saw you. But now, I get to see exactly what I'm unwrapping."

My breath caught as I stood up, and he finished undoing the knot at my side. When my dress fell to each side of my hips, I felt as if I were completely naked in front of him, though I was still wearing clothing. The hungry, dark look in his eyes, nearly sent me over the edge.

And when he studied my body, I felt as if I were enraptured, treasured, his.

He reached out, and ran one knuckle underneath my breast, and then over my nipple. It immediately pebbled, and I sucked in a sharp breath, the sensation of his touch going straight to my cunt.

"Aston."

He looked up at me then, that familiar smile on his lips.

"I love it when you say my name. Just my name."

I swallowed hard again, as he cupped my breasts, and let my head fall back.

"Aston," I repeated.

He tugged at my dress, and it pooled at my feet on the floor.

"You're so beautiful. You take my breath away."

I opened my eyes then, studying him.

"It's really hard to think with you touching me. Or with you even in the room for that matter."

"I'm going to take my time with you."

I shook my head. "Maybe not the first time. I don't think I can wait that long."

He laughed then, a deep laugh that went straight through me. "Oh, this is going to be fun."

And then his mouth was on mine again, and I was tugging at his shirt. He let me take it off him, one button at a time. And then my hands were sliding over his skin, over the slight hair over his chest.

"I can't breathe, I'm so hot."

"Yes, you are."

I laughed. "That's not what I meant."

And when he slid his hands between my legs and cupped me, I sucked in a breath.

"Yes. You are."

I swallowed hard, and then he tapped two fingers over my pussy, and my knees went weak.

Before I could breathe again, I was on my back, my heels still on, and he was kneeling between my legs.

"I need to taste you."

Blushing, I let my thighs fall to the side, as he gently tugged on the edge of my panties.

"Did you wear these for me?"

"And for me," I said truthfully.

"Such a good girl," he whispered, and then he slid my panties to the side, baring me to his face.

He studied me slowly, gently sliding one finger along my swollen folds, then the other. He was taking his damn time, and I moaned, my hips lifting without thinking. He pressed his arm over my hips, keeping me pinned, and when I opened my mouth to protest, he leaned forward and took me in his mouth. I buckled off the bed, as his tongue lapped at me, gently, slowly, as he continued to eat me out. I couldn't breathe, couldn't think, and then two fingers were spearing me, and my knees went weak.

"Aston."

He hummed against me, curling his fingers just right

to play with the sweet bundle of nerves inside me. I nearly shot off the bed like a rocket, my thighs clamping around his face as I came, my hips rocking along him.

He continued to move his fingers in and out of me, two and then three, and not stopping, as my wetness covered his hands, and his face. I should have been embarrassed about how hot I was for him, how drenched I was making him, but I couldn't think. The sound of ripping hit the air, and I realized that he had torn my panties off me. I could have complained as those were nice panties, but I didn't care. Instead he had his arms wrapped around my thighs, as he continued to lick at me.

"I can't. Not again."

"You will," he growled against me, and then he continued to feast, like a man starving in the desert. And miraculously, I came again, my toes curling in my heels, the sounds I was making echoing off the walls.

And when he finally stood up, between my legs, I looked at him then, and nearly came again. His mouth was wet from my orgasm, and he was licking his fingers one by one, and then licked his lips.

"So fucking sweet."

I swallowed hard, and then he hovered over me, kissing me. I could taste myself on his lips, and I arched underneath him, my pussy against his still-clothed cock.

"That's it, move for me. Get me wet. You're a dirty girl, aren't you? Wet for me."

"Aston."

"That's it, keep going, drench me."

I was blushing, as I wasn't usually into dirty talk, but

there was just something about Aston Cage that did everything to me.

He shoved off my bra, unclasping it as he did so, and then he was sucking on my nipples, licking and squeezing and biting my breasts so I knew that I would bruise in the morning, but I didn't care.

"I need to be inside you," he growled, and when he stood up, I swallowed hard.

"Yes. Aston. Same. I need you inside me." I slid my hand between my legs, playing with myself, and he smiled.

"That's it, play with yourself as I get this cock out for you."

"Okay," I whispered, not sure what else I was supposed to say, I couldn't really think.

But before he took himself out, he undid my shoes, gently rubbing his thumb on the arches of my foot as he did so. I moaned, wondering exactly what I was feeling. When he stood up again, and undid his belt, and shoved down his pants, I nearly wept in pleasure. He was hard, thick, and he sprung out of his boxer briefs, looking as if he were ready to come right there.

"Are you ready?"

I nodded, reaching for him. "In me already. I can't think."

"I need to get a condom."

I shook my head. "I'm clean. I'm on birth control." I paused, wondering what the hell I was saying, but I didn't care in that moment.

His hand around his dick, he paused, and nodded

slowly, before he swallowed hard. "I've never had sex without a condom before."

We stared at each other, the moment pulsating between us heavy. "I'm safe."

"Same."

And for some reason I trusted him, it made no sense, but it did. I just wanted to feel him.

"I want you bare," he growled, and I nodded tightly, needing him. I lay on my back, with Aston between my legs, and as he kissed me slowly, his hand over mine between my legs, he worked my fingers inside of me. I couldn't breathe, the connection so fierce, and when he gently probed my entrance with his cock, I swallowed hard.

"Aston."

"That's it, keep repeating my name." And then he shoved deep inside me. He was buried to the hilt in an instant, his thick cock stretching me to the point of pain, and I didn't care. He was so thick, so deep, that it took me a moment to catch my breath.

"Are you ready?" he asked, pausing.

"Yes. Please move. I need you to move."

"You feel so fucking good. I can feel every inch you."

And then he began to move, slowly pounding in and out of me, as I reached for him, my fingernails clawing at his shoulders. He bit down on my flesh again, biting at my breast, sucking, and I couldn't think, just moving with him thrust for thrust. When he moved again, I wrapped my legs around him, trying to keep him close, deep inside. But he pulled out of me, leaving me bereft.

"Hands on the wall," he growled, and he flipped me over on my stomach and gripped my hips. I crawled forward, with him behind me, and I put my hands on the wall, my knees shaking.

"That's it, feel me." And then, without any warning, he shoved deep inside of me, and I groaned, arching for him.

To keep myself steady, I nearly clawed at the wall, and he had one hand on my pussy, playing with my clit, the other around my throat.

"You're so fucking beautiful."

"I can't think…" I swallowed hard, and came again, not even realizing that his voice could do that to me.

"That's it, squeeze me. I'm almost there."

"Aston."

I knew I needed to say something other than his name, but that was the only thing on the tip of my tongue. But when he pulled out of me again, I was afraid it was over, and yet I knew I could barely move. But instead he sat so his back was to the headboard, and then pulled me over him.

"Finish me, ride me. Take control. You've got this, Blakely."

At the sound of my name on his lips, my eyes filled, and I lowered myself over him, knowing this would take him even deeper.

This was the most intimate I had ever felt, we were face to face, my breasts pressed against his chest. He gripped my hips and nodded slowly.

"I've got you, Blakely. You're safe with me."

Tears slid down my cheeks, and I rolled my hips, slowly setting the pace. He just nodded, and kept going, his jaw tensing as he was nearly there.

And when he pressed his lips to mine, and I cupped his face between my palms, he came, groaning my name, and I let the tears fall.

I hadn't planned for tonight. I hadn't meant for any of this. And I was truly afraid with this one moment, with the tears running down my cheeks, I was well on the way to falling in love with Aston Cage.

And that would be my sweetest mistake.

Chapter Eleven
ASTON

Rule #4: Cage First. Always.

FOR THE SECOND MONTHLY DINNER, WE WERE ONCE again at my place. We would begin to alternate locations, as well as perhaps even go to restaurants in the future. But for now, my home had the most room.

"I'm not quite sure I enjoy the fact that we have a spreadsheet for meals," Dorian grumped, as he poured himself a drink.

I shrugged, and looked over at Sophia and James who were looking over the cheese board, and figuring out what was what. "If we don't, we'll miss something."

"And what, we have to check in with the lawyer once a month with a selfie or something?"

"It's what they want. At least he doesn't have to come to these dinners with us."

"Thank God," Kyler said as he came out from the

bathroom, drying his hands on his jeans. "Your towels are really fancy, and I didn't want to ruin them," he said with a laugh.

And I shook my head. "Please ruin them. Those are gifts from Mother, because apparently hand towels for Christmas were exactly what I needed."

"And so you put them out so that way when she came over and saw them, you were in the clear."

I nodded, a smile playing on my face. "You got it in one."

Kyler shrugged. "I think Mom got me towels one year for Christmas, but it was because I was moving out and didn't own anything of my own really."

I sighed. "She got them for me this year. So please, use them, abuse them, and then I can toss them into the rag pile for cleaning."

"What's wrong with the towels?" Sophia asked, her brows raised. "Do they have embroidery on them or something with little flowers?"

"Yep," Kyler and I said at the same time, and the other man, my younger brother, just winked at me.

"Little pink flowers with monogrammed initials," he said with a drawl.

"Oh." Sophia pressed her lips together, and I knew she was holding back a laugh.

"You didn't say the best part," James put in, before tossing a cracker and some form of cheese in his mouth.

"What?" Sophia asked, and I sighed, lowering my head. I really didn't want to get into this part, but thankfully Dorian answered for me.

"It's not just *his* initials."

"What do you mean?" Sophia asked, and everyone stared at me.

"My mother sent me embroidered towels with not only my initials, but my former fiancée's initials. *After* we broke up. After the wedding was firmly canceled."

James and Dorian just laughed, as Kyler and Sophia looked at me as if they couldn't quite believe it.

"You were engaged?" Kyler asked.

"Yes. I'm no longer engaged. However, I don't believe that Mother really believes that."

"Does Blakely know?" Sophia asked, and my gaze shot to her.

"Yes. We've discussed it." I tilted my head. "So you're friends with her as well?"

"Yes. She's come over to dinner sometimes when I'm there with Isabella, and we've had girls' nights. So yes, we're friends. I am just glad that she knows."

"Why would it matter?" Dorian asked, and I gave him a look. He ignored me of course.

"Because secrets are bad." Sophia looked at all of us, eyes wide. "We're all in this room together because of a major secret."

"Okay, you got us there," James said. "But those two have been dating what, a month? When do you lay out all of your past relationships?"

Sophia looked around the room and shook her head. "You know, family conversations were a lot easier when I wasn't outnumbered."

Kyler just beamed. "You see? This is how I felt my

entire life. Surrounded by women." He tilted his beer up at us and nodded. "Thank you for letting the pendulum swing our way."

"I don't know if I like this very much," Sophia said primly, before letting out a soft laugh. "But yes, after a month I would like to know if the man I'm currently seeing and most likely sleeping with has had a past serious relationship. I mean, you were going to get married, that seems pretty serious."

"Seeing as I told Blakely, it's not really a problem. And Meredith isn't a problem."

"Except for the whole embroidered towels thing," Dorian said dryly.

I rubbed the back of my neck. "Please, throw them in mud or something. Mother's already seen them, so I guess I don't even need them in there."

"It's okay, I'll most likely spill something later, and use them to clean it up," Kyler said, a grin on his face so similar to Dorian's it was a little shocking.

"So, there's five of us here," James said, pointing to all of us. "Three from one side of the family, two from the other. I guess we should what, check in with the lawyer so that way we can say that we did it?"

At that abrupt change of topic, I glared at James. We had been having a good time, and now everyone looked a little edgy. "Yes, we can check in with the lawyer. However, I did put out some food for everybody, so we should still fucking eat." I hadn't meant for the words to snap, but I was already tired of being put in this situation, and I didn't want to deal with my brother's attitude on top of that.

"Hey, I don't mind good food. I'm just surprised that I was actually in town for this," Kyler said as he strolled over to the food spread and popped a grape into his mouth. "And I do love cheese boards. Actually, I just love any food."

"Well that hasn't changed since you were a kid," Sophia said with a laugh. "I don't know how this is all going to work. However, can't we just think about this as a family dinner without the fact that we're forced into it?" Sophia asked. The pleading in her tone hit me.

I gave a tight nod. "I get it. The whole reason that I even said I'd have them at my house to begin with was that I want to make sure that I get to know the people that my father hid from us for so long. And apparently that makes me far more sentimental than I thought."

"Honestly, I'm surprised it's you saying it out of everyone," Dorian said, and I flipped him off.

The others laughed thankfully.

"I don't know how this is going to work for three damn years," Kyler said, before he strolled into a nearby chair.

"Well you're out of town more than all of us." I paused. "Other than Hudson."

Kyler raised a brow. "Because Hudson lives in this mysterious town that we own."

"We only own parts of it."

"Well, I guess I'm going to have to visit sometime,"

Kyler said, though I wasn't quite sure if he was serious or not. I couldn't get a beat on Kyler. But then again, I didn't always understand the brothers I had grown up with either.

"Come on, let's go sit down and get comfortable," I said, as I gestured for everybody to take a seat in the room large enough for us. We each leaned down to grab a few bites to eat, though everything felt awkward as hell.

"So how is this going to work in the future?" Sophia asked as she perched on the edge of a chair. She played with a grape between her fingers and winced. "I'm not being confrontational. And I know we have a spreadsheet about who can go where for the next couple of months, but is it only family? Or can we invite friends. Or should we do a dinner with all of us at one point? I mean, it's vague and yet specific at the same time, and I don't know if I like it."

"I sure as hell know I don't like it," Kyler mumbled. "And this is all because you want to invite Cale?" Kyler asked, fluttering his eyelashes at his sister.

The prim and proper Sophia flipped him off, and Dorian barked out a laugh, while James and I grinned at each other.

"I've met this Cale, he seems like a nice guy," I put in.

"I liked him," Dorian added.

Kyler sat up and frowned. "Wait, they've met him, and I haven't?"

Sophia rolled her eyes. "They were in town. You're never here, little brother."

Kyler glared. "I really wish you would stop calling me that."

"I can't help it. I now have too many big brothers, so I have to make sure you know that you're still younger than me."

"You know you're going to hate that when you start to reach monumental ages," Kyler snapped back. "And then I'll lord it over you."

"I wouldn't do that," I said dryly. "Mostly because I'm pretty sure all of our sisters could probably kick your ass once you start making fun of their ages."

Kyler tilted his head, studying me. "You're sure free and easy with the 'our siblings' part."

"Is that a problem? I figure that the more I try at least, the less I feel like I'm going to want to find Dad's grave, dig him up, and beat the shit out of him."

"That was very violent," Dorian said, as he finally broke the awkward silence that had filled the room. "And graphic."

"What? You've thought it."

"I was more thinking about lighting it on fire, but sure, we can beat up the bones or something," James added before sipping his drink.

Kyler and Sophia looked at us like we were crazy, before they both shrugged in unison. It was quite funny to see.

My newest brother turned toward the window, staring off into the distance. "I haven't really thought of the man often. Mostly because I don't want to. I could give two shits about him."

I let out a breath. "I don't want to continue to do this for *that man*. I want to do it for us. For our legacy."

Dorian studied me. "Really? You really think that we have a legacy anymore?"

"We should make our own." I paused. "I don't want Dad to fuck up our lives any more than he already has."

Kyler growled something under his breath, but I couldn't quite understand what he said.

"I do like the fact that we're trying. I don't want the money." Sophia paused as we all looked at her. "I don't. I did well enough when I was a dancer. I saved everything that I could. And my studio is in the black, thank God." She knocked on the wooden seat.

I smiled. "That's always good. And I bet it helps that your sister's an accountant."

"Always."

"I'm sure you're great at business, and this is being completely patronizing, but if you'd like us to ever look at anything for you, we do this for a living," James put in.

Kyler just shook his head, a smile playing on his face, and Sophia beamed. "Totally not patronizing at all. Because one day if I do want to expand, or change things up, I would love somebody who actually knows what they're doing. I really just lucked into this career of mine."

"So says the woman who tortured her body and broke toes and spent far too long learning dance and making connections in order for it to happen. You know enough," Kyler mumbled.

Sophia melted. "You know, sometimes you are nice."

"Only sometimes," Kyler joked.

"Whenever you're ready to expand, or franchise or do

whatever you want, we're here," I said. "And frankly, I get it not being about the money. I just don't want him to have any say in our business. I don't want him to have the power to break our enterprise in a thousand pieces just because he can. And do it from the grave." My hand tightened around my glass, and I forced myself to calm down. "Well he does like control, even when he said he walked away from the business."

"How did that work anyway?" Sophia asked.

"What do you mean?" I leaned forward, drink in hand.

"So I understand all of the positions you, James, and Flynn have in the company, but Dad just walked away?"

"Not exactly," James said with a sneer. "He *said* he would, but he ended up trying to handle things a little backhanded."

"Much like he did with the will," Dorian said as he drained his drink and went to pour another one. Kyler gave him a look, and Dorian nodded. I assumed that meant that Dorian would be getting him a drink. I was amused at the fact that the two didn't have to speak. Maybe we were getting something out of these mandatory dinners.

"I honestly feel like we had two different dads," Sophia said, and I frowned.

"I'm pretty sure the whole reason that we're here is because we had the same dad," James added.

She bit her lip, thinking. "I meant the way he treated us. I have no idea how he even made the logistics of two families work."

"See that's what I've been trying to figure out," I said, shaking my head.

Sophia leaned forward. "When we were younger, he was constantly traveling for work."

"Same with us and we believed because Mother decided to lie for him," I added.

"It's just weird that we knew our dad as one thing. A traveling salesman of sorts, who was home sometimes, but then we thought that Mom and Dad were just going through marriage problems," Sophia said.

Kyler didn't say anything, but his face darkened.

Sophia continued. "We were told that they needed time apart and were separating, and they would come back together."

"When in fact he was probably with our mom," James said with a sigh.

"Either way he's a damn liar," Dorian growled. I nodded and drained my drink. When Dorian raised a brow, I shook my head. He may be the resident bartender of the family, but I didn't want to drink. Not now.

"But how do we not know he was *The Cage*," Sophia asked, exasperation in her voice.

"That I don't know. But it's not like he was in the news or anything. He was big in his business circles, but he wasn't famous famous."

"And he shunned the media," James said slowly. "Which I always thought was odd for the ego on that man."

"It turns out it was for a reason," I said with a snarl. "Because the face of the company was grandfather, then me. Father always found a way out of it. And spent far too much time at Cage Lake." I paused. "Or at least he said he did."

"When I was younger, I thought it was because Dad wanted to do better for the company, to focus on what we were doing, but I was wrong," James said, his voice low.

"He didn't shun the limelight for too long," Kyler blurted, and then he looked at all of us, the anguish on his face surprising me.

And that's when it clicked. The reason I couldn't get a beat on Kyler.

"You knew," I whispered, as everyone went silent. "When did you find out?" I wasn't angry, I *couldn't* be angry, not with the look on Kyler's face. But what the hell.

Kyler just set his drink down, squeezed his sister's hand, and then walked casually out of the house. The door slammed behind him, and we sat there in silence, feeling as if another blow had just hit, and we were still echoing with the reverberations.

Sophia stood up, her hands shaking. "I should... I should help him." She looked at all of us, tears in her eyes. "I knew he hated Dad. But I never knew why. I'm sorry."

I stood then, Dorian and James following me. Without thought, I pulled Sophia into a hug, doing the big brother thing as if we had all along.

"Go help him. We'll figure it out. Remember, Dad's the liar."

She nodded against me, pulled back, and then wiped her face. "I'm sorry we're not staying for dinner."

"Well, if the lawyer asks, you did. After all, we already sent him proof," James said dryly, and then Sophia fled after Kyler, and I stood there with my brothers, wondering what the hell was going on.

"So, baby brother knew." Dorian tipped back his drink, before setting the glass down on the side table. "No wonder his music gets a little angstier every once in a while. Dear old Dad sure liked to fuck with all of us."

"I want to be angry and a little annoyed that he knew and didn't tell anyone, but then again, what did Dad do to make sure he kept quiet?" James asked, and my gaze shot to him. "I have no idea. But I have a feeling we're just scraping the surface of Dad's secrets."

James sighed and gestured toward the table. "Let's eat, since you have everything out, and we can discuss business."

Dorian blinked. "Oh joy. I'm excited."

"You are welcome to leave," I said. "Since it seems that our second dinner is going to be a little shorter than the first."

"No there's food. I'll stay and listen. Maybe you're going to need my expertise."

James laughed, and Dorian flipped him off, before I took a seat at the table, my brothers following. "You know, you have to head to Cage Lake next week," James said after a moment, and I sighed, knowing he was right.

"Going to go visit Hudson?" Dorian asked.

"Yes, and I have to meet with the resorts. A few business dealings. I could just go there and back in one day."

"Or you could take a couple of days off."

I stared at James as if he'd lost his mind. "Excuse me?"

"Go on a Friday, enjoy the weekend."

"Why are you telling me to take a vacation? You know we're busy."

"It's just a weekend. And maybe you could take Blakely."

Dorian choked and slammed his fist against his chest. "That was so subtle. But yes, you should totally take Blakely on a weekend trip."

"I have no idea why you two think that my relationship, whatever it is, with Blakely has anything to do with the two of you."

"You're going to be wrong there," James added with a sigh. "However, maybe you should just enjoy yourself."

"Where is this coming from?" I asked, honestly confused.

"Because Dad keeps ruining everything. Look what he did to Kyler. We don't even know the half of it. You need to go up to the town in order to get work done, and I know something weird is going on in your head about this relationship with Blakely."

"I have no idea what you're talking about," I said, my tone icy.

"You don't have to lie. You could just stay silent, but we both know you've got something in your head about being the leader of this family, and whatnot."

"I don't know what that has to do with me and Blakely."

"I just don't want you to fuck things up like Dad did."

James winced at his words, and Dorian cursed under his breath. I looked between the two of them, wondering if they had been talking about me behind my back. Or if I was just seeing things.

"Well, it's good to know exactly what we all feel about Dad and what we do with him and his legacy."

"That's not what I meant. But there's something going on in your head. So take this time. You're allowed to you know."

"So you want me to take Blakely and show her our small town, and what, make her fall in love with me?" I asked, not liking the tone of my voice.

"Or maybe you could just take that stick out of your ass for once and relax. I wasn't there the time you met her, but I heard about it. I heard that you smiled more. So just do something. Don't let Dad ruin everything."

I looked between the two of them, and I didn't want to listen. However, I couldn't get the thought out of my head. A whole weekend with Blakely. In the mountains. Just the two of us.

It was a dangerous temptation. One that wasn't going to end well. Because what we had between the two of us wasn't serious, it was just beginning.

The Cages didn't make serious work. I knew that. The family knew that.

But maybe I could take a weekend.

Chapter Twelve
ASTON

Rule #5: Never let the world see.

I STILL COULDN'T QUITE BELIEVE THAT WE WERE IN MY SUV, driving up the winding roads to our mountain town. It wasn't fully in the mountains like Vail or Aspen, but it was enough that the altitude could affect some people. Although, I knew visitors to just the mile-high city sometimes had to take oxygen because of the change in elevation.

I had been born and raised in the two parts of Colorado that called me home. So, of course, this was just home.

Now, the surprising part might've been the fact that I was taking a weekend off when all I wanted to do was bury myself in work, so I didn't have to think of reality. But that was only part of it. No, the other part was all about who was sitting next to me.

Blakely hummed along to the popular song playing on the radio, her sunglasses perched on her nose as she tilted her face up to the sunlight. She was so damn beautiful. It sometimes hit me, and it should probably worry me a little bit more than it did. Because it was hard to think when she was around sometimes. I still didn't understand why this was happening, or why she was by my side, but for some reason, my brother's little niggling of a recommendation via taunting had settled in, and I couldn't go back. When dinner had ended, however abruptly, I had immediately pulled out my phone to text Blakely.

ME:
So, what are you doing?

BLAKELY:
I almost feel like you should ask what I'm wearing.

BLAKELY:
Is everything okay? I thought you were at dinner tonight.

I had rubbed the back of my neck, annoyed with myself with even doing this. But maybe my brother had been right.

ME:
Dinner is not working out. Can I come see you?

I should just go home. I should ignore whatever was rising inside of me. Blakely was a complication. I knew that, she knew that.

> **BLAKELY:**
> Of course. Although I'm having girl dinner.

> **ME:**
> Do I want to know?

> **BLAKELY:**
> I have rotisserie chicken, a baguette, some bread, grapes, and a handful of mini-Oreos. You make the decision.

> **ME:**
> It sounds delicious. Do you have enough for two? I can pick something up.

> **BLAKELY:**
> I'm sure I can scrounge something. You're welcome to come over.

And so I had arrived at her door, my stomach in knots for some reason, and she had just smiled up at me. And of course, my lips had brushed against hers, and then the door had closed, and suddenly I had been on my knees in front of her, eating my way through our appetizers.

She had come on my face, and both of us had been drained by the time that we finally got to her version of girl dinner. We had been sitting in her kitchen, me in just my slacks, her in my button-down shirt and panties—the hottest fucking thing I had ever seen—when my brother's idea popped into my head.

"I'm being forced to take a vacation next weekend."

Blakely had blinked up at me. "Oh? Do you not take them?"

I had shaken my head. "Never. Which is probably an

issue. But I'm heading up to Cage Lake." I paused, trying to collect my thoughts as I popped a grape into my mouth.

Blakely smiled, her fingers playing with an Oreo. "You do work an insane number of hours. Of course, all of you guys do. You should go up to this infamous family town where you guys are kings."

I snorted, shaking my head. "Not even in the slightest. But you should come with me. See what the town's really like."

She had frozen, ever so slightly, and stared at me. "You want me to come with you? That's an overnight trip, Aston Cage."

I had just stared at her, my eyes narrowing. "It is. A little scary, isn't it?"

"We haven't exactly discussed what this is between us." She gestured between the two of us. "I am not quite sure if I should be flattered you want to take me to your town with your name slapped on it or be scared."

I frowned right back at her. "I don't know what it is between us. Rushing into labels and wanting to figure out exactly where I am, ended up pushing me into an engagement I wasn't ready for."

Something flashed over her face, just an instant, but she blinked it away so quickly, I couldn't tell what it was. "That makes sense. I don't want to push you. But I also want to see the mountains."

My chest had warmed at that, and I knew. "I have a place up there. In fact, we all do in some way or another." I paused. "At least the brothers I grew up with. Hell, I

THE FOREVER RULE

wonder if any of the new ones want something up there? I have no idea how that's going to work."

"I don't even want to go into the ins and outs of that will. Just seeing Isabelle's eyes go blank when she tries to go through the paperwork makes me want to run away."

"I don't blame her. I still don't know what the hell my father was thinking." I had waved that off. "Sorry. As for this weekend. Come with me. We'll do what we're doing now."

"Eating practically naked in my kitchen?"

"We can do that. Or we could eat completely naked."

"I don't think that's sanitary."

"Touché. And as for what we are to each other. I don't know. But I'm exclusive." I blurted out that last part, wondering why the hell it felt as if I were a teenager trying to figure out the rules.

Her teeth had bitten into her lip, and I had swallowed hard at the sight. "Me too. And I don't know what this is or where it's going, if it's going anywhere. Everything's changing so quickly, and I'm just going to go with the flow. Which is very unlike me."

"Two peas in a pod there. So you'll go with me?"

"What time will we be leaving?"

"Well, we may have to ask your boss if you could leave early on Friday."

She cringed. "Okay, that's awkward."

"No, it's not. We're allowed to work remotely. Just take that day. The boss isn't going to care." I had made sure that wouldn't happen.

And when Blakely had finally said yes, I had reached

over the table to grip the back of her neck and pulled her into a deeper kiss. She had moaned into me, and we had indeed gotten naked in her kitchen. However, the laughter that had burst from her as we had both cleaned up after had made the hard tile underneath my ass worth it.

So now, we were winding our way up through the mountains, and I was feeling awkward and yet, the most relaxed I had in a while. Didn't know what that meant. Maybe it was the fact that we were going back to Cage Lake.

Cage Lake was situated between two large peaks. There was tons of hiking, fishing, with a large tributary that was practically a full river, carving one side of the town boundaries, and the lake on the north side.

"Okay, after this ridge, we're going to hit Cage Street."

Blakely slowly lowered her glasses. "Really? How many of these places are called Cage?"

"I don't want to discuss it," I said, my lips twitching.

"All of them, right?"

"Enough of them that it's actually a little embarrassing."

"For a man in real estate, staking your claim sure does make you blush."

I shook my head as we rounded the curve. "I don't need to stake my claim at all."

Before I could say anything else though, Blakely looked out the window and gasped, and a sense of ease settled over me. The beauty of the town was breathtaking. Yes, the town came with its own burdens, and its own memories, but for a man who wore suits every day, I was comfortable here. Hell, I was wearing jeans and a flannel. When Blakely had first seen me, her eyes had practically bugged out of her head, and then she had just reached around, and slid her hands into my pockets.

"I like it."

"Well, you in jeans that grip your hips? It's going to be very uncomfortable with zipper marks on my dick this whole drive."

And now, she was seeing the town that I loved. I wasn't like Hudson who could live here full time, but I loved to visit. There was one main road into the town, and that got you to the lake. It was, of course, called Cage Street. It was very long, and windy. To the west of us, there was a large forest with tons of trails, with the resort settled against the most northern mountain. On the south side, that was the main river, and there were other trails and fishing spots. And branching off Main Street were multiple streets filled with homes and businesses that had grown over time. Hell, at first, we hadn't even had a main. Now the first business you saw when you took that right into Main Street, was a welcome center, and the admin building right behind it. There was also a clinic, a coffee shop, an actual mercantile, a hardware store, bakeries, and more. It was your typical small town that was anything but typical. Because most of the places had our names all over it. It was embarrassing, but hell, it was our family legacy. We were fighting for it for a reason.

"This is adorable. How many people live here?"

"The population changes all the time because of tourist seasons. And there's a lot more homes and town homes than there was when I was growing up." I paused. "I don't even know the population anymore. Hudson might."

"He lives here, right?"

"His home is on the west side of the lake, but nearly on the opposite end of mine."

"For a reason?" she teased.

I shook my head. "No, we just each split up the land and built our own places. There's still spots for the others that we can make work which isn't going to hurt the land. Then again, there's places that we could also add that they might like."

"I like that you're thinking about them."

"I do too. It's weird, but we're making it work. Somehow. At least I hope."

"I have to have hope. My best friend is your half-sister."

"That is very true." We passed by the streets that bisected Main Street, and I found a parking spot near one of the small restaurants that had popped up over time. This one was an Italian place, and I had never been here before. However, it had our name on it.

"Cage really isn't Italian, is it?"

"I don't ask these questions. I'm not in charge of the town."

"I don't believe that at all."

I rolled my eyes, though she couldn't see it through my sunglasses, and we got out to finally stretch our legs.

"Well, as I live and breathe," an older woman said. I looked over at a very familiar voice, and smiled such a wide smile that I had a feeling I even surprised Blakely.

"Hello there, Ms. Patty."

The woman with bright red hair, and even brighter red lips, opened up her arms, and hugged me tightly. And then I leaned down so she could press those bright red lips against my cheek, inevitably leaving her mark.

Blakely's eyes filled with laughter, and a little fear as the boisterous woman pulled back.

"I didn't know you were going to be here today. Did someone come out and clean your house and freshen up everything?"

I nodded. "Hudson took care of it. You know him."

The older woman just waved that off. "Who knows with that brother of yours. And I hear there's more brothers, and even sisters. Cage women. It's about time we start to add more to the pool." Then her eyes filled with curiosity as she looked at Blakely. "Is this one of your sisters? Or perhaps a new Mrs. Cage." Her gaze went right to Blakely's left hand, and I had a feeling this small-town life wasn't going to settle in for long.

"This is Blakely. Not a sister." I held back a visible shudder.

Blakely full-on laughed. "It's nice to meet you. Although, I do know his sister."

"Oh, really. I need all the gossip."

Blakely met my gaze, and I saw the wince she tried to hide. My whole life was under a microscope these days, all about gossip, and perhaps coming to this small town where everybody knew the Cages and all of their mess, wasn't the best idea.

"I don't know about that. I'm just really excited to see the town. Maybe you should be the one to give me all the gossip."

"Oh, I have a lot of it. I've lived here since I was a little girl and got married right up at that resort up there. The Cages take good care of us. My husband's the mayor, you know."

"And he's not a Cage?" Blakely asked, and this time I laughed.

"No. Somehow, we're not the mayor of this small town. Although, I think Grandpa was at one point."

"He was. And I'm sure one of you guys will be again. We're really easy here. And we all make sure that whatever businesses pop up are good for the economy, and all of the land here is owned to a point that nothing can be built up that we don't want here. We want to keep this feeling like it always has, with a little bit of flair."

"You took the words right out of my mouth, Ms. Patty."

"Now you head into the restaurant right here and have a great lunch special. Although, Cage Italiano? You guys could do better."

"I don't know who made that up. Probably Dad," I said. I tried not to speak through gritted teeth.

Ms. Patty grinned. "He did love branding the place. But it's what gives us character."

People were walking past us, calling out their greetings, and I did the same. Because while tourists came and went, the people who had lived here all their lives stayed the same. They got older, got married, had kids, but they were the ones that had been here when I had visited. Had never quite lived, which maybe was the problem. I liked my expensive suits and drinking bourbon out of a lowball glass, while sitting in a high-rise. I liked my fast cars, and dining with white tablecloths. But I also liked sitting on the ground, fishing pole in hand, trying to catch my lunch, knowing that my brothers would be better at it than me. Maybe I just liked memories that came when we were happy here. But then again, Dad wasn't always here. No, he was down south, raising his other family.

I pushed those thoughts aside as we said our goodbyes, and I introduced Blakely to a few other people. I saw those curious glances and winced.

"Now that Ms. Patty and a few others know that I'm here, everyone's going to know that I brought a woman to Cage Lake."

"And you've never done that before?" Blakely asked, her voice soft.

"No. And I didn't think it was going to be a problem."

"Is it a problem?" Blakely asked before we walked into the restaurant, and I knew if I said the wrong thing here, it would screw things up for far too long.

I reached out and pushed a strand of her hair away from her face, ignoring the curious looks from onlookers. "It's not a problem at all. It's just something I'm getting used to."

"Okay, then. I'm getting used to it too."

"Well good. Now, let's go see what this special is. And then I'll show you my town."

"Your town."

"I meant because I spent summers here, not because my dad branded it."

"Just a little bit of a problem," she teased, and slid her hand into mine.

I didn't want to think too hard about it, because I knew for a fact that things didn't work out. My family was living proof. But I can enjoy the time we had together for now.

And as I introduced her to countless others who came to sit with us, I took a deep breath, and let the day wash over us.

We were deep into our salad when a familiar voice echoed to the room.

"And you don't even say hi," Hudson said as he came forward, waving at the hostess.

"I'm not going to say stay, have to pick up an order, however, I'm just here to razzle my brother."

"Have fun," the manager said. I didn't bother standing up, but Blakely smiled over at him, and I did my best not to feel jealous. I didn't know why the hell I would.

"We were going to come to you after we ate. It's a nice place."

"Yeah, Dad started it up, but the manager knows what they're doing and has good food. I'm sure that Flynn takes care of it. You know him."

"I do." I frowned, gesturing toward Blakely. "I actually don't know if you've met or not. Which is probably an oversight."

"We haven't," Hudson said as he held out his hand, the rough calluses there evident underneath the overhead lighting.

Blakely smiled. "Hi, I'm Blakely."

"I've heard a lot about you," Hudson said, and I raised a brow.

"Oh, really?"

"You know the group chats, they get interesting. At least the group chats without you," he teased, and I settled back, watching my brother flirt with the woman I was currently sleeping with. And yet, there was nothing serious about it, and though a little bit of jealousy nagged at me, I ignored it. Because Hudson was laughing. He had indeed taken a seat, and joined us for lunch, ignoring the fact that I had just wanted to be with Blakely, but then again, I wanted to be with my brother too. He didn't come down enough. He didn't smile enough.

But he was smiling now.

"Okay, I'm going to need to hear all of the childhood stories. Ms. Patty already said she'd tell some. But I'm sure you have some."

Hudson smiled again, and this time, it truly reached his eyes, startling me. "Oh, I've got stories."

"And I'll go get the check," I said, as Blakely laughed.

"This town is just so interesting. I love the fact that you guys have this whole history here, and downtown in Denver."

"That's us Cages, shrouded in history," Hudson said,

and Blakely and I both noticed the tone. But she didn't say anything, instead went into a story about the time she tried to ski in Vail, and nearly broke her wrist.

"Aston here's a great skier, and we do have all access to the resort."

"Thankfully, it is not time for skiing, and I will never be on little blades, little pieces of wood like that again."

"Maybe snowboarding?" I teased.

"God no. That's just asking me for a broken nose or something."

"You know Aston could teach you. It's just pizza and French fries like they teach you in ski school," Hudson said.

"We can go down the bunny hills," I said, laughter spilling out.

She glared between us. "I thought Hudson and I were supposed to gang up on you," she said pointedly, and I shrugged.

"We're brothers. We can't help it. But I can teach you to ski if you want."

"Let's not take that up as a challenge. I like my bones where they are."

"Well, a woman who knows what she wants, I like that." Hudson turned to me. "Your house is all aired out for you. And I put some groceries in the fridge, though I know you're going to be eating in town often."

"Thanks for that, Hudson. You didn't have to do that."

"I don't mind. Needed something to do when I'm trying to ignore work."

I knew Blakely had questions about what Hudson did, but she didn't ask. Instead, my brother's gaze went distant, and he said his goodbyes abruptly before leaving.

"Did I do something?" Blakely asked, as I put money down for the check, and we headed out of the restaurant.

"No, that's just Hudson."

"That's not ominous at all."

"We Cages have baggage, some of us more than others." I shrugged like it meant nothing, but maybe it meant everything.

"I'm glad you brought me here though, it's beautiful."

"I'll show you around more."

"Really?"

"Of course. Do you want to see my house first? Or a little bit more of the town?"

She was so beautiful, and it took me a moment just to breathe it in. I had to be careful though, and I couldn't let it get too serious. As long as we kept things calm and casual, there would be no broken hearts when it ended.

"Show me around. And tell me one embarrassing story from your childhood."

I sighed. "As long as you do the same."

"I just told you about the skiing."

"Oh, no, you told me and Hudson that story, and it wasn't part of our deal yet. So, I'm going to need another story."

I took her hand in mine, as I said hello to a few other residents, and we made our way down Main Street.

"You go first," she said quickly, and I sighed, but couldn't help the smile spreading on my face.

"Okay, I think I can come up with something."

After all, the Cages had their secrets, but a slightly embarrassing story from my childhood wasn't one of them. Thankfully.

Chapter Thirteen
BLAKELY

Dear Diary,
I'm not quite a small-town girl...but I could get used to this. To him.

With Aston's arm around my waist, we walked down the block toward the other businesses.

"A few of these are new, like I said, so I don't know exactly where everything is."

I looked up at him, knowing that he would make sure that I didn't run into poles or trip over a curb. That was odd to think that I trusted him so completely, but maybe again, I was trusting whatever this was in our relationship to begin with. Because if this went wrong, it was going to damage so many things, and yet it was hard for me to even contemplate that, since I was doing my best not to think about it at all.

"Maybe we should have gone to the welcome center and picked up one of those maps."

He leaned down and kissed the tip of my nose as we turned the corner.

"Maybe. Although I don't think I've ever gotten a map from the welcome center."

"I'm sure that one of you Cages has the town all drawn up somewhere. Complete with a color-coded guide."

I looked up at the closest store and froze, my jaw dropping, and Aston groaned.

"Really? Who named this one?" I asked as I looked at the adorable coffee shop, complete with the beautifully scripted sign of the name of the place.

"I have no idea. It's apparently changed hands since I've last been here."

With a laugh, I pulled him into the Caged Bean, and couldn't help but look around, elation sliding through me.

I hadn't known how today was going to go. After all, I should've been at work. I should have been working with my team, going through paperwork, but as most of my team was off today for their own reasons, I had somehow found myself on a weekend trip with a man that could be considered my boyfriend. However, it wasn't as if we used those labels.

A man that, if we broke up, it wouldn't only damage my heart, but it could damage the relationship he was making with his sisters, and my relationship with a business that I was falling in love with.

Me making these choices was probably the worst thing I could be doing, and yet, here I was, continuing to make these choices.

"You must be a Cage," an older woman with short black hair, full-sleeve tattoos, and a nose piercing said as she came forward. "I'm Melody, the manager here." She held out her hand to me, and I shook it, before she did the same with Aston.

"Yes, I am a Cage, how could you tell?" Aston asked, his voice deep.

The other woman laughed, as others turned to look at the tableau in front of them. "You all look the same. But I don't think I've met you."

"Aston Cage, this is Blakely."

The other woman grinned at me. "It's nice to meet you, both of you. And welcome to my establishment."

"I have to ask, did you come up with the name?" I asked, laughter in my tone.

Once again Aston groaned.

Melody gave a good-natured laugh. "Of course I did. You don't think the Cages came up with all of these names, do you?"

"Honestly, I was pretty sure my dad did most of it," Aston said dryly.

Melody waved him off, before gesturing toward the bar. There was an actual bar with stools in a coffee shop along with small tables scattered around. It was quite cute in here, with black and wood furnishings and embellishments. It looked a little rustic, a little modern, and yet welcoming at the same time. It wasn't soft, but the aromas of coffee and sugar and other flavorings made my mouth water.

"Your dad did some, but this one was all me." She winked. "Honestly, I really enjoyed trying to think of something ridiculous. But your name helps."

"I feel like I should be offended by that," Aston said as he helped me onto my stool.

"Don't be, it'd be worse if your name didn't allow for so many cute little titles."

"I can't wait to learn them all," I said, sort of enjoying the way that Aston looked slightly uncomfortable. Mostly because the man was always so rigid and focused. When I had seen him in those comfortable jeans and flannel, I had nearly come on the spot. He was so damn sexy, and different than what he usually looked like. Don't get me wrong, I loved looking at him in the suit, because he looked fantastic in one. But in jeans? It was just a new level. And now watching him learn to relax around people he didn't know and wasn't trying to work with, was an all-new level of appreciation.

"We just opened in the past six months, but we've been doing good. Your brother, Hudson, has been wonderful. He painted that mural back there."

My eyes widened as I looked over at the back wall at the beautiful abstract photo that looked as if it was a tree reaching for the sky, and yet possibly a woman weeping. I couldn't quite tell and I had a feeling if I studied it for hours, I would see more and more details that stood out.

"I didn't know he was a painter," I whispered, and Aston cleared his throat.

"He is now. He was always good at it, but I'm glad he has time to breathe up here and settle into it."

"He's doing good work. Though I think he's working on a project up at the resort."

Aston nodded, as I turned my attention to look at the menu. "Yes, and I'm glad one of us is here now to work in person."

"You guys take care of the town, and you're not tyrants."

A man with dark hair and a big beard snorted behind us, and I turned. "Sure. The prodigal son arrives, and the world is going to bow down at the Cage's feet."

"Weston," Melody said with a sigh. "Stop being a grump."

The other man grinned, and it brightened up his face completely. At first, I thought he had been an older man, slouching and annoyed with the world, but instead, he was much younger, his eyes bright, and with a humor there that I wouldn't have expected from that gruff introduction.

"I can't help it. It's just my nature."

"Weston here is our local mechanic. He makes sure everything around here is up and running. Which is no small feat during winter."

"It's what I do. Thanks for the coffee, Melody. And it's nice to meet you, Blakely." He glared over my shoulder. "Aston."

Aston narrowed his gaze at the other man. "I wasn't aware we actually were introduced."

Weston just winked, though his eyes weren't filled with humor. "I'll bring the twins by a little later?" he asked.

"Of course. Now get to work. And I'm going to introduce this Cage to what he's been missing."

Weston grunted, and headed out, as everyone else went back to their coffees, and I finally took a look at the menu.

"You have an iced coffee tasting?" I asked, as I clapped my hands in front of me. "We just had a very large pasta lunch, and yet, I'm going to need this."

"I don't know if I've ever seen an iced coffee tasting," Aston said softly beside me.

"They're not that uncommon at smaller places. You're not going to see something like this at a chain, of course, as soon as they hear about it and figure they can make money, they'll hop right on the train and ruin it," Melody grumbled.

"So you don't want the Caged Bean to be a nationwide phenomenon that spreads the name all over the country?" Aston asked, and I bumped his side with my elbow.

"You know who can make that happen," I said with a laugh.

Aston gave me a look, and I blinked innocently up at him.

Melody however, just shook her head. "No, thank you. I'm sure the Cages are spreading enough around."

There was something in her tone though that worried me, but I couldn't tell exactly what she meant by that.

Aston's laughter cooled ever so slightly, but then he cleared his throat. "So we just pick our favorite four?"

"Yes, sir. Now have fun."

"Oh, I'm sure we will," I said softly, as I looked down at the options. "So what are we going to have?"

"And you want to share something with me?" he asked, his voice a purr.

I swallowed hard, aware we were in public. "If you'd like."

"Let's share something, and then head up to the lake." Again, his tone. This felt like a whole new side of Aston. Like he was trying. Trying what, I didn't know, but I was so in over my head.

I cleared my throat and went through the options with Aston, both of us keeping it light, trying to breathe.

In the end we had a toffee nut latte, a Belgian waffle latte, a lucky latte that had actual Lucky Charms inside it, and a strawberry and rose flavored latte that tasted much better than it sounded. After we left the place and said our goodbyes, we walked back to the car, and I felt beyond full.

"I have way too much energy now, thanks to all that caffeine, and I probably shouldn't have had the breadsticks and then a tray of coffees."

Aston kissed the top of my head, and my stomach fluttered. "Well, looks like we're going to have to work that off."

I blinked up at him. "Is that the line you're going

with?" I asked, although something did tighten deep inside.

"It's not a line. It's a promise."

And then he pressed his lips down to mine, right where everyone could see, and I felt claimed, needed.

I took a step back, my breathing quickening. "Show me your house? We can look at the rest of the town and the lake later."

And with that, promise sizzling between us, we practically ran to his SUV.

I might've been able to notice the beautiful architecture, the trees and path around the lake. But my pussy throbbed, and I pressed my thighs together, trying to focus, and yet nothing was calming.

"I'll show you the area, the trees, the resort, everything later."

"I'm okay with that."

"Good."

And then he dragged me inside, the door slamming behind us. His lips were on mine, and I couldn't breathe, couldn't think.

"The luggage is in the car," I whispered.

"It's in the garage, safe from bears."

I paused. "What?"

"Don't worry. I'm going to be the only one pawing you tonight."

That he could have such humor in a time like this surprised me. Again, a whole new side of Aston. And it worried me, because I was getting to know different facets of him that made me want him even more.

And that meant there would be no going back soon.

But then his hands were on my shirt, pulling it over my head, and I couldn't think about anything else but him and his touch.

He pulled me into his bedroom, and I would probably notice the decor later. I didn't even know what color the walls were, because all I could do was look at the color of Aston's eyes. The deep blue pools of them bringing me in as we stripped each other.

Soon we were naked, hands roaming all over one another. He gripped my ass and spread my cheeks, his cock hard and thick against my stomach as he rocked.

"You're so beautiful," he growled.

"I can't think straight," I whispered, my mind going a thousand different places.

"Then don't think."

Again his lips were on mine, nibbling slowly, and then more. But there was something I needed to do, something I hadn't done since that first night. I slid to my knees and he groaned.

"Is the carpet soft enough?" he asked, and I hadn't even realized it was carpet below my knees as I gripped the base of his shaft.

"I'm fine, let me take care of you."

"Only this once, only until I can't think."

"My mind is already blurry," I whispered, and then I took him deep into my mouth. He wrapped my hair around his fist, and I lapped my tongue around the tip, playing with the slit at the edge. It was salty, the fluid bursting on my tongue.

"You on your knees, my cock sliding between your lips? The hottest fucking thing I've ever seen."

I looked up at him then, widening my jaw so I could take him in deeper. He groaned, and then gripped my hair hard enough to keep me still.

"Are you ready?" he asked, his voice low.

In answer I hummed against his dick, and he smiled. That wicked smile that nearly sent me over the edge and yet I was the one gripping him. I slid one hand between my legs, sliding over my clit. I was already so wet, that little bud swollen just from his kisses.

I pulled away suddenly, needing to catch my breath, and he frowned down at me, worrying his gaze.

"Are you okay?" His voice was like a shot of warmth directly to my core. How could a voice do that?

"Yes, I just needed a moment."

And then I was back at it, my head bobbing as I slid over his cock, needing him, needing this slight control in a situation that I never had control of.

When his balls tightened in my hand, he pulled away suddenly, it was all I could do not to gasp. He was somehow on his knees, his hand around my waist, and then he was rolling us, him taking the brunt of the action. My back hit the carpet, and it was indeed soft, as his lips trailed over mine, and then down my neck. Hands on my breasts he plucked at my nipples, and then kissed between them, underneath the globes, and then slid his mouth over the tips.

"So beautiful." His voice was a caress, just like his hands. He continued to trail kisses down my skin, gently, a little more, to the point that it was all I could do just to breathe.

And then his mouth was on me, his tongue sliding between my lips. When his tongue lapped against my clit, I arched up, the sensation far too much. My toes curled, the arches of my feet aching.

"That's it, that's it," he groaned against my pussy, and then I was coming, riding his face as he continued to eat me out. As reality started to clash back down, warmth in my extremities as my legs literally twitched, I found myself lifted into the air. I hadn't even realized he had stood.

"Aston!"

"Mine," he claimed. And then my hands were on the wall, and he was sliding into me.

I gasped, the intrusion hard, sudden, and everything that I needed.

"That's it, take me."

I pressed back into him, meeting him thrust for thrust as he pounded into me, and both of us gasped into each other. With one hand on my hip, he slid the other up to my breast, cupping one and then the other, and then his hand went to my neck, keeping me in place. It was the most erotic image I had ever seen as I turned to look into the mirror. He was so strong, so big, it was all I could do not to fall in his arms. And yet I trusted him to keep me steady.

And then he pulled out, and I turned in his arms, wrapping my own around his neck. He lifted me, and then I was on him again, his cock even deeper this time.

"Aston!"

"That's it, take all of me."

"Always."

I nearly came again, but before I could, I was on my back and he was lapping at me again. This time the orgasm hit full force, and I wrapped my thighs around his neck, needing it to stop, needing it to begin, needing it to continue. It was a circle of time and I never knew where I was. When we were on our sides again, he slid behind me, his cock between my thighs as he gently lifted my leg up. He cradled me in this position, his body so big—and yet it felt like the safest place in the world.

"Tell me when to stop," he whispered, a sheer need and desperation mixed with worry in his tone.

Tears slid down my face but had nothing to do with pain. And everything to do with him.

"Don't stop."

And then he took my mouth and worked in and out of me. It wasn't hard; it wasn't fast. He was taking sweet time with me, sweet care. As if I were the most precious thing in the world. And when he finally came, I followed him, his hand between my legs, his mouth on mine.

After, I lay in his arms, nearly ready to shiver, but then he was gone. Bereft, I looked up at him, wondering why he hadn't said a damn thing, only then he was back again, a warm cloth in his hands.

"Let me take care of you," he whispered again, and I was lost.

And the man I was falling in love with, far too fast, far too deep, took care of us both, and then held me, as I finally came down from whatever high we had each taken each other to. It felt like the same exhilaration from our first dance. The right high that felt as if the world was ready to burst around us. Yet the fall had come far too hard the first time.

It might break me. Or maybe it was exactly what I needed.

Chapter Fourteen

ASTON

Rule #6: (Added by Aston) Remember who you are vs. who you need to be.

IN THE MONTH SINCE WE HAD RETURNED FROM OUR weekend away, things had shifted. I wasn't quite sure how it had happened, but here we were, somehow in a relationship.

Things now felt, perhaps not settled, but firm? No, that wasn't the right word either. More like steady. Which, for a man who wasn't sure he even wanted a relationship, sounded far more unsteady than the word represented.

In that month, Blakely, had gelled with her team and her admin, Garcia, already her number one fan. The entire team was already on their third project, with the microloan program enhancing even more. None of that was in my purview, but James was singing her praises.

We spent more time at my house than hers, but Blakely said it was only because of my shower. It wasn't my fault that I had two shower heads, and then a third that happened to be removable. I held back a smile at the memory of our testing that out.

We'd had dinner with Cale and Sophia, which had been awkward at first, because the connection was two ways. Sophia my sister, and Sophia the sister of Blakely's best friend. In the end, labels hadn't mattered. We'd had good dinner and ended up at a piano bar afterward, singing along with the piano man as everybody was wont to do.

Afterward, Blakely and I had spent the evening tasting every inch of each other at her house, and then eaten sundaes in her bed, courtesy of some of the hot fudge I had used on her breasts prior.

"Sophia and Cale seemed really happy," she had said, and I had nodded, my gaze on her breasts.

"They do. And I don't know how protective I'm supposed to feel about Sophia's boyfriend."

"Eyes up here, I don't think even you can go for round three right now."

I had looked down at my not-so-quite-limp dick, and grinned. "I could probably find a way to enjoy this hot fudge."

She shook her head. "No. Sweet things do not go down there. Breasts are okay, nowhere below the belt."

We had left, and then indeed enjoyed hot fudge above a certain equator.

And in that month, we had had one more monthly

dinner, where seven of us had joined in, though Kyler hadn't come at all. I wasn't sure exactly what I was supposed to say to the brother who seemed to have known the secret all along.

However, the dinner had gone off quite well at Dorian's place. Hudson had even come down from the mountains, joining in for the first time. While checking in with the lawyer each dinner felt as if we were on some form of house arrest, most other things felt normal. Just family dinners. Instead of having to deal with our mother at our *other* required dinners, we were learning the other half of the family at equally required dinners.

But in that month, things felt right. I had never expected Blakely, not once, but twice in my life, and now here we were, feeling as if things could be more.

Or perhaps I was just thinking too hard. I didn't know where this was going, but it felt like it could be going somewhere. It sure as hell felt different than the last time I had been on this path. Of course, it wasn't Meredith's fault that I had fallen out of love with her before she had even broken it off. She had been the one to see the signs it seemed, though I still didn't know exactly what her game had been the night she had come to my house. But she had left me alone since.

But now, I wasn't near Denver to figure out what Meredith had wanted, not that I cared. And I wasn't near Blakely.

How the hell was I already missing Blakely? How had she become so important to me in such a short amount of time. Or perhaps in the nearly two months we had been in each other's lives once again, that wasn't such a short period of time.

My phone buzzed, and I looked down at the text from my brother.

> **FLYNN:**
> Are you planning on gracing us with your presence anytime soon?

I looked across the expanse of the restaurant that the dinner conference was being held at and narrowed my gaze at my brother. He just grinned, while James stood beside him, rolling his eyes. Even though James wasn't the one texting me, I knew they were equally making fun of me.

> **ME:**
> Is there a reason you two are watching me and not working on getting the contact we needed?

The fact that all three of us were at the same conference was unusual. We usually took turns, or when our father had been alive, he had done most of it. Or perhaps there hadn't been any conferences at all and he had just been with his second family. The mechanics of how that man could keep so many secrets still eluded me. I could barely keep up with the work I was trying to do, and spending time with Blakely, and our new family. But maybe it was because I actually cared about the people in my life.

I paused at that feeling. Yes, I cared for Blakely. Was

it love? No. Clearly not. It was way too soon for that, and I wasn't even sure that would be appropriate in this situation. It would get far too complicated if it was.

I once again pushed those thoughts from my mind, and focused on the fact that we three Cages were at this conference. We needed to ensure backers for an upcoming project, and that meant Flynn needed to be his normal people person self, and James needed to act as the steady rock. While I had to be the face of the company, The Cage. I had to put on my shield and ensure the naysayers that we had not fallen or crumbled when the secrets of my father's past had come out. We hadn't lost a single client when the news of a second family had broken. But it had been a precarious situation that we were still dealing with the ramifications of. And the vultures were circling, ready for us to make a mistake.

It didn't help that a certain so-called rival was also here.

I nodded at my brothers, and then went to go speak with the client, doing my best to keep my attention on him, and not the asshole older gentleman that was walking toward us.

Mr. Howard of Howard Enterprises shouldn't be here at all. He should have lost his title and so much more when he had fired Blakely as he had. But then again, we wouldn't have Blakely with us if he hadn't made such a misstep.

"I'm really looking forward to seeing the documentation you have," Patricia Novel said and I forced my attention back on her. As a woman who had not only come from money, but married into it, she had decided to put her incredible wealth toward philanthropic work. And that meant not only with charities, but with businesses that could provide help for others. And that's what we were trying to get her to do. We had worked with her before, and things had worked out well. However, she had come in through my father, and now we needed to ensure that the connection stayed the same with the second generation.

"We have everything set for tomorrow for the presentation. However, you know Flynn and James, they already have a few things I can send you right now."

Flynn who had been coming by, just grinned. "You know we do."

"You Cage brothers, you always know how to step up to the plate."

James had his phone out, and I had no doubt that he was already sending over the information that had been at his fingertips.

"You know I say Cage brothers, but you have sisters now, don't you?" the other woman asked, and there was only curiosity in her tone, not any slyness. A few others stopped what they were doing to listen in, but there was no hiding it. There never had been. Not since the news had broken.

"We do have sisters. So I guess our moniker has to change," I said, keeping my tone light.

"I would think so. You needed more estrogen in your household anyway. I don't know how your mother did it."

I had a feeling my smile added a slight bitter edge to it, but I masked it quickly. "She persevered. Somehow."

"And we were perfect angels," Flynn added.

The older woman threw her head back and laughed, and attention was on us once again, but this time for a different curiosity.

"I've always liked you Flynn."

"And I've always liked you. I'm really sad that you're married though. I can't whisk you away."

"You're lucky that you golf with my husband and he knows you're kidding," she said with a laugh. "And I know you're just buttering me up because you want to work with me, and I get it. But I've always really liked you."

"And I don't joke the way that I do with just anyone," Flynn added, and I had a feeling that he felt bad about teasing the way he had. We had to schmooze and put on fake laughs for most people, but not for her.

"We do like you, you know," I said softly, and the other woman's eyes softened.

"I know you do. So, you three Cages work together. This company is still thriving despite what that old man of yours did," she said, the biting tone making us all stand up a little straighter. "Are any of the others going to work with you? I don't need to know the details of the will or inheritance," she said, waving off any speculation. "I just know how family can be."

Her smile went wistful, and I remembered in that moment, that she had had four children, three of them dying in a plane crash when they had been teenagers, on their way to visit relatives. Her remaining son was now happily married, and had given Patricia grandchildren, but I couldn't even imagine the loss.

"We're figuring out the family part," I answered.

"One step at a time," James put in. "Although we did hire one sister," he said.

The other woman's eyes brightened. "You did? Is she here?" she asked, looking around.

I shook my head. "No, she's a forensic accountant. This isn't really her scene." Though I didn't know Isabella's scene completely, I had a feeling a meeting like this wouldn't be it.

"Well, when I come down to Denver, I'm going to have to meet her and the rest. I really like you Cage brothers, and I should meet the rest of them. Including that rockstar," she said, this time the laugh full out.

I sighed, as both James and Flynn chuckled. "It puts our meager standings in *Forbes* and other circles to shame, doesn't it?" I asked wryly.

"He does have good music, and my granddaughters love him. Maybe you can get me an autograph? Make me the best grandma ever? I'm still competing with their mother's mother. That old bitty got them horses for Christmas. Actual horses."

I pressed my lips together, as James assured her that we would get Kyler's autograph. I wasn't quite sure how we were going to do that, but we'd find a way. If anything, I would ask Blakely. She was on better terms with him than we were for now.

We finished up our conversation, laughing along the

way, and we went to go speak with a few other people. As James and Flynn went in opposite directions, each on a mission, the hairs on the back of my neck stood on end, and I looked over to see Mr. Howard staring at me.

"I knew she was working for you the whole time. Espionage? Really?" the other man asked.

His voice was low, but deep enough that it could carry. I was not about to have Blakely's reputation or the Cage's impinged with this asshole.

"You know she wasn't. You know that you're just jealous of her talents, and our business. We aren't rivals, Howard. We never were. Only in your mind."

"I'll have her arrested," the other man snapped, and I smelled the bourbon on his breath.

"You can try, and I will take you for everything you're worth."

Howard's gaze narrowed. "So you're fucking her as well. I knew you were. It couldn't just be one dance like I said. Fucking the help? I should have known."

I moved forward, hands clenched, but then James was between us, my usually quiet brother literally growling.

"You're going to want to step back. Blakely works for me, not Aston. And if you say a single word about her again, in front of me, or anywhere that I hear about, I'll sue you for all that you're worth. Then I'll let Aston have what's left of you."

The other man gulped, and I glared over James's shoulder. We were creating a scene, the exact thing I did not want, but as the older man seemed to realize what was happening, he finally left, and James let out a breath.

"You okay?" he asked, as Flynn came toward us.

"I'm fine, but I need a breather. I'm going to go out on the balcony, and just get some air."

"Don't worry about it. We've got it. No one overheard by the way, they were trying to, but you were in the corner enough," Flynn reassured.

"I'm going to have to tell Blakely about this," I whispered.

"Yes, you will. Because secrets suck," James put in, and then my brothers left me to my own devices, and I walked out on the balcony.

We were in the Hamptons of all places, and I really just wanted to go home, and deal with the altitude, and the crisp air there. It just didn't smell the same here. I wanted to be with Blakely, and that should have scared me more than anything. That she would be the first thing that came to mind. But then again, maybe it shouldn't have scared me.

"I knew you were here," a familiar, and very unwanted voice said from beside me, and I stiffened, wondering why the hell this night was out to get me.

I turned to see Meredith walking toward me, or rather staggering. She had a martini in hand, her dress fitted to her like a glove, but not overly ostentatious. Instead she just looked as if she had walked off a catwalk into the event.

"Meredith. Can I get you some water?"

She shook her head, and then seemed to think better of it and reached out. As I didn't want her to fall, because I wasn't that much of an asshole, I gripped her elbow, keeping her steady.

"Let me get you some water, Meredith."

However, I knew touching her was a mistake, as she set the martini glass down in the same moment that she plastered herself to my front.

"Meredith. Seriously?" I asked, trying to gently pull her away from me. There were others on this balcony, and we were creating quite a show.

"I miss you," she whispered, her words slurring. I'd never seen Meredith drunk before. What the hell was going on with this woman?

"You broke up with me," I reiterated. "We haven't been a thing for a long while. Let me go get you some water, and we can forget this ever happened."

"I made a mistake. I was scared before."

This woman had an MBA and was brilliant at what she did. And yet right now, I couldn't see any of the Meredith that I knew before. Something was wrong, but I did not need to be in the middle of it.

"I'm with Blakely now," I said softly, knowing our voices were carrying no matter what we did.

"But I love you," she blurted.

I closed my eyes for a moment, hating this. My chest tightened, and I realized that I would've loved those words before. Maybe it would've triggered something for me when I had needed it. And yet they did nothing for me now.

"You're better than this, Meredith."

Her eyes narrowed to slits, and I tried to step back.

"Don't you think I know that? I made a mistake. Please." And before I could say anything, she pushed herself closer to me, arms wrapped around my shoulders, and her lips were pressed to mine.

Chapter Fifteen
BLAKLEY

Dear Diary,
Sometimes you just have to break things before they break you.

"I'M SO GLAD THAT YOU'RE HERE WITH US," EMILY exclaimed as she wrapped her arm around my waist. I did the same, and we leaned our heads together, waiting for the others to arrive.

"It's been a hot minute since we've been able to just take a night off and have girl time," I answered.

In fact, I wasn't sure all of us had been together for a girls' night since before their father had passed. It had been a few months, and I knew they were all breathing in their own ways but having this moment just to relax felt wonderful. So much had happened since that night. And not just with our promotions. There were different relationships, so many secrets revealed, and new jobs. And not just for me.

Isabella came forward, her gaze on her phone, and I scowled at her.

"You better not be working," I teased.

She looked up at me, eyes wide. "Of course not. It's kind of bizarre that I get weekends off to be honest."

"It's because you're working with a company that actually supports you," Sophia replied as she came forward, Phoebe at her side.

"I kind of hate the fact that they do run a smooth business," Isabella said, as she crossed her eyes.

The door opened, and our last member of our group of six entered. Greer waved at us, looking a little nervous.

I didn't blame her, because this was her first time with our girl group. However, as she was married to Ford, technically she was now their sister-in-law. Phoebe ran over to the other woman and hugged her tightly.

Greer smiled at all of us. "I'm sorry I'm late, I was delayed." From the blush on her cheeks, I had a feeling we all knew exactly how she was delayed.

"I don't really want to know more about Ford's love life, sorry, but I'm not related to your other husband Noah," Phoebe said, her voice filled with laughter.

Greer rolled her eyes. "Well, having two husbands does mean it takes forever to get out of the house." She held up her hand. "And not just because of *that*," she said with a laugh.

Everybody joined in and we made our way to the front desk.

Tonight we were doing a smash room before we headed to dinner. It was something that none of us had done before, and I had a feeling that some people in our group had a little more rage than others, so tonight would be good for them.

"Your admin couldn't come?" Sophia asked as she came to my side. Isabella and Emily went to the front desk, while we stood back. We were a larger group, and we didn't want to be in the way.

I shook my head. "Garcia has a date tonight that she did not want to cancel."

Sophia let out a content sigh. "I'm really glad that you're making friends with people at work. I realize that work friends and real-life friends are a different connection, but it's good that you have that support system."

I looked at Sophia, at her bright eyes and blushing cheeks. She looked so damn happy. Of course, Sophia always looked as if she were going through a thousand emotions at once. She had been a talented dancer, and still was, and worked with children and young adults daily. But teaching others how to dance wasn't what was making her eyes bright I didn't think.

"I do have a good place to work, and I enjoy the people I work with. Much like Isabella seems to be doing, but I want to know why you can't stop smiling," I teased.

"Oh I want to know too," Phoebe said as she came forward, Greer by her side.

"It's nothing," Sophia said, ducking her head.

I bumped her hip with mine. "So, things with Cale are going well."

She blushed even harder. "Yes. He's just so nice. I mean, he's not perfect, none of us are, but he just does things that make me feel cherished. And he's hot," she blurted, and I burst out laughing.

I beamed. "As I've met him, I totally agree."

Sophia hugged me tightly, her smile widening. "You know, I was going to ask how things were going with your man, because you can't stop smiling, but then I realized he's my brother, and I don't know if I want to know all the details."

I ducked my head, my teeth biting into my lip. "We're just taking it slow. After all, it's a little complicated." I lifted my head, looking at each one of them. "For many reasons."

"That just means we have more of a reason to kick his ass if he hurts you," Isabella said, her voice prim and proper.

I rolled my eyes. "You really shouldn't say that as we're about to go and get a sledgehammer or something. Do we use sledgehammers?"

"They're going to have all the instructions for us," Isabella explained. "And I don't know about you, I could really hit something right now." I lifted a brow, and she shrugged. "Past resentment. Don't worry, I don't hate your boyfriend."

Everybody laughed, and it was Greer who squeezed my elbow. I looked over at the other woman, and she smiled softly. "I really like Aston."

"You don't have to say that just because I'm dating him. Though now that I think about it, you've known him longer than all of us."

"I have and I would tell you the truth if I felt like there was something different about him. Or if I thought you weren't a good fit."

I smiled, feeling oddly at ease with that promise. "We're just taking it slow. I mean, a lot has happened in the past few months."

The other woman's hip bumped me. "That's an understatement, although you did get to see Cage Lake. Isn't it beautiful?"

"I really want to see this infamous small town that happens to be branded with our name," Emily said as we waited for the attendant to explain things.

"I really don't know if it exists," Isabella said, and I knew she was just teasing me. "I mean, maybe you Photoshopped all those lovely images of that mountain."

"Yes, I spent all of my free time to add in random Cage landmarks just for you," I said dryly.

"That sounds like something you would do," Sophia added with a laugh.

The attendant came over, and the woman with bright purple hair styled in some form of Mohawk, two nose rings, and a full-sleeve tattoo smiled at us.

"Hello there, and welcome to Break It."

"Thanks for having us," Emily said, bouncing on her toes.

"Okay, you already went through the waivers before you came, so that's going to handle the housekeeping beforehand. When we get into the room you can choose from baseball bats, sledgehammers, crowbars, and even more. You guys also added on a few items so in addition to your own personal crate of things to smash, we have a few special things for you. You're allowed to throw things against the wall, stomp on them, crash them, do anything you'd like. Isabella here also sent over a playlist, so we're going to fill the room with the music of your choice and have fun."

I looked over Isabella and shook my head. "Really? *You* picked a playlist?"

"I can do music."

"I helped," Sophia whispered, and Isabella flipped us off.

Laughing, we headed over to the locker room, each of us pulling on coveralls, a face shield, gloves, boots, and loop earplugs so we could still hear the music and each other, but we'd be able to protect our hearing just a bit.

"You'll have exclusive use of the room, and about an hour and a half just to smash to your heart's content. Afterward we do have pizza and soft drinks, but I know you have dinner plans."

"Pizza is always an answer though," I added, feeling elated to be able to smash something.

"Okay, let's go through a few more instructions, and then have at it."

By the time we were ready, I was amped up. Metallica was already blaring through the room, and I bounced on my toes, the others looking as if they were just as wired.

While things seemed to be going well in my life, being

able to get through all the resentment for the past year felt good.

Yes, I was falling in love with a man that made me smile, and put me first when we were together, but I didn't know what would happen after this. I didn't know who we would be together. Or, maybe I was always thinking too hard about what that meant. What we meant.

While I loved my job now and my team, I still hated the fact that every once in a while, I had to see news or paperwork over my former team. It just reminded me of every single thing that I had been put through and hadn't even realized that I had been ignoring. I had lowered myself and my talents in order to fit in the box they had placed me, all because I had been too scared to take a chance. But now here I was, taking all the chances, and I had to hope that I wouldn't break in the end.

Isabella took the crowbar first, as I picked up a baseball bat, and we each took our weapons, grinning at each other.

"Okay, let's break things," Emily said, sounding so much like a cheerleader, it was a little disconcerting.

So...we broke things.

The exhilaration of smashing random objects with other objects shouldn't feel this good. But I felt like I was on that office movie where they were beating up a printer that annoyed them. In fact, I was enjoying beating up a piece of office equipment, just remembering the fact that my old printer never used to be able to connect to the network. No matter what I did, I swore the printer had it out for me.

Sophia and I took turns with a barrel, though I knew Sophia wasn't really putting her all into it, she was there because we were there, and I didn't mind. In fact, it only took about thirty minutes for me to realize we were just having fun laughing with each other, although Isabella kept hitting a little bit harder. I wanted to tell her everything was going to be okay, even though I didn't know exactly what was going on in my best friend's heart right then. But she kept smashing things, kept hitting, and when she finally stopped, her shoulders heaving, we all looked at her.

She looked at us and shrugged. "I was just imagining my old office. I'm okay. Promise."

I raised a brow, and then Isabella blinked away tears so quickly I nearly missed it. "And maybe I thought of Dad."

Everybody was silent for a moment, as Emily let out a long breath.

"I thought I was the only one."

"I don't want to hit him, I just don't want to think about him," Sophia added.

"I don't think about him. Although, I think about Mom more."

"I'm not speaking about Mom," Isabella snapped, before she let out a deep breath. "I'm sorry. Maybe I need to hit more things."

"Maybe we should go get dinner," I put in.

Isabella looked at me then, tilting her head. "Are the

Cage brothers upset with their mom? Or is everything hunky-dory on that side."

I cringed and looked over at Greer.

"I wouldn't say hunky-dory," Greer added. "Not that I know what that word means."

We all let out a soft laugh, though there wasn't much humor in it.

"I know there's strain there, and it's not perfect. You should talk to them."

"About their mom? Or about the fact that our moms seemed to have found a way to hurt all of us at the same time," Isabella asked dryly.

"We don't talk about it," I said, feeling a little hurt by that. Because no, Aston and I didn't talk about his parents. At all. We talked about my family, and his work, and what we wanted with our futures in terms of our careers, but we didn't talk about the big thing that stood between us and was obviously so heavy over his shoulders.

"We don't talk about your father, their father," I corrected. "I don't know if we should, I don't know if it's my place. But you should all talk. That's what those dinners are for."

Sophia just shook her head, as Emily and Phoebe held onto each other, and Isabella's fists clenched.

"We do those dinners because we have to. And while I can't blame any of my siblings, on either side, for what happened, I'm not okay with it. I don't want to talk to Mom. And I don't want to talk about Dad anymore. I just want it all to be over. And it's never going to be over. Because they've royally fucked us."

"I wish I knew what Aston thought, but he doesn't tell me." I blurted out the words and didn't realize that they were there until everyone stared at me. "Sorry, I shouldn't center this around me."

"No, I'd love to talk about anyone but myself," Isabella said. "Are you okay?" she asked softly. "Do I have to hit my brother?" I asked.

"No, no violence." They all stared pointedly at me, and I looked around the smash room. "Other than right now." The soft laughter didn't fill the silence. "Everything's fine. I mean, it's not like we're too serious."

"Are you trying to tell us that, or yourself," Emily asked, not unkindly.

"I don't know. I just, I don't want to make something out of nothing." I cleared my throat and rolled my shoulders back. "And since we ended this on such a weird note, let's go get dinner, and stuff our faces."

"I might have to eat some pizza before we go," Phoebe added. "I'm starving."

"Honestly same," Sophia said, her hand on her stomach. "I skipped lunch again."

"Sophia," Isabella chided.

"Class ran over, and then I had to deal with a few yelling parents." She held up her hand. "It's part of my job. And it's okay, I'm going to eat two dinners, like a little hobbit, and everything will be fine."

I sighed, as we made our way into the locker room to

change back into our normal clothes. Isabella tugged on my wrist, pulling me back.

"I'm sorry if I pushed," she said.

I shook my head. "You didn't push."

"I did. But you're my best friend, and I want to know about the guy you're seeing. I want to know what you feel, and what he feels. Just like old times."

"And I want to tell you that," I whispered.

"But you can't, because it's Aston. Because he's my brother." She shook her head. "And that's such a weird word to say. Kyler was my only brother for all of my life, and suddenly I'm surrounded by testosterone."

"So much testosterone," I whispered. "But it's okay. We do talk. You listen."

"I still have so much anger. And Dad's not here, and I'm not talking to Mom, so I keep pushing it at them. So I'm sorry. I want you to tell me everything."

"There's not much to tell right now."

"Do you love him?" she asked point blank, and I swallowed hard.

"I don't know." My voice was so small, that Isabella hugged me tightly.

"It's okay not to know. And we can talk it out. Or you can talk it out with your parents, or someone. But you should. Because I love you."

She kissed the tip of my nose, and I rolled my eyes.

"I love you too. But not like that."

"No, you like another Cage," she teased, and I shook my head, and we went to go get ready.

I pulled my phone out of my locker and frowned at the four messages from Garcia.

"Are you okay?" Sophia asked, and I nodded, pulling out my texts.

"Garcia texted a few times. I hope she's okay."

And then it felt as if ice slid through my veins.

> Garcia:
>
> I didn't want to send this. I don't think it's my place, and I don't think I'm doing you any good.
>
> GARCIA:
>
> But others have seen, and I don't want you to be in the dark. I'm here if you want to talk. I'm sorry.

And below that was a screenshot of a social media post, that made my knees go weak. Isabella's arms went around my waist, as the others came forward.

"What's wrong?" Sophia asked, as Isabella snatched the phone from my hand, letting me lean on Phoebe.

"I'm going to kill him," Isabella snapped, and Greer took the phone from her.

"There has to be something wrong. This isn't what it looks like," Greer said softly, and Isabella put up her hand.

"You may have known him longer, but I don't think we can deny what's going on in this photo."

They started arguing with each other, but I knew they weren't mad at one another. No, they were mad at the man in the photo, with the woman crawling on him, with their mouths pressed together.

Aston was supposed to be on a work trip, and we were supposed to talk to each other tonight before he came home.

But instead, he stood on a balcony, with Meredith holding onto him, and with a kiss that seemed to shatter everything inside.

And as a single tear finally fell, I knew no amount of rage rooms were going to help. Nothing would.

Chapter Sixteen
ASTON

Rule #7: (Added by Aston) Break the rules.

My head ached and all I really wanted to do was take a shower and get into bed. The day had been long, full of travel delays, dead phones, and a lost charging cord. And, on the way home, it seemed that I hadn't put the charging cord back in my car. Meaning I still had a dead phone as I walked into my house.

I was supposed to have been home six hours ago, but a thunderstorm in Dallas, complete with a lovely tornado, meant the entire country was dealing with weather-related issues with their flights. I was just glad everybody was safe, but I was exhausted.

I rubbed the back of my neck and plugged in my phone. I probably needed to look at the codependent relationship I had with it because I immediately relaxed when I saw it charging.

My brothers were still on the east coast and would be coming back tomorrow. At one point when I was on my layover, I was truly afraid they were going to make it home before I did. However, I was home, and I just wanted to talk to Blakely. I rubbed my hand over my chest, wondering why she was the first person I thought of.

Things were happening quite quickly, and I knew that, but after the night before, I felt like I should say something.

I had pushed Meredith away as soon as her lips had pressed to mine, and then she had wiped away her tears and shook her head. When she had looked back up at me, her eyes had widened so much, she looked even more surprised than I had.

She had bolted away, leaving me standing there wondering what the hell had just happened. I had no idea who had seen or what I was supposed to fucking do, but then I needed to go back into the meeting space and talk with more people. I hadn't been able to get a hold of Blakely the night before, since she hadn't texted me back, and with my phone and plane issues, I had no idea what else I had missed.

I stripped off my button-down shirt, leaving me in just my undershirt and pants, having toed off my shoes when I had walked in.

I hated traveling in a full suit, but I had had a meeting right before I needed to head to the airport.

My phone finally turned on and I pulled up my notifications, wincing at the number of texts and emails I had.

THE FOREVER RULE

I shot a quick email to the family group, minus Mom, letting them know that I was there. I was finally home.

I paused after I did so, knowing that we probably needed to make a full siblings chat. That made my lips twitch, as an unsettled feeling washed over me. Adding Blakely to the group, even by accident, all those months ago was how we had met. Sure, we probably would've been introduced to each other at a later point because she was friends with Isabella, but it wouldn't have been the same. I hated when people said that everything happened for a reason, but maybe it did. No, my father being a cruel and uncaring person when it came to family matters wasn't for a reason. And the night I had had previously shouldn't have been for a reason.

I frowned when I looked at my text to Blakely and realized she hadn't responded.

I checked the time, and figured she might be sleeping, but I was worried now. I quickly pressed her contact, dialing out, but after waiting, it went to voicemail.

I blinked wondering maybe she was on another call? No, maybe I was just thinking too hard. I called again, immediately it went to voicemail.

An odd feeling washed over me, and I texted her quickly wondering what the hell was going on. Why was she ignoring me?

> **ME:**
> I'm home, had phone issues all day. I missed you.

There, that was the most I'd ever put in a text

message about what I felt. The fact that I didn't know what I felt meant I needed to worry about other things later. But for now, I was worried.

The doorbell rang, and then somebody banged their fist on the door as soon as my thoughts went into a tailspin about Blakely. Alarmed, worried somebody was hurt, I ran to the door. As I pulled it open, I blinked as Isabella stood there, fuming. Her eyes narrowed, hands fisted at her sides, she glared.

"You asshole."

I blinked at her, wondering if this woman was honestly going to hit me.

"Isabella? What are you doing here? And what the hell?"

She stomped right toward me, and though she was much smaller than me, I was slightly afraid of her.

"I can't believe you. Just when we were starting to trust you, just when we were letting our family trust you, you do *this*? I should have known, with the way Dad was. I should have known you'd be just like him."

I staggered back, confused as hell, then her words finally hit. "Holy fuck, who told you about the kiss?"

"You don't even deny it. Of course, how could you deny when there's photographic evidence?" She held up her phone, and I blinked, reality crashing in so swiftly, it was like a punch to the gut.

"How? It's not what you think."

"No, that's what they all say. But I'm pretty sure that's your ex-fiancée and you with your arms around each other kissing at a work event, one that the family business was invited to. I cannot believe I get to work with philanderers of course, it must be in the genes. I hope it doesn't trickle down to our side of the family because I don't want to be a cheating asshole."

Isabella kept going and I saw the tears glisten in her eyes. She might be angry, might be snapping out, but there was far more emotions than just the shrewishness that she put on as a good front.

I held her phone in my hand, staring at the photo that somebody had put on social media. Someone had taken a fucking photo of the moments where Meredith had lost her mind.

I shook my head, handing over the phone, now realizing why Blakely hadn't texted me back. Why she was ignoring my calls.

"Did you show this to Blakely?"

"I didn't have to. Her admin sent it to her because she was afraid that everybody else would know and she would be left in a dark. Because she actually *cares* about Blakely."

"Stop, just stop," I said as I pulled Isabella into my house. She tried to get out of my grasp, but I was stronger.

"Get your hands off me."

"I'd rather not have this fight on my porch."

Considering I already dealt with a fight with not only Meredith but also my mother on my porch at one point, I didn't like this becoming routine.

"It's not like that," I said quickly as Isabella pulled her arm from my grasp and shook her head.

"It's not like what? That you decided to be just like Dad and have another woman when you're on one of your work trips." She used her fingers to make air quotes, and I pinched the bridge of my nose.

"Meredith was drunk, and she kissed me. I didn't kiss her back and I pulled her off right away. And then for some reason, she burst into tears and ran away before I could figure out what's going on. Something's wrong with Meredith, and I know she doesn't want me back, but something happened, and yet, it is not me. *I didn't kiss her.*"

The last sentence was practically a shout, and Isabella stood there, and I could not tell what the hell she was thinking.

"I would never hurt Blakely like that. And I'm not our father." Even as I said the words, bile coated my tongue. I wasn't our father. I didn't cheat. I didn't lie. But in every other way I was my father. I was *The Cage*. Multiple people said it. Every single time I was out, news articles said it, and it was how we kept our family reputation until Dad had tried to bulldoze it with his casualness of cruelty.

"I care for Blakely."

"Care," Isabella whispered, but there was no ire in her tone.

"Care," I repeated, "I don't know exactly what I feel because I haven't let myself, and that's something I need to talk over with Blakely." I cursed under my breath and began to pace. "If she even fucking lets me."

"You didn't cheat," she said after a moment, the

confusion lacing her words sending anger through my system.

"No, I don't cheat. Cages don't cheat."

She raised a brow and pointed between us. "I think you and I being half-siblings is sort of the error to your ways."

"*Real* Cages don't cheat. I don't know what the fuck my father was thinking, but I am not him." Even as I said the words, it didn't feel right. No, I wasn't Dad, I didn't cheat. But maybe my father hadn't cheated until he had met Isabella's mother. Maybe I was wrong, and it was in the genes. I knew nothing I was thinking was making sense, and yet, that little inkling of doubt kept seeping in.

I was my father's son, and maybe that cruelty came with time.

"I can tell what you're thinking," Isabella whispered after a moment, "but dear old dad was a bigamist. Except for the whole legal thing."

"I cannot believe the moms kept secret families for so long."

"Blakely said you don't talk to yours."

I met Isabella's gaze and nodded. "Not anymore. I'm done with her. Which I know doesn't make any sense because I'm going to have to deal with her soon when it comes to business and my brothers. But she *let* this happen. She lied to us just as much as Dad did."

"Hence why I'm not talking to my mother either. Not that Sophia and the others understand that," Isabella ground out.

"Look at us, having common ground."

"I don't like it," my sister said, although I wasn't sure if there was humor in her words.

"I didn't cheat on Blakely."

"Then go tell her that."

"Just show up at her house?"

"Do the big gesture, grovel, do something." She paused and rubbed her hands over her face. "And I'm sorry I immediately thought you were like Dad. I guess I'm not actually grieving the man, I'm just pretending he didn't exist."

I moved forward, and tentatively put my hand on her shoulder.

Her hands fell and she looked up at me. "What?"

"I don't want to grieve him. I want to move on, and I'm sorry."

"It's not your fault. I guess you aren't Dad." Without thinking, I pulled her into a hug, and Isabella stiffened before hugging me back.

"This is weird," she said after a moment, and I laughed, even though there was barely any humor in it.

"Very. We're going to have to figure this out, Isabella."

"I know. I thought we were off to a good start, at least with some things." She pulled back and cleared her throat. "But I guess there are a lot more potholes out there."

"I need to figure out how the hell I'm going to grovel."

She studied my face. "Tell her the truth."

"If she lets me." I let out a breath. "If it's all right with you, I'm going to change, and we can deal with the family things later. I have a feeling there's going to be a few more obstacles in our way before we navigate how to live with this new reality."

"I'm not sure any of us are ready for that. Now go to her and tell her the truth. Blakely is a lot calmer than I am," she added dryly.

"I've noticed that." I let out a breath. "I didn't mean to hurt her."

"Were you going to tell her about the kiss?"

I nodded immediately. "Yes, but I was going to do it in person. That way she could actually see my face. I didn't realize I had paparazzi."

She cringed. "Nothing is private anymore. I'll let myself out. Do good things, Aston. For some reason I believe you can."

And with that, my sister left, and I quickly changed, not knowing how the hell I was going to fix this. It took the entire car ride to Blakely's house for me to realize that I had no idea what I was going to do.

I pulled into her driveway and was grateful that the lights seemed to be on in her living room. She was home, hopefully she was awake, and hopefully she would listen.

I knocked quietly on the door not wanting to wake her in case she was actually sleeping, but she opened it quickly, and my breath caught in my throat. Her hair was piled on the top of her head, her eyes swollen, and her pajamas were of the comfy sort. Her cardigan wrapped tightly around her.

"Hi," I said, my voice cracking.

"What are you doing here, Aston?"

"I'm sorry."

Blakley tilted her head and gave me a slow blink. "Sorry for kissing your ex-fiancée? For leading me on?"

I shook my head quickly and reached out to her. She took a step back, and I held back the curse. "Meredith kissed me. I did not kiss her at all." I explained the entire evening, going over every detail, and Blakely stood there, silent.

"I was going to tell you as soon as I got home because I wanted to see your face when I did so you could see my face. I am sorry you found out that way."

"I want to trust you, I think, but seeing that kiss just threw me for a loop."

"Honestly, why wouldn't you believe it? My entire family is drenched in this mess because of cheating, and we've spoken of Meredith before, so you understand how she's like. At least recently. I hope you never have to cross paths."

Something skittered over her face, and I frowned.

"What is it?"

She sighed and pulled me inside the house, closing and locking the door behind us. "I should probably tell you that one time when we were out to dinner, Meredith cornered me in the bathroom."

My eyes widened and I moved forward. "What the hell? Did she hurt you?"

She shook her head. "No, but she claimed that you two were meant for each other. I told her that she needed to think better about herself and the choices she made, but I suppose she didn't take that to heart."

I ran my hands over my face before moving forward tentatively. "Isabella said I should grovel, and I will."

Blakely's eyes widened. "When did you speak to Isabella?"

"Right before I came here when she yelled at me."

"She came to your house?"

I nodded. "Yes. I deserved it. Especially if all you saw was the photo, and no explanation."

Blakely ran her hand over her face. "My best friend is insane."

"She loves you."

When she let her hands fall, my heart kicked. She was so damn beautiful. "She does, and I love her."

For some reason, the word love echoed between us, but I didn't say anything. I couldn't because I had no idea what I felt. This had started casual, and it should have stayed that way, but it wasn't. And that worried me.

"I didn't kiss her and I'm sorry that you were hurt."

"I may be making a terrible mistake, but I believe you. It just felt like a slap, and then I got in my own head. Just like before, when you didn't call, even though that was for a good reason."

"I'm still an asshole who should have called. Both times."

She stepped forward and I wrapped my arms around her. She hugged me tightly and I kissed the top of her head.

"I promise to never let my phone die again, and I will tell you the next time a random woman kisses me." She punched me not so softly, and I grunted. "Too soon?"

"Far too soon. What are you going to do about her?"

"Isabella?" I asked, knowing full well who she meant.

"Sure. Her first."

"Isabella, I don't know. Meredith, I don't know."

"If something's wrong, maybe she just needs a friend."

I pulled back, my eyes widening.

"And *you* want to be friends with her?"

She grimaced. "Maybe not, but maybe she needs one. I don't know. Everyone keeps saying the way she's acting is out of character, so maybe something's wrong. I just hate feeling like this and I never want to feel like this again. It was like a slap and a punch all at once, and that scares me because I've never felt this way before, for anyone. And then the rug was pulled out from under me, and I was lost, and I don't want to feel that again either."

Ease settled over me and I nodded wondering if I would do it again. I might not cheat like my father—if you could call consensual relationships like that cheating—but I'd hurt her. Because I'm my father's son. Because I couldn't promise I wouldn't.

Instead of saying anything though, I just held her, and got lost to my own thoughts.

I wouldn't break my promises, not when it came to fidelity. But I hadn't called when everything had changed the first time, and I hadn't called the night before.

So perhaps I really was my father's son, at least when it came to promises.

And that worried me more than I thought possible.

Chapter Seventeen
BLAKELY

Dear Diary,
Is it okay to believe in forever?

MY PARENTS WERE IN LOVE WITH MY BOYFRIEND.

I was quite confident that I had never thought that particular phrase before in my life, nor would have even *suggested* it in the past. However as we sat in my parents' living room, Aston smiled, and my mother practically swooned.

An arm wrapped around my shoulders, and I leaned into my dad's hold. He had that same forest scent that he always did, that mix of cologne and his deodorant that reminded me of my father.

I knew I was lucky in the way that I had grown up. Two loving parents, who cared about me. Yes, Mom had worked long hours, and Dad had been gone for forty-eight hours at a time, and yet, I had never felt the lack. I had grown up in my mom's office, and in his fire station.

In Aston's family parents had been there. Yes, his father had been away half the time it seemed once he had started his second family, but he had worked with three of his sons. Had done some summer vacations with them in Cage Lake. Just like he had with all of Aston's full brothers. I remembered Isabella telling me that their father would do smaller family vacations, but nowhere near the mountains. Nowhere near a small town that bared his name.

I wasn't quite sure how all twelve of the siblings had come out somewhat whole, or sane. Not that I knew all of Aston's brothers inside and out, but from what I could tell, they were good people. And Isabella's full siblings had been in my life since I had known Isabella, and they were also kind. Even Kyler, who growled more often than not.

But then again, he had been the only boy growing up in a household of girls.

I had been the lucky one, and I hadn't even realized it.

"Well that's a sight to see," my dad whispered in my ear, and I sighed against his shoulder, watching my mother animatedly talk to Aston, her hands moving in the air as if she knew that if she had to sit on her hands, she probably wouldn't be able to complete a sentence. Aston looked fully engaged, leaning forward and smiling as my mother spoke.

He was in the middle of the conversation, *truly there,*

although something had felt off when he had picked me up. Or maybe I was just so nervous about this family dinner where he was meeting the parents, that I had put undue pressure on myself.

"What's a sight?" I asked, pulling myself back into the present.

"You brought a man home. This is a big deal."

I was grateful that we were far enough away that I didn't think Aston had heard, but I still hissed lowly. "Don't let him hear you," I whispered.

"What? It is a big deal. You brought him over so we could check him out and vet him. I approve of your decisions, though I haven't approved of the man yet."

I looked up at him, my eyes narrowing. "Excuse me, you are not here to vet him."

"Who says I haven't already? I did warn you I would. All before your what, second date?"

My chest tightened, and I took a step back. "Please tell me you didn't ask your friends."

"What, I could have. I didn't, but I could have. And you know your mom could have easily. Just a few click of the buttons."

"And then illegally do a full background check? No, neither one of you would do that." I paused. "Would you?"

"If I thought he was going to hurt you? In a second." The seriousness of my father's tone made me sit up a little straighter.

"It's not like that. He's a good man."

"And I'm glad. I would hate to have to go to jail for murdering a Cage."

That made me smile, and I shoved at him gently. "If he hurts me, I will be the one who takes care of it."

"And while I believe you would try, you would have to get past your mother first." He paused. "And Isabella."

I pressed my lips together, both of us on the edge of laughter. Because that was true. Isabella was always in our corner, even though she didn't always let us be in her corner.

"She's a good friend."

"And Aston's sister. Small world."

I shook my head. "So small it's a little worrying. But I'm glad we're here for dinner. Although I am really nervous."

"That boy better be more nervous."

"That *boy* is in his thirties. I think you can call him a little more grown up than that."

"Maybe. But since you're my little girl, I'm going to have to use the words that I want."

"Dad," I said, exasperated.

"What? You really can't blame me. I've never got to interrogate a boyfriend before."

"Excuse me? You interrogated the boy that came over to drive me to swim practice. A boy I wasn't even dating."

"But you could have been. I didn't know. I needed to ensure that he knew he had precious cargo."

I rolled my eyes. "And that boy was not into girls. Remember? He's happily married to his husband."

"And I didn't know that at the time. All I knew was

that some stranger was about to take my baby girl out in a car, all while we weren't there."

"Because he had a license, I didn't, and both of you worked way too many hours."

"I really don't like this logic of yours. You're starting to sound like your mother."

"That better not be a bad thing," Mom called out as she came forward, Aston behind her. Dad and I had been so engrossed in our conversation that I hadn't realized that the other two had joined us.

"Oh. Hi," I blurted.

My dad cleared his throat. "I love you, Piper."

My mom raised a brow. "Okay. You say that as if you've done something wrong."

"Never. I promise."

"I don't know if I trust that," Mom said, her eyes dancing.

"Well, I would love to know who this swim club partner of yours was," Aston asked, and I groaned.

"Dad."

"What? It's a legitimate question." My dad looked at Aston, and grinned. "His name was Shane. And he did the 200 IM, and 200 butterfly. Meaning he was really broad-shouldered."

"Are you serious right now?" I asked, this time glaring at my father.

"I just want him to get a full picture."

"I'm glad you interrogated him. It's the only right thing to do."

I poked at Aston's side and glared. "Oh no you don't.

He was just a friend, nothing more. And as soon as I got my license, I drove myself."

"I always find it strange that swim team practice was so early in the morning, and at a different location, so there was never any buses. It was always carpool and parents."

Dad shook his head at Mom's words. "But our little girl did pretty well."

I pinched the bridge of my nose. "Okay, let's go eat. I'm tired of this conversation."

"Oh no, we're just beginning. I'm going to need to know every sport and club that you did. And see if there are photos."

"Aston, you really don't."

He smiled then but didn't reach out to touch me. He didn't wrap his arm around my shoulders, didn't smile in the way that he usually did.

Was he distant? Or was I just thinking too much. He'd been so animated with my mother, but perhaps I was merely seeing things now.

"Okay then, we do have lunch on the way. I made Greek wraps, not fully gyros because I don't have the seasonings quite right, but I made tzatziki sauce." Mom beamed, and my stomach rumbled.

Aston's lips finally twitched into a semblance of a smile, as my dad licked his lips.

"Don't forget the Greek potatoes. And salad. Okay I'm starving. Let's go."

We walked into the kitchen and pulled everything off the warmers and took the salad out of the fridge. Of course, my father decided to tell a few more embarrassing stories, and I did my best to ignore it. Mostly because this is what you did with parents. At least that's what I had heard. Because my father was right, I hadn't brought anyone over before. But I had with Aston.

This was a big step, something I didn't realize was so monumental until we were in the middle of it.

I wasn't quite sure if I would ever get an invitation to a full Aston family dinner, not with his mother. But I wanted to get to know his brothers more. And yet, sometimes it felt like we were moving so fast that it was hard to keep up.

"The olives don't have pits, so you're safe with your salad, Blakely," Mom said, and I winced.

"Is there a story there," Aston asked, as my dad laughed.

"One time when we had this, I didn't realize it had pits, and decided to almost break my tooth, and choke at the same time. And then I did it again later. But it was really good salad."

"And I don't mean to laugh," my dad said, clearly still laughing.

"I was fine though, not really hurt. But now we buy the pitted olives."

"I don't blame you, I love Kalamata olives, but they can crack a tooth."

There was something different in his tone, but I wasn't sure what it was. Maybe he was just nervous that he was meeting my parents.

"So, I know your half-siblings quite well," Mom said,

apparently jumping over the ledge into a difficult conversation.

Aston cleared his throat, nodding.

"I assumed you would have. They've been in your life quite a long time."

"They have. They're like family," my dad said, and there wasn't any pointedness in his tone. Just honesty.

"So you have six full siblings?" Mom asked, and I held my breath, wondering if this was an okay conversation.

"I do. Flynn and Hudson are the twins, then it goes Dorian, James, Theo, and Ford."

"I don't know how any of your parents were able to handle so many of you. Blakely was enough."

I snorted at my mom's words and shook my head. "Thank you for that."

"It's the truth. Then again, our jobs took us out of the house often enough, that any more of you would mean you'd probably end up taking over the world," Dad said, not unkindly.

"That is true. And then when Isabella and I found each other, we did contemplate taking over the world."

"I wouldn't be surprised if Isabella could do that," Aston murmured.

"And I can't?" I asked, brow raised.

"Touché. I'm pretty sure you could."

"Thank you," I said primly.

"So, Blakely, have you met all of the brothers?" Mom asked, and my stomach tightened just a bit. And I had no idea why.

"In passing, but not all at once."

"We have a Cage family dinner in a couple of days, you should join us," Aston suggested, and I blinked at the suddenness of his words. Because I hadn't known they were having a dinner at all. Or maybe once again I was thinking too hard.

"Oh, that would be awesome. A little daunting though. There are so many of you."

"Ford won't be there, just because he has a job offsite that's overnight, but the rest of us will be." He paused. "It isn't one of the required ones, and we're just used to doing dinners this way. At least just to catch up with each other."

"I think it's quite nice that you still have your traditions with the siblings you grew up with, and you're finding your path with your new ones. It's okay that not everybody is in one room at the same time," my mom said, her words kind.

Aston nodded, but I wasn't sure what he was thinking.

"But really, you should come to dinner. See how annoying we all are in a big group."

"I think I could handle that," I said, smiling at him.

Before he could say anything, his phone buzzed, and he winced.

"I'm sorry, that's the emergency vibration tone."

He pulled his phone out of his pocket, cursed under his breath, and apologized again before leaving the dining room.

I frowned after him, wondering what was wrong, and not just with whoever was on the other line.

"So you get to meet the family too," Mom stated, her voice low.

I turned to my parents and nodded. "Yeah. I mean, I've met them before, but I guess this will be different."

"Just like he's here. I'm happy for you, baby."

The smile on my face was true, and yet, that distance felt off.

Before I could dive deeper into my odd feelings, Aston came forward, a grave expression on his face.

"Are you okay? Is it your family?" I asked standing up.

"I have to head out. I'm sorry," he said, looking over my shoulder at my parents. "An emergency with a client. But I'll call you later?" he asked.

I nodded, and he reached out, squeezing my shoulder. He didn't kiss me, didn't say anything but a murmured goodbye. He didn't lean down and kiss me, not even a brush of lips against my forehead. It was so different, it nearly felt cold. But maybe it was just because my parents were here.

"Crap, I drove us here," he mumbled.

"We can get her home. Go help who you need to," my mom said, her voice soft.

"We've got our girl, don't worry."

Aston smiled at all of us then, the brittleness of it setting me on edge, and then he was gone, leaving me without a true goodbye.

"I hope whoever was on the other line is okay," Mom said softly.

"I hope so too, but Aston can handle it. He can handle anything." And then I took my seat again, but I was no longer hungry.

My parents continued their conversation, and I answered back at the appropriate times, but my heart wasn't in it. I knew Aston's time wasn't his own. I knew he ran a very successful and demanding business. But something felt off tonight.

And after my parents dropped me off, and I got ready for bed, I held the phone in my hand, waiting for it to ring. Waiting for a text.

But the call never came.

Once again.

Chapter Eighteen
ASTON

Rule #1: There is no such thing as forever.

I WAS AN ASSHOLE.

Although, this really wasn't a new development. I was the asshole in business, the one who had to get shit done, I was the asshole with my brothers, the eldest who had to rein them in. And according to my mother, I had been born an asshole.

I didn't know what I had done as an infant to her, but things hadn't changed since.

Now, I was the asshole for not calling.

It had been late when I had finished dealing with my client. The same client who realized that they were potentially going to end up in prison because of money laundering, and I hadn't wanted to wake her.

My head wasn't on straight, my thoughts on other things.

I had texted the next morning, and even seen her at work, but we hadn't had a full conversation since I had left her at her parents' house. I had no idea if they even liked me.

I had hoped the event had gone well.

Except I wasn't thinking about my client, I wasn't thinking about the fact that my client's brother was the one who had tried to destroy their company, and now we would all be dealing with legal issues. No, I was thinking about the letter I had found in my mailbox before I had gone to pick up Blakely.

The letter that had been addressed to me from my father.

The letter that the fucking lawyer had sent out on a time-released schedule.

And according to him, a letter was going to be sent to each child.

Twelve letters, and I was the third.

Phoebe and Ford had already gotten theirs according to the lawyer. But that was all he could tell me. I didn't know when anyone else would get theirs, and I was a little concerned that I hadn't known that Ford had gotten one. Maybe his had been just as cruel.

He wouldn't even be at our dinner to broach the subject. I wasn't sure that Phoebe trusted me enough for me to ask. In the end, I only had my letter, and everything that made no fucking sense.

Now I was in my own head, and not focusing on what

I should. Not knowing if I was good enough for the woman who looked at me with stars in her eyes.

I had invited her to dinner, and so she would be there, because Blakely didn't run out on promises.

No, that was me.

I didn't call. I texted, but I hadn't called. And I had left her behind at her parents' house, and this was just after the incident with Meredith.

I was surprised I hadn't gotten a text saying that Blakely was done with me.

Then again, maybe I was expecting one because I wanted one. It would be easier if she left.

I rubbed my temples and sighed as Theo got to work in my kitchen.

"Why are you dancing?" I asked dryly, trying to push my own melancholy and self-deprecating thoughts out of my mind.

"Because there's music on, and I'm cooking. You have a classically trained chef in your kitchen making a family dinner, when I could be actually making money on this."

"You're the one who offered. Any one of us could have cooked, and I could have ordered in."

"I'm tired of catered food. I want something that's ours."

"So what are you making?"

"Well, a few things because I was in the mood. We're going to have a miso butter roasted chicken with an acorn squash panzanella, and also because I'm in the mood, we're having a cedar plank salmon."

I blinked at the menu, wondering what Theo was

dealing with at the moment if his menu was this complicated. "Two proteins? Look at you being all fancy."

"Shut up. I'm also making a garlic aioli, complete with vegetables and seafood we can dip in."

"Okay, that sounds great."

"A creamy squash risotto, that also brings in the miso. And of course a tomato tart with a chickpea crumble."

"How many leftovers are you planning?" I asked with a laugh, feeling marginally lighter. "Do you think Dorian will like any of that?"

"Dorian can go fuck himself."

"I can do what now?" Dorian asked as he walked inside.

Theo beamed. "Just telling you to fuck yourself."

"Oh that's so wonderful. Thank you. And I'll try anything once. You know that."

I rolled my eyes, as Theo continued to lay out the menu, complete with a mushroom and thyme mini pot pie to go with the individually baked mini fruit pies for dessert.

"How the hell are we going to eat this much food?" I asked, shaking my head.

"Easy, you're going to want to stuff your mouths because this is going to be the best food you've ever had in your life."

"I knew I liked this guy," Dorian said as he reached over to grab a vegetable off the tray. Theo slapped his hand.

I just grinned. "Well then, at least you're beating up on someone else other than me."

Theo ignored Dorian's pleas. "I don't beat up on you but stay out of my kitchen."

"You know it's my kitchen, right?" I asked.

"It is mine when I'm cooking."

"Don't you need a sous chef?" Dorian asked, and Theo raised a brow.

"It won't be you. You burned water."

Dorian rolled his eyes. "I burned the pan. I forgot that I was boiling water to make eggs. It happens."

"Oh God, not the pan story again," Flynn said as he walked into the kitchen, James by his side.

"It was one time," Dorian spluttered.

Hudson followed them and shook his head. "Dorian trying to help cook again?" It was nice to see him since we barely saw him these days.

"I don't know why we keep bringing up the story. I'm sure you've all burned things yourself."

"Hush," Theo said as he tossed salt over his shoulder. "We don't bring that kind of negativity into my kitchen."

"But apparently we throw salt in my kitchen?" I asked.

"Hudson, come help me cook. You're the only one I trust."

"I'm kind of hurt," Flynn said, rubbing a hand over his shoulder. "I mean, I look just like that asshole, and you would think that I would be able to help as well."

"I like Hudson better," Theo said, grinning, and I left the chef and his sous chef in the kitchen as the doorbell rang.

"I'll go get it," James said, and I shook my head.

"No, we're only missing one person."

"Do you think she's ready for us?" Flynn asked, but I didn't say anything. Because I wasn't sure I was ready for this. Dorian gave me a look, and I ignored him before going to answer the door.

As soon as I opened the door, my heart stopped. Just in that instance, all thoughts of family squabbles and fathers who tried to rip your heart out fled.

Because Blakely stood there, in a soft pink dress, one that brought memories to the surface. Oh, it was a different dress than the one I had seen her in at the gala, and yet it was such a similar color that it made my mouth go dry.

"You're here."

She tilted her head, worry in those bright eyes of hers. "You invited me. Was I not supposed to come?" she asked, her hands tightening on her purse.

I reached out for her, bringing her inside. When I brushed my lips against her temple, she relaxed, and yet I couldn't help but tense in her stead.

"No, I'm glad you're here."

"Are you?" she asked softly. But before I could answer that, if I even had an answer, Dorian was pulling her out of my arms, and placing a very loud and smacking kiss on her cheek.

"Blakely! It's my favorite person. You have tamed the beast."

"Oh, you've probably made a grave mistake in coming," Flynn said as he lifted his chin in hello.

"Would you like a drink?" James asked, and Blakely just blinked, as everyone seemed to be speaking at once.

"I can get her a drink," I growled, annoyed with myself more than anything.

Blakely stood still for a moment, a deer in headlights, before a sense of calm washed over her, a small smile playing over her face. When she smiled like that, it felt like time stood still. And that was a damn problem.

"I'd love a glass of wine. Anything you have."

"We're having mostly poultry and fish, so go with white or sparkling," Theo called out from the kitchen, and I shook myself out of my own thoughts, and went to go get her a sparkling wine.

Soon, the woman I couldn't stop thinking about was surrounded by my brothers, and even the quiet Hudson asking questions.

It would've probably felt like an interrogation, except for the fact that everybody was laughing, and she was asking the questions right back.

The table was overflowing with food, and I sat next to Blakely, using my fork to spread my meal around on the plate so it looked as if I was eating. Oh, Theo noticed, and so did Blakely, but I wasn't sure anyone else had. Theo would yell at me later for being so disrespectful to his meal, but Blakely? I didn't know what the hell I was doing.

And that seemed to be the tone of the day.

"I saw your painting, Hudson, I didn't get to tell you when we met up at the lake. But it's gorgeous."

Hudson set down his beer and shrugged. "It's okay. It could use a few more finishing touches."

"You always say that, and yet I think it looks damn good," Flynn put in.

Blakely looked between them, frowning.

"What? Do I have something on my face?" Flynn asked.

She shook her head, her cheeks going pink. "No, it's just the fact that I see you nearly every day at work, and I know you and Hudson are identical twins, yet you two are nothing alike."

"Because I'm more handsome," Flynn said. "By the way, we're not at work, my humor doesn't count as an issue, right?"

"I'm pretty sure that the fact that my best friend is your sister and works with you, and I'm dating Aston, we're past that point."

"And I'm the more handsome one," Hudson said deadpan.

Blakely smiled. "Totally. It is the beard."

A slight jealousy crawled through my system, and I pushed it away.

"I'm going to have to grow a bushy beard. I don't know if I like that," Flynn said as he ran his hand over his face.

"Aston's going to need a beard," Theo said, studying me with worry in his gaze. "Do you think you can grow one."

"I grew one before you even hit puberty and your balls dropped. So I'm pretty sure I'm fine."

"If you could refrain from talking about my balls at the dinner table that would be great," Theo said with a laugh.

"I'm just surprised you are the one that brought it up," Dorian said, staring at me. "After all, you told us to be on our best behavior."

I rolled my eyes, the slight humor sliding through the gloom. "You have already discussed accidental boners, girlfriends who tried to key your car, and the one time we had to help you out of handcuffs. I think we're well past that."

Blakely snorted beside me, and I looked down at her smiling face, once again that kick in the gut surprising me.

"When you first mentioned the handcuffs, I didn't realize it was because *he* was handcuffed to a bed."

Dorian fluttered his eyelashes. "What? I wanted to see if it was fun."

"I don't need to know any more," Blakely said with a laugh, and they continued on with their teasing of each other.

Soon we were cleaning up, with Theo putting Dorian and Flynn on dish duty. When Blakely got a call from one of her team members, she went out onto the back patio, needing to handle it. Hudson was already out there, also dealing with something from the town, and I stood between the back French doors where she had just walked through, and the kitchen where my brothers were all working.

"So you going to tell us what the fuck is wrong?" Dorian asked, his voice low.

I stiffened, shaking my head. "I'm fine."

"You aren't fine. Don't fuck this up with her," Flynn whispered. "And I'm not talking as someone who works with her. I'm talking as your brother. A guy who likes Blakely."

"It's none of your business."

"It is, and that's the problem," James added.

"What's going on in that brain of yours?" Theo asked.

I swallowed hard, hoping to hell Blakely's call lasted a bit longer. And then I pulled the envelope out of the drawer nearest to me. I could have kept it anywhere, but I kept it in the junk drawer, where it needed to be.

I handed it over to Dorian, without thinking, and then pulled back. As my father clearly hated me, he hated Dorian the most. So seeing that familiar handwriting had put a gray pallor on Dorian's skin.

James moved forward, and cursed, pulling out the letter. "What the hell is this?"

"Apparently we're each getting letters from beyond the grave." I explained about the timing, and the lawyer, and while they each wanted to get into the group chat to ask what the hell Ford was thinking not warning them, I had a feeling that Ford and Phoebe had different instructions or were still dealing with the ramifications of Dear Old Dad's honest cruelty.

"I'm going to kill him all over again," James growled.

"What does it say?" Dorian asked, his voice slightly fearful.

James cleared his throat, his hands tightening on the paper.

"And do it fast," I said, nothing left in me at the moment.

Aston,

If you're reading this, I'm dead. Or I've decided it was time to tell you.

Now that I'm gone, either physically or metaphorically, you are The Cage. But are you really?

You have always been a disappointment to me. Never truly able to step up into the paths that your grandfather and I had chosen for you. If you would have been paying attention, you would've learned long ago about your other siblings. But no, you were so busy trying to move out of my shadow, you never could see what was right in front of you.

It's your fault that your siblings will be hurt. Because if you had been smart enough, powerful enough, you would've known.

I was the one who built this company to what it is. And the changes you have been making have been breaking my heart. You're so worried about keeping the environment safe you're not thinking about what we could truly do with those plots. What we could truly become worldwide instead of stuck in this state. We could have been something more, but no, your job as The Cage will never slide you out of the shadow of who your grandfather and I were.

You know my rules. I pounded them into you far before you even tried to take my mantle. A mantle you will never have.

But the rules I had kept our lives separate. It kept the secrets that needed to be.

Do not let your brothers ruin this company. Do not let the other Cages in. And while the will is forcing you to become acquainted, remember that you are The Cage. Perhaps not The Cage I wanted, but The Cage.

I was the small-town dad when I needed to be, and the elite father when you were around. And that's how it should have stayed.

But, with time comes reflection. And if you had been a better son, I wouldn't have had to try to make so many. I wouldn't have had to try with another woman. But you are my greatest failure. Well, my first failure.

So just know that genes run true, and if I could fail, me with all of my talent and all of my power could fail...

You will too.

So keep to the rules, and when you inevitably screw up, remember that the rules could have saved you.

Loren.

"Are you kidding me?" Flynn asked. "That is the ramblings of a delusional man. You don't actually believe that do you?" he asked, and I shrugged, my jaw tightening.

"I need to go," Dorian said, as he pushed past me, not saying another word. James looked between us, cursed, and followed Dorian out. Because while those words in that letter were terrible, and perhaps true, it was nothing to what my father had done to Dorian.

Theo pressed his lips together and didn't say a thing. And I wasn't sure there was anything else to say.

"Do not believe this. He's just a ranting old man who's dead. And yes, we're playing his little game by getting to know our siblings, but I want to. I want to fucking know them. Don't let Dad ruin this. Don't let him in your head."

"He's already there. Do you know how much work I've had to deal with the company and dealing with the fallout of his mistakes? And when I fuck this up with Blakely, because I will, it's going to fuck things up with Isabella too. So no matter what I do, I'm going to hurt this family."

"You're not making any sense," Theo whispered. "Just don't screw up things with Blakely. I see with the way you two are. You love that woman."

"How do we even know what love is? We're Cages."

"You don't believe that, look at Ford."

"Ford was the one who got out. Maybe he was the smartest one of us all."

Before they could fight with me any longer, the back door opened, and Blakely and Hudson walked in. The tension in the room was palpable, and I knew that everyone could feel it. But when Blakely looked at me, I didn't have any words to say. There was nothing.

"I should head home," she said, her voice oddly shallow.

What had she heard? What was she thinking? I hated that I couldn't read her mind. Nor did I know what the hell I was doing.

"I'll walk you to your car."

She stared at me, her eyes pleading, but my brothers didn't say a damn thing. At least not until she went to get her purse. Then they said their goodbyes, although we didn't explain why Dorian and James weren't in the room.

As I walked her to her car, I knew I needed to say something. To fix this. But maybe there wasn't any fixing. Maybe if I fixed things the way they should be now, it wouldn't hurt later.

I leaned down and kissed her temple, and she stared up at me, confusion in her gaze. "What's wrong? What happened?"

"Nothing."

"You're lying. Something happened before dinner with my parents, and something just happened when I was out on the porch. What's going on, Aston?"

My throat tightened and it took effort to grind the words out. "It's a family thing."

She nodded, swallowing hard. "I get that. But you can talk to me you know. We've been together for how long? I thought you trusted me enough to talk to me. Or at least talk to your brothers. Don't push me away."

I slid my hands into my pockets and stared off into the distance, my father's word's reverberating within my mind. "Maybe I need some space."

"What?" she asked, the break in her voice nearly killing me.

"I need to figure out where my head is at. And while I'm doing so, I might hurt you. So it'd be good if we just took some time."

"Why won't you *talk* to me? You always push me away, and I can't take it anymore."

"Blakely, I…" My voice trailed off.

"You know what, no." I met her gaze, and there were no tears, just a lifted chin, and resignation in those eyes. "Just don't call. It's what you're good at. Take your time to figure it out. Because I can't do this. Because I know if I'm the one that pushes you, I'll be the one that breaks. And I'm better than that. I truly hope you figure out what's going on, Aston. Because you're not going to talk to me. And I'm not going to fight when all I'll do is end up broken."

Some part of me screamed, shouted for me to reach out, to hold her, to tell her everything. But the other part, the one that sounded suspiciously like my father, told me to stay put. That this was the easiest way.

And so I didn't say anything, and when that single tear tracked down her cheek, I didn't brush it away.

Instead she got in her car, and drove off, and I let it happen. But it was for the best.

It needed to be.

Chapter Nineteen
ASTON

Rule #8: (Added by Aston) Forever might never be enough, but it's always worth trying for.

I couldn't quite believe that I was watching her drive away. Again, that part inside of me screaming to go after her, to get my head out of my ass, couldn't make me move. Instead all I could do was repeat the words my father spoke.

It was better this way. I could get my head on straight, and I wouldn't hurt her more than I already had.

I made my way back inside, only to come face to face with Hudson.

He glared at me and folded his arms over his chest. "Are you serious right now?" My taciturn brother whispered. His voice was laced with an edge that should have worried me.

"I just had a really shitty day. Don't get on me."

"Oh, we're going to do that," Dorian snapped, and I realized that everyone had come back from their perspective corners to stand in my living room, glaring at me.

"I don't have time for this."

"I think you have all the time in the world if you're going to push the woman that you love out of your house and your life," Theo snapped.

"I don't...love her. It's not like that." And yet I could hear the lie in my tone.

I hadn't let myself even think the word love. I liked being with her. I liked seeing her smile and I loved seeing how she grew. But I didn't love her.

Could I? No, because if I had, I wouldn't have pushed her out.

"I need you to fix this," James said softly as he moved forward. "Not because she works for me. Not because she's one of the best managers we have ever had, not because you ruining this could literally break the family because of Isabella's loyalties, but because you need her."

I ran my hands over my face moving toward the side bar. "I need a fucking drink."

"No, you need to be clearheaded for this," Flynn argued.

"You're looking at me as if you have never even thought of the fact that you could love her, and that worries me," Dorian added, and it surprised me that it was him saying these words. The one of us who was the actual player of the family. "Don't let Dad get in your head. He's a fucking asshole who doesn't deserve a single breath that we give. No space in our minds, no space in our days. It doesn't matter what the raving lunatic has to say."

"Everything he put in that letter was just about him," Flynn continued.

"And it was all bullshit." Hudson shook his head. "He's the one who lied, cheated, and somehow ended up with two women who were apparently just fine with having secret families. Because the only secrets they kept were from the kids, not each other."

I began to pace, my heart racing. "But don't you see? If I let this get any more serious, and when it blows up spectacularly, I am going to hurt this family."

"It's already beyond serious," Theo said, shaking his head.

"You brought her here to our family dinner," James whispered. "I've seen the way you two are with each other. You guys can work on the same floor, bump into each other, and be completely professional where I'm pretty sure most people don't even realize you're dating. You don't keep it a secret, but you act like a rational human being. Where is that rational human being right now?" James shoved at my shoulder, surprising me.

"I am being rational."

"Do you not hear yourself?" Hudson asked. "You're so scared of what could be, you're making it all worse. Go get her back. Fix this. She's the best thing that ever happened to you. Dad was the worst thing. I don't know what kind of sick games him and the moms were thinking of but fuck them. Fuck what they think. When my letter shows up, I'm going to burn it. I don't really care what he thinks about me. Because I was always the disappointment. The one who didn't go into business, the one who decided to serve my country instead.

"And I'm the one he's hated since he first looked at me, even though he loves my twin," Dorian put in.

Flynn reached out and gripped his shoulder. "I'm sorry."

"It's not you, twin of mine," Hudson said, that familiar smile in his voice.

"We are all disappointments to him in one way or another," James said with a shrug. "But he's dead. The only way that I really care about him, is the fact that we have to deal with his will. And I would throw it all in his face and ignore it, but I don't want to give him the satisfaction of being right."

"But what if he is right?" I whispered.

"He's not," Theo said.

"Go get her back. Go apologize. Grovel. Do what you did the first time you fucked up," Dorian snapped.

I looked at all of them and realized that I was the idiot. It hadn't even taken me ten minutes to realize that I made a mistake, and I needed to fix this.

"Go. Go get your girl. Because I really don't want to have to hire anyone else," James said as he gave me a pointed look. "I mean you. Replacing you. Because we are keeping Blakely."

"Damn straight," Flynn added.

Panic racing through me, I grabbed my keys, and headed toward her house.

I was driving so fast I was pretty sure I was going to

beat her there, as I tried to figure out what I was going to say.

Only there weren't going to be any words to express my regret. I had hurt her. Again. Yes, the first time had been out of my control, the second time because of a photo I hadn't even realized had been taken. It wasn't third time's the charm, it was three strikes you're out. And I knew that beyond anything.

I loved her. And it had taken me making the biggest mistake of my life to even realize that. I pulled into her driveway, and my heart squeezed ever so slightly, seeing her shadow in her front window. I needed to fix this. I needed to be The Cage. The one who was determined and knew what the hell he wanted.

Or perhaps that was the problem. Because The Cage was just a façade. And my father had never known what he wanted. He had taken everything to try to find it, but he hadn't.

But I had, I needed to atone for everything that I'd done.

And now I stood on her doorstep, hand raised to knock, when it opened.

Blakely looked at me, eyes swollen from tears, her cheeks wet, still wearing her pale pink dress. "What are you doing here?" she asked, her hands at her sides.

"I'm sorry."

"You're getting really good at saying those words. Just go away, Aston."

"No, please. Hear me out."

"I did. When you rambled about whatever was going

on in your head, and when you pushed me away. It's been what, forty minutes? And you've already changed your mind. Maybe you should deal with it. Because I'm worth more than your misgivings."

Panicking, I swallowed down the bile in my throat, before I finally cursed under my breath. "I just don't want to be my father."

Her eyes widened slightly, before she took a step back. "I don't want to make a scene for my neighbors, so come in. But what are you talking about?"

Grateful that she even let me in, I swallowed hard, and took those steps inside.

"My father ignored my mother. And his other so-called partner. Even with that deal with them that I never understood, he ignored them. All he wanted was the power and the connections that came with it. He liked his secrets, liked lording them over everyone. I just hadn't realized that he had so many more secrets than I thought." I reached forward and brushed the tears from her cheeks with my thumb. The fact that she didn't pull away I took as a good sign. And hopefully not a goodbye.

"Aston..." she began, but I took a step back, handing over the letter that ruined everything.

"Read this."

She gave me a strange look before taking the letter in hand and began to read. Color dotted her cheeks as she continued, and I cleared my throat.

"I don't want to take you for granted. And I feel like I do. I want to show you how much I care about you, how much I fucking love you. But I don't want to become my father, so I hurt people along the way."

Her eyes widened even more, and I realized that I'd just blurted that I loved her.

"You are not your father. Your father would never say that he loved you. You told me that. You love me though?" Her voice broke, and I sucked in a breath.

I nodded, moving my hands back to her face. "I do. I didn't fucking realize it because I didn't know what I was looking for. But I do. And I want to believe that I'm not my father. But sometimes I get so focused on making sure that this family and this legacy isn't what he made it, that I lose track." I had let my hands fall, and nearly began to pace. But I didn't want to lose her gaze.

"That is not what your father tried to do. I don't know what his end goal was, but you're trying to protect your family, and yourself. You just have to stop pushing me away when you get scared. Because I love you too, you asshole."

A smile slid over my face, even as my heart raced. "You love me?"

"Of course I do. Everything wouldn't hurt this bad if it wasn't love. I've never been in love before, so I didn't realize it either, but I do love you. So, don't push me away when you get angry. Whenever your father does something to annoy you, even from the grave, talk to me about it. But the next time you do anything close to what you did, I'm done. I love you, but I also love myself."

I moved forward and cupped her face once more

before bringing my lips down to hers. I tasted the salt of her tears and nearly fell to my knees.

I had hurt her, the person that I loved, and I hadn't even realized how I was doing it until it was almost too late. And when I pressed my forehead to hers, I let out the breath I hadn't even realized I'd been holding. "I love you."

"I really like when you say that. But you can't use it to grovel the next time."

"I'm not going to need to grovel."

"Oh you will. Because we're both going to make mistakes. That's part of the rules."

I leaned back, tilted my head. "Rules?"

"Of being in a relationship. You're going to make mistakes, but you figure out how to fix them without hurting the other person. I've watched my parents navigate two careers that take up so much space in their lives that it sometimes felt that there wasn't enough space for each other or me. But they made it through. And we can too. As long as you talk to me."

I stared at her, my heart racing. "Okay. I promise. I'll do better. I won't be the asshole that I know I'm being."

"Good. And I'm really delighted that you came here because we have that gala this weekend, and I really don't want to go alone again."

This time my smile widened even further. "I met you the last time. You know, I think we should make sure this gala ends a little bit better than the last time."

Her smile softened as she wrapped her arms around me.

"Good. Because I want to enjoy myself with you, and not be worried that I'm going to ruin everything."

"No, and I'll do my best not to ruin it either."

I slid my fingers down her bare arm, and she raised a brow.

"Is there something you would like?" she teased.

And as I gently pulled down the straps of her dress, she rolled her eyes, before I took her lips with mine.

"Oh, I think there's something that we could both want."

"WHY DOES THIS FEEL DIFFERENT AND YET THE EXACT same," Blakely asked as we walked inside the large ballroom. Everyone wore tuxes and ballgowns, with far too many diamonds and jewels. What a pretentious way to donate money for a reputable cause. But others wanted to be in their finery, and we let them. It wasn't the same organization as before, but we Cages needed to show face, and donate. And Blakely was here as my date.

"Well, this time I get to monopolize all of your dances, and not have to worry if I'm going to scare you away."

"I think after meeting your entire family, I'm not going to be that scared."

"Well I'm scared," Isabella said as she stood on my other side, her green dress flowing around her in waves. She had piled her hair up on the top of her head in some sort of updo and added subtle makeup.

"I don't think I've ever seen you in a dress, dear sister."

She glared at me, but I saw the fear in her gaze. "I still don't know why I'm here."

"Because you're a Cage," I said as I squeezed her hand. "And our world is starting to realize that, so you have to deal with what we do."

"And that means getting in fancy dresses and schmoozing?"

"I'm going to have to do it too, and I'm just dating him," Blakely said, and I squeezed her hip.

"Hey, I thought you liked schmoozing me."

"Please don't finish that sentence," Isabella said, as she pinched the bridge of her nose. "I should just go. I've showed my face, did the Cage thing, but I'm going to go."

"Oh, I don't think so," James said as he moved forward. "Flynn is off talking with a potential client, which I think you're going to want to hear about," James said, looking at me, before turning back to Isabella. "And, while you are a Cage, you're a Cage that works with us, so now you're going to have to deal with everything that comes with it."

"Why can't anyone else be here. There's a lot of us. Sophia would be great at this. She used to have to do those things when she was in the ballet."

"I'm sure we'll bring Sophia to these too," I said, holding back my laughter. "However, you work with us. So you get first dibs."

"Come on little sister, I'll take you to the punch."

"We are the same age and my birthday is before

yours," Isabella snapped, and I just shook my head as those two walked off, and Blakely shook beside me.

"Hold back your laughter. Isabella won't appreciate it," I murmured.

"Getting her out here was like pulling teeth. But I'm sure she'll figure it out."

"You know, she didn't really need to be here," I said softly.

Blakely's eyes twinkled. "Oh, I figured. But it's a good way for her to get to know you guys in all aspects. You know, Emily would actually love this."

"Is it weird that I feel like I don't even know her at all. She's so much younger."

"You know Phoebe and she's even younger."

"I've known her longer." I rubbed the back of my neck. "I mean I really do need to get out of my head about whatever Dad said and worry about the family that we have."

"You are the big brother. And I think you're doing a pretty good job about it."

"And I can do a better one. Because once those letters start to arrive, I have a feeling Dad's going to do his best to try to hurt each and every one of us."

"And we're not going to let him. Because you have me on your side too."

I leaned down, and brushed my lips against hers, my heart swelling.

Out of the corner of my eye, Blakely's old boss walked by, whispering something to his wife. That glare on his face looked like it needed to be ripped off, but

Blakely squeezed my hand, and just smiled over at him, before her attention went to someone else. She ignored him completely, and I couldn't have been prouder.

Because, she was right, just like my father, that man did not have the right to have any space in her life. It looked like the older man wanted to say something, most likely a little cutting, but we moved past the couple, and toward Flynn and the woman that he wanted to introduce us to.

And that was that. No huge blowup, I didn't pound my fist into the man's face. And Blakely didn't even have to say a word. She ignored him like he didn't matter. Because he didn't.

She was with us, the Cages, and that was just fine with me.

Not to mention that the so-called rivalry stood no chance. We'd outbid them on each and every proposal they'd tried in the past few months and would continue to do so until they got the hint.

The Cages played to win.

"I see you're here," a cold voice said from beside me, and I realized that maybe I had thought those words too soon. I squeezed Blakely's hip as we turned to the side. "Hello Mother."

"Aston." She looked at Blakely, and nodded tightly, and didn't bother to say anything to the woman that I loved. Ice practically slid off this woman, and I had to wonder exactly what had happened to her to make her this way. Had she always been this way? Or had Dad's constant infidelity and lies done it. It was hard to feel sorry for her when she acted like this, but I did. Because I didn't want my mother to hurt.

"I didn't know you would be here tonight," I said. "You look lovely."

"I'm here with Dorian. I didn't want him to bring some floozy."

I raised a brow and looked across the ballroom. I hadn't even realized Dorian would be here, but there were shadows in his eyes, and I had to wonder exactly what had happened.

"It's good you're here, the world needs to see The Cage. Don't embarrass us."

I shook my head, wondering why she was like this. "I'm not The Cage, Mother," I said pointedly, and her eyes narrowed. "I'm Aston. I'm not Dad. And I think Dorian's doing just fine without you. But you're welcome to go stand with him. It's good that you actually like one of your sons."

And with that, I nodded goodbye, and pulled Blakely to the dance floor. Mother just stood there, fuming, but Dorian was now talking animatedly with Isabella and James, so my mother had nowhere to go, other than to speak to people she didn't want to.

"Well, that was fun," Blakely said, with a roll of her eyes.

"Family, am I right?" I said, and she just laughed.

"I love your brothers and sisters. So I'm glad you have the multitudes that you do."

"I don't know what's going on with her, or how she keeps getting colder, and maybe we'll figure it out, or maybe we won't. But I'm done trying to act like Dad to make her happy. Which, sounds far weirder than it should be."

Blakely held back a laugh, her shoulders shaking. "Thankfully I know what you mean," she said with a laugh, as I twirled her on the dance floor. And as the music changed, we continued to dance, doing the one thing we hadn't been able to the first time we'd been here.

Just be.

I had almost lost her, had almost pushed her away because of the man they had wanted me to be.

And I wasn't going to be that anymore. I was going to be who Blakely needed me to be.

Who I needed me to be.

Whatever Cage that happened to be in the moment.

Chapter Twenty
BLAKELY

Dear Diary,
 It turns out, if you take a chance. Sometimes it works.
  Sometimes...not so much.

I HUMMED ALONG TO THE MUSIC IN MY HEAD AS I walked through the empty building on Avalanche Street. I knew it was named Avalanche for the hockey team, and not an actual Avalanche, but that still worried me some. Cage enterprises had been looking at numerous places for their next endeavor on my project list, and we were thinking of purchasing this one.

We.

It was so odd that *I* was a *we* now but I was going to lean into it for the time being

However, the building that I now stood in was a little

older but was going to be the home of a future business that one of our loan recipients was going to use. The best part, it was going to be a multiple loan partner establishment. The women had come together with a proposal, and the Cages were going to be the ones that helped fund it. I was really excited to see what they did, because it was going to help the community. However, I probably should have waited for Aston to drive me to the place, rather than meeting him here. The clouds overhead were getting dark, and while there hadn't been any rain in the forecast, it was Colorado. And that meant weather had no reason.

Aston had texted saying he was on his way, so hopefully we'd be able to get back to his place before the storm.

Everything just felt spectacular. Which probably meant that I needed more sleep. But for the past week, we hadn't been getting much sleep. Between meetings, each other, the business, and countless other things, I had been too wired and now here I was, bouncing on my feet as I waited for Aston to come.

I still couldn't quite believe that things were working out. I loved him. And he loved me. And if I kept saying that, I was going to become a Disney princess and start twirling around even though I wore jeans and a top. I was pretty sure Disney princesses wore jeans these days. It was all in fashion.

I rolled my eyes, knowing that I needed to focus on my checklist, before Aston got here. Lightning crackled in the sky, but it was far enough away. I checked my phone, but he hadn't texted any updates. That meant he was driving.

I really hoped that it didn't start raining while he was driving. If anything, we could just wait out the storm here.

I bit my lip as worry slid through me, hoping he wasn't driving through the rain. When the door opened, I smiled brightly, turning toward it, but it wasn't Aston.

Instead, Meredith stood there, her eyes wide, and I stiffened, wondering if I needed a weapon.

The last time I had seen this woman, she had tugged on my arm and said horrible things. And then she had thrown herself at Aston, and we hadn't heard from her since.

While he had said it was out of character for her, I didn't know her enough to know what was in character.

"Excuse me? We're not open." Which should have been obvious since the place was empty and full of cobwebs. There was only the master lock on the outside, so I hadn't locked it fully. The neighborhood was safe enough, but now I was kicking myself for leaving it at least somewhat open.

Meredith looked around the place, and licked her lips, before holding up both hands.

"My office is across the street, and down a few buildings. I saw you walking in, I swear, I wasn't stalking you." She winced. "Although, you don't have to believe me. You can look me up on my profile to see where I work so you can see the address. Or ask Aston." She paused. "Not that he would want to hear from me either."

"Is there something I can do for you Meredith? Because we're not doing this. I'm not going to continue whatever this drama is you think that we have."

The other woman swallowed hard, her face paling. "I'll leave. I promise. I just wanted to say." She sucked in a deep breath. "I just want to say I'm sorry."

My eyes widened, and I wasn't quite sure I had heard her right. There were only a few feet between us, and yet I could practically sense the nerves rolling off her.

"I've just had a really shitty year." She let out a hollow laugh that held no humor. "And I realized that my shitty year shouldn't have affected you. But it did because I made it so. I tried to fix my old mistakes from before, and just ended up making more."

"I'm really not following," I said, wondering exactly why she was here apologizing. While I appreciated it, it felt off.

"I thought I could step into the person that I had once been, and fix things, but it turns out that I can't do that. And I'm so sorry, Blakely. I'm sorry that I hurt you in the process. Because I did. Some part of me wanted to, because I was hurting, but the real me wouldn't have wanted to."

Everything she said sounded true, I heard the sincerity in her voice, but I was still so confused. "You see, when Aston and I were engaged and we were trying to plan the wedding, my family was trying to make it this *event*. In the middle of things, my mom and his mom were fighting, his dad was ignoring us." She paused. "Which in retrospect makes a little sense. He was really good at ignoring things."

I laughed with her despite myself. "So it seems. I never had the chance to meet him."

A splash of humor filled her gaze before she blinked it away. "You weren't missing anything. He never liked me. Of course, he never really liked anyone. Though he might've liked his other family." She paused. "But I'm off-topic here." She let out a deep breath, rolling her shoulders back. "As we were planning the wedding, I found out I had cancer."

Of every single thing she could have said, that hadn't even crossed my mind. "Meredith...I'm so sorry. That's terrible. I want to ask if you're okay now, but I don't want to pry."

She wiped away a tear and rolled her eyes. "I need to stop crying. I'm trying to apologize to you and explain. This is not about me. But I'm fine now. I had to deal with a few things and turned my pain inward. I pushed everyone away, not knowing what I wanted. Yes, I broke up with Aston. I didn't want him to see me like that. Which makes no sense because I know he would've been great."

Part of me wanted to reach out and hold her, to help pull that pain away, but I knew neither one of us would truly welcome the action in that moment. "He would've stood beside you. He's a good man."

"The best. But he didn't love me. Just like I didn't love him." She shrugged, that sad smile on her face. "And he would've stayed with me throughout all of it, and then when could he have walked away? He couldn't leave the sick woman, and then the woman who bravely fought and beat cancer. *I did beat it.* I'm in remission. I have wonderful doctors and thankfully my body reacted well to treatments."

"I'm glad to hear that you're okay. That must have been so scary. Do you have anyone?" I couldn't imagine pushing everyone away in that moment. Though, in the end, I couldn't imagine her pain at all.

A small smile covered her face. "My mom. When she's not planning a wedding, she's pretty great. She didn't understand why I pushed Aston away, and when I was sick and trying to just wonder exactly what I was supposed to do, she kept prying into why I would let a good man go. But that's the problem, he was a good man. Is a good man. And somehow, it twisted inside me that he was such a good man that I made a mistake by letting him go. And I'm not going to have any excuse other than when I realized my mistake I tried to fix it. Only I hurt a lot of people along the way. I'll apologize to him too. In fact I was trying to do that first, I just don't know how to contact him without sounding like the horrible reject that I am. Blakely, I'm sorry. Everything that I did was unlike the person that I was, but that means it's the person that I am now. And I don't want to be that person anymore. So I'm sorry."

It took me a moment to get through everything that she had said, and while part of me didn't want to believe her, because it was such an outrageous story, I saw the sincerity in her eyes. She was scared and was now owning up to it. "I can't speak for Aston. But I'm sorry you went through all that. That you didn't have anyone really to lean on for it." At least at first.

"I made my own mistakes, and I'm living up to them. I lost a lot of people because I didn't want them to know. Which sounds ridiculous. I'm sorry for being a jerk. And honestly, I can see you two are great together. I'm oddly just not good at not winning? Which is not the greatest thing to know about myself."

"He's not a prize to win over." I pause. "Which makes me sound like I don't like him. I love him." I paused. "I do. I love him."

"I'm glad. And I can see he loves you. I'm sorry. So sorry for what I did.

"Well, I'm going to head back to my office and then try to forget that I'm such an idiot. Or maybe I should remember that way I don't do it again."

I moved forward without thinking and wrapped my arms around her. She stiffened for a second, before she hugged me back, laying her head on my shoulder.

"You shouldn't be the one comforting me."

"I think, you're the one who needs this more." And I squeezed her tightly, before letting her go. I hadn't even realized I was letting tears fall before I wiped them away, and she did the same.

"I don't want to be the terrible ex. I don't need to be your best friend, because I realize that would get tricky, but I promise to never stand in your way. And if I ever see some woman making cat eyes at him, I'll block the way for you."

That got a laugh out of me. "I can do that myself, but you really can't help them. Aston's beautiful."

"I want to say yes, but since I just tried to say that I was doing better, I'm not going to put my foot in my mouth anymore."

Laughing, I shook my head. But before I could say anything else, a huge crack of lightning shattered into the sky, the sound eliciting a scream from both of us. Meredith reached out and gripped my hand, as the electric pole in front of the building snapped.

In an instant, I tugged at her arm, and we dove back behind the lone counter in the room, as the pole slammed into the sidewalk, shattering the glass fronts.

"Cover yourself, Blakely!" she shouted, as we covered our faces from flying glass. Smoke filled the building immediately, and the scorching sound of fire from the transformer hit my ears.

"We need to get out of here."

"Is there a back door?" Meredith asked, and we each coughed, both of us looking around.

"I think so. I don't know this building. We were just checking it out."

"Okay let's go," she whispered, and I realized that she had glass in her hair, and a cut on her face. Since my face hurt as well, I figured we each looked the same.

We gripped each other's hands, bending down so that way we were as close to the ground as possible. Getting out the front way wasn't going to work, so we had to use the emergency exit. Only when we pressed the back door, it wouldn't budge.

"No no no no no," I shouted, alarm spreading through me.

"Is it not opening?" Meredith asked, coughing.

"Help me push it. It's either rusted shut, or something's blocking it. But we have to get out."

"Okay, we need to call 911."

"Yes. And let's just keep pushing," I said, knowing that we needed to get out of here quickly. If we didn't, the smoke was going to get us before anything. I wasn't even sure that the flames were coming into the building, but it wasn't raining yet, just lightning on this side. And that was dangerous in any weather.

"I can't get it," Meredith said, kneeling down.

I pulled out my phone and dialed 911, but the busy signal was the only thing I heard.

My brain went oddly blank before calming, as if I knew pure panic would break me. Because I was indeed panicking. "They're going to be able to see the fire. They're going to get us. We just have to keep pushing," I said, trying to remember everything that my dad taught me, and keep calm. But there was nothing calm about this.

Meredith and I shoved again, each one of us pounding on the door and screaming, and all I could do was think about the moments that would never come. I tried to push those thoughts from my mind, but there was nothing.

Just screaming.

And then the door was being pulled open from the other side, and I fell into Aston's arms, Meredith coming with me. I only saw Aston's shocked face for an instant, before he was pulling us both out of the building, other people shouting around him. Smoke billowed behind us and I tried to suck in clean air even through the rain.

"Blakely? Meredith?" As Meredith tried to pull away, he tugged her closer as well, moving us toward where an ambulance was pulling in.

"What the hell happened?" he called out over the rain.

I tried to catch my breath and answer, only I coughed loudly instead.

"We need help over here!" Aston yelled, as I threw my arms around him, hugging him tightly.

"You saved us."

"Blakely. My God. How did this happen?" He looked over my shoulder and stiffened as he looked at Meredith, and I realized that he was probably thinking the wrong thing. He hadn't realized who had fallen into him at first and now he leapt to the wrong conclusions. I pulled away and gripped Meredith's hand.

"A transformer blew because of lightning and somehow the whole place caught on fire. The door wouldn't open and I was so damn scared. We had just been talking before. Setting things straight. We're good now. I promise." And I promptly burst into tears as Meredith hugged me. Aston looked between us, confused as he held my shoulder, before moving to the side so the paramedics could check us out. When he took my hand, he didn't let me go, and I just looked over at Meredith, realizing that perhaps trauma could bond you more than I thought. Because I was never going to forget today, even as the paramedics poked and prodded.

"Blakely?" a deep voice asked, and I looked over to see a familiar firefighter from my dad's old station.

"Mr. Snow?"

"Oh hell. Are you okay?"

"I'm fine. Really." I coughed, making that a clear lie.

"Keep the oxygen on your face," the paramedic warned, and then pointed to Meredith. "You too."

Fireman Snow looked between me and the building the firefighters were currently working on and let out a breath. "I'm calling your father."

I groaned, knowing that soon the entire station was going to be checking to make sure Baby Blakely was fine, but that didn't matter. I just leaned into Aston's arms as he held me, my other hand still in Meredith's.

"I love you so much. Never do that again." He kissed the top of my head, as we tried to explain what had happened.

It turned out Aston had finally made it to the street to meet with me, only to see it catch on fire. He had run around the back as the front was blocked. He'd used a crowbar to get the door open as the authorities pulled up. When we explained that Meredith had been there to apologize, he just shook his head, listening. I knew we'd have to explain again, because I wasn't going to let him blame Meredith. It was literally lightning. But for that one moment, he had been scared it had been his ex. But it hadn't. No, it had been a single storm that still raged around us.

"Okay, so we're not going to buy that building," he said with a laugh. But again, no humor in that.

"I don't think so." I held onto him, the shakes finally hitting my body from the adrenaline.

"It was not up to code," Meredith said in her most prim voice, and somehow, I was laughing and coughing, holding onto Aston, and wondering exactly how this was my life. But then again, the man that I loved was holding me, and we were safe.

And I was never going to take that for granted again.

Chapter Twenty-One
ASTON

The Rules According to Aston Cage: Make your own rules.

The Rules According to Loren Cage:
Rule #1: There is no such thing as forever.
Rule #2: Never lie to your family.
Rule #3: Only lie to your family if #2 is unavoidable.
Rule #4: Cage First. Always.
Rule #5: Never let the world see.

The Rules We Needed:
Rule #6: (Added by Aston) Remember who you are vs. who you need to be.
Rule #7: (Added by Aston) Break the rules.
Rule #8: (Added by Aston) Forever might

never be enough, but it's always worth trying for.

The Rule that Matters: Make your own rules.

"I STILL CANNOT BELIEVE YOU WERE IN AN ACTUAL fire." Isabella held Blakely's hands and from the look on Blakely's face, my sister seemed to be squeezing her hands a little too tightly.

"You might want to let Blakely go so she can feel her fingers later."

Blakely gave me a thankful smile, as Isabella released her.

"Sorry about that. But seriously, thank you for saving them. Even your ex. Because she sounds like a really nice person now that she's doing better."

Since the fire the day before, Isabella seemed to have been off kilter. Hell, everyone seemed to be. I had met with Blakely's parents at the hospital so she could get checked out, and as many of the firefighters who had once worked with or heard of Blakely's father had come to check in. Then, the Cages had shown up en masse.

In other words, we had taken a full waiting room, and had made sure that Blakely and Meredith were never alone.

The fact that Meredith's parents hadn't shown up because they were out of town, worried me. However, I had a feeling that with the way that Blakely and Meredith had bonded in an incident I never wanted to think about again, my ex wasn't going to be alone for long.

I wasn't quite sure how I felt about that, but in the end it didn't matter. Because they were both fine.

"I just opened a door," I said, though it was much more than that. I had ended up needing stitches on my hand from a cut I had hid from Blakely at first. Having to use a crowbar to pry open the door had scared the shit out of me, but I had heard them banging on it, and knew that they had no other way out.

So now my hand was wrapped up, and Blakely seemed in better condition than I was. Then again, I couldn't help but hold her, wanting to make sure she was actually real.

I could have lost her when I had just found her. And I never wanted to have that feeling again.

"I'm really okay. And I could use something to drink. Since you blocked me on my way to the fridge," she said, and Isabella rolled her eyes.

"I just need to make sure you're okay and relatively unharmed. Of course, the bandaged one behind you won't let me ensure he's fine as well." My sister glared at me, as Emily and Sophia pushed me down on the couch.

I let out a grunt and glared at them. "Really?"

Emily shook her head. "You won't rest. You have stitches. You're supposed to be resting."

I held up my arm. "On my hand. Not my feet."

"Just let them do it," Kyler said from his perch on the

armchair. "It's really hard to fight against them. I just let it happen."

"You should listen to him, he grew up with us," Isabella said, and I met the gazes of the others in the room.

Somehow all twelve siblings, plus Blakely and Cale, had fit into my living room. We had invited Blakely's parents as well, but they had declined, saying that it might be a few too many Cages all at once. I didn't blame them, and it was nice to have the siblings all in one place. We really hadn't been like this since everything had happened.

"Okay, so we're not buying that building," James said suddenly.

Blakely snorted. "That's what Aston said. Though it was really cute, but clearly not taken care of."

"We'll find another place, and make sure it's inspected before we walk into it," Flynn said dryly.

"The problem is, it *was* inspected," James growled. "They're fired, don't worry," he added as I narrowed my gaze at him.

"It was an odd set of circumstances with the storm and everything, but the emergency exit? That's a worry." I shuddered and was grateful when Blakely sat down next to me.

I kissed her temple, and she wiggled closer. "I'm fine. I'm safe. Just breathe."

"I'll breathe later," I grumbled, while Dorian and Theo came into the living room, their hands full of platters.

"We're just going to eat in here," Theo stated, as it wasn't really a question since he was already making it happen.

Kyler hopped off the couch, and Hudson followed him, and soon we were overflowed with fifteen kinds of appetizers and finger foods.

"I cook when I'm nervous, just let it happen," Theo said pointedly, as Emily rubbed her hands together.

"Having a chef in the family might be my favorite thing ever." She looked up at him and beamed. "I know you're busy, but I really would like to learn how to make a soufflé."

Dorian snorted, as Theo just grinned. "Brother dearest over here is laughing because he cannot make a soufflé. But I can help. But can I ask why that in particular?"

"I don't know, I just always wanted to make one after watching Dr. Who. And my favorite restaurant that I went to in Paris was all about the soufflés."

Theo rubbed his hands together. "Oh, I know exactly what you're talking about. And yes, we'll make them."

"You're going to create a monster," Isabella said, but there wasn't too much humor in her tone. She kept looking over at Blakely, and then off into the distance. Something was going on with her, and we would figure it out. Once we could all just settle.

As I stared around at my family, everybody speaking to one another, as if we hadn't all been forced together in an odd sense of genetics and circumstance, I realized that maybe all of us in one room wasn't that bad.

Ford and Cale were in the corner laughing about something, as Sophia came up to both of them, and leaned into her boyfriend's hold. The two of them seemed happy, and I liked the way that he treated my sister. Just like I liked the fact I could freely say *sister* and not feel like I was out of my element. At least too far.

I was never going to understand my father. And I knew that every single person in this room could walk away from what that man had built at any moment. But in the end, it had forced us to get to know one another. I knew that no matter how many forced dinners we had, it would be on our terms. As much as we could make it happen.

I wanted to get to know my family. And I did not want to be my father. I would follow the rules of the will, but those were the only ones.

And in the end, we were about to make rules of our own.

I knew that not everybody was happy with the situation, and there was going to be resentment bubbling up soon, and we'd deal with it. I wasn't resentful of the people in this room. Not with what they represented.

My mother might change her mind at some point, and stop being so icy cold. But I did not care what my father thought anymore. Not when I had almost lost the woman that I loved, not once, but twice. And I never wanted to feel that again.

"You're off in your head," she whispered, and I kissed her temple.

"Just thinking." I cleared my throat and held up my glass. "How about a toast?"

"Should we take a picture for the attorney?" James asked.

I rolled my eyes. "You know what, let's do it, just so we can get ahead on the game."

"I'll send one from my phone too, just to annoy him." Kyler grinned as he said it, and I had a feeling that the brother I knew the least was probably going to keep us on our toes.

We all held up our glass as they each took a photo, and then I cleared my throat.

"Okay, an actual toast. To the Cages we are, not the Cages he made. And to figuring out how the fuck to make this work, without His Lordship ruling over us."

"Hear hear," Dorian said.

"So eloquently put," Isabella added.

We each held up our glasses, before taking a sip, and I looked down at Blakely and raised a brow.

"I'll figure out a better toast next time."

"I like that you're already thinking of next time."

"As long as you're there, I can do it."

My brothers made oohing and aahing sounds, with Dorian gagging in the back, but I just leaned down and pressed my lips to hers.

"I love you."

"I love you too, Cage."

"Please call him Aston, there's way too many Cages in this room. You might get confused," Dorian said with a laugh.

"I'm pretty sure I can't confuse him for anyone. Just saying."

"That was far too sappy," Isabella said with a laugh that didn't reach her eyes.

And as I held up my glass again, we all took a sip, and then I kissed Blakely on the temple again and settled back as my family figured out their new routines and did the one thing that we had never been allowed to do.

Tell our secrets.

Chapter Twenty-Two
ISABELLA

Lost in the darkness. Lost in the light. Where does the path end? Or where does it begin?

I inhaled deeply, letting the mountain air soak into my pores, and hopefully remind me exactly why I was here. Of course, I didn't have a good answer for that.

Eyes closed, I didn't even know why I was out here. Maybe I just needed a breath, a moment. I didn't feel like there were enough of them to get over this.

My phone buzzed, and I was surprised that I had service out here. I looked down at the screen, and shook my head, knowing I needed to answer.

"Sophia? What's wrong?"

"When are you coming home?" she asked, her voice soft.

I wish I knew. "Soon. I think. I don't know."

"Take as much time as you need. Or we can come to you. I miss you."

"I'm fine, Sophia. You don't have to worry about me."

"The thing is, I do. Because no one else will. Or at least you won't let anyone else."

"That's not true." Was it? I was afraid that she was right. I was getting far too good at pushing people away.

"I love you with all of my heart, and I just want you to be happy, okay?"

"I am happy," I lied.

"I can come to you."

"No. Stay with Cale. You guys need to celebrate."

My lips tilted up into a smile, just thinking about the way that my family was growing. Everybody seemed so content. Like they were all moving on, while I was standing back, screaming into the abyss wondering what I was supposed to do.

I was supposed to be the strong one, the one to be there when people needed someone to lean on, and yet I knew if they tried, I would crumble. And I would hate myself in the end.

"Cale says we can both come up there."

"He's a good man, Sophia. I'm happy for you." And I wasn't lying. He was a good man to her. Just like my best friend falling for my half-brother seemed like the perfect match in heaven, and my baby sister falling in love as well. Everybody was moving forward, and all I could do was scream.

"You don't have to do this on your own."

"I know. And I'm not alone," I lied.

"Do you want me to talk to her?"

"No. I can handle it. I always do."

"You adding that last part doesn't make me feel very happy."

"I'm not broken, Sophia. Maybe a little bruised, but not broken. I'll handle it. And then I'll come home. I promise."

"I will take you up on that. And, if I don't hear from you in the next couple of days, Cale and I are going to come up there. We won't force you to come back, but we're going to see you. Because I love you, big sister."

"I love you too, little sister. And you don't have to worry about me."

"And you don't get to tell me what I get to worry about. It's that lovely thing about choice and humanity."

"I feel like I taught you too well."

"Funny, because it probably should have been Mom and Dad who taught us."

"I don't want to talk about them," I blurted, and Sophia's sigh over the line matched my own.

"Okay. I love you."

"I love you too."

I slid my phone back into my pocket when we ended the call, and I kept staring out into the cloudy sky. Large white cotton balls in the air made shapes I couldn't quite sketch out. I wasn't fanciful, I didn't see art in the air. I was the analytical one, the type A bitch according to my former boss. And I didn't know what else I was supposed to do. I couldn't see shapes and dreams in the sky; I couldn't see promise.

I just saw a vast expanse that wouldn't let me go.

After what he did, after what they did, I wasn't sure what I was supposed to do.

But I needed to go back. I needed to stop hiding from what had happened, and what would happen next. I wasn't sure who I was anymore or who I could be. And that broke me more than I thought possible.

With one last look at the cloudy sky that didn't tell me answers and only gave me worries, I finally turned back toward the walking path.

I took one step, as the earth began to shake, and I held up my hands to steady myself.

"What the hell?" I blurted, panic rising in my throat.

Rocks began to slide underneath my feet, the soil beginning to weaken, and I reached out, grabbing for the nearest rock.

My feet fell from beneath me, as part of the cliff I had been standing on disintegrated alongside me. A scream ripped from my throat, as I grabbed for that rock, and a root, and tried to lift myself up. But the wind knocked out of me, and I couldn't even scream fully.

My phone fell out of my pocket, the resounding plastic and the glass and metal against rock echoing in my ears even though I knew I couldn't hear it above the roar of part of the mountain falling down.

And when I realized that there was nothing beneath my feet, and I wasn't strong enough to pull myself up, my fingers dug into the soil, my body sliding down the side of the rockface. Pure panic slammed into me and tears threatened.

"Reach for my hand, damn it!"

The growl of a voice nearly made me fall and I clung to the side of the cliff harder, finally looking up into the eyes of a bearded man holding out his arm.

"Come on. I don't have a firm grip and we're both going to fall off this fucking mountain if you don't *move*!"

Scrambling, my fingers bleeding, I reached out trying to grip his hands. My fingers brushed his before I fell down another inch, and a scream ripped from my throat.

"I can't reach!"

"I've got you. I've got you." He kept repeating the words as I tried to climb, tried to save myself.

Then his hand was on mine and we were both shouting, muscles straining. Somehow I lay beside him on the edge of the hillside, both of us breathing heavily, the cuts over my body beginning to sting.

Before I could say anything or even think for that matter, the man sat up and looked down at me.

"You. It had to be you."

I swallowed hard and looked up into the eyes of Weston Caldwell and held back the tears that threatened that had nothing to do with my aches and pains.

"*You.*"

Don't miss the next Cage Family romance with Isabella and Westin in: An Unexpected Everything.

AND IF YOU'D LIKE TO READ A BONUS SCENE FEATURING ASTON AND BLAKELY, YOU CAN FIND IT **HERE.**

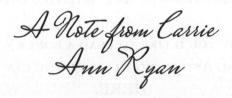

A Note from Carrie Ann Ryan

Thank you so much for reading **The Forever Rule**.

The Cages are already digging their ways into my heart and I am overjoyed you're going on this journey with us! Aston and Blakely butted heads the entire time I wrote them, so being able to finally give them their HEA is so relieving.

Yes, each of the Cages are getting their HEAs.

No, they aren't what you think.

And yes, Isabella is next with An Unexpected Everything. And her hero is everything unexpected.

This series is small town meets big city with all the feels and all the heat and I cannot wait to figure out what happens next!

Thank you so much for being here!

The Cage Family
Book 1: The Forever Rule

A NOTE FROM CARRIE ANN RYAN

Book 2: An Unexpected Everything
Book 3: If You Were Mine

Don't miss the next Cage Family romance with Isabella and Westin in: An Unexpected Everything.

AND IF YOU'D LIKE TO READ A BONUS SCENE FEATURING ASTON AND BLAKELY, YOU CAN FIND IT **HERE.**

If you want to make sure you know what's coming next from me, you can sign up for my newsletter at www.CarrieAnnRyan.com; follow me on twitter at @CarrieAnnRyan, or like my Facebook page. I also have a Facebook Fan Club where we have trivia, chats, and other goodies. You guys are the reason I get to do what I do and I thank you.

Make sure you're signed up for my MAILING LIST so you can know when the next releases are available as well as find giveaways and FREE READS.

Happy Reading!

Acknowledgments

I've been waiting for this series for years and I'm overjoyed that it's finally starting! I have more than a few people to thank and I know that there are far more than just this list, so THANK YOU for being here.

Brandi - thank you for all of our text messages and for our ramblings. Yes, we needed a flow chart for this book but it was worth it. And yes, readers should probably thank you for keeping some of the darkest thoughts at bay...for now.

To Ann, Lauren, and the Crew at Milk & Cookies - Thank you. You took my love of spreadsheets and calendars and made it shine. I cannot wait to see what happens next!

Amy - thank you for asking for flow charts and maps. And also not laughing at my AMAZING drawings. I mean, they were color coded and I made little mountain peaks. That should have been enough for the Cages!

To everyone who helped shape this book, THANK YOU. This world might be scary and feel solitary, but I'm not alone because of you.

Also from Carrie Ann Ryan

The Montgomery Ink Legacy Series:
Book 1: Bittersweet Promises (Leif & Brooke)
Book 2: At First Meet (Nick & Lake)
Book 2.5: Happily Ever Never (May & Leo)
Book 3: Longtime Crush (Sebastian & Raven)
Book 4: Best Friend Temptation (Noah, Ford, and Greer)
Book 4.5: Happily Ever Maybe (Jennifer & Gus)
Book 5: Last First Kiss (Daisy & Hugh)
Book 6: His Second Chance (Kane & Phoebe)
Book 7: One Night with You (Kingston & Claire)
Book 8: Accidentally Forever (Crew & Aria)
Book 9: Last Chance Seduction (Lexington & Mercy)

The Wilder Brothers Series:
Book 1: One Way Back to Me (Eli & Alexis)
Book 2: Always the One for Me (Evan & Kendall)

ALSO FROM CARRIE ANN RYAN

Book 3: The Path to You (Everett & Bethany)
Book 4: Coming Home for Us (Elijah & Maddie)
Book 5: Stay Here With Me (East & Lark)
Book 6: Finding the Road to Us (Elliot, Trace, and Sidney)
Book 7: Moments for You (Ridge & Aurora)
Book 7.5: A Wilder Wedding (Amos & Naomi)
Book 8: Forever For Us (Wyatt & Ava)
Book 9: Pieces of Me (Gabriel & Briar)
Book 10: Endlessly Yours (Brooks & Rory)

The Cage Family
Book 1: The Forever Rule (Aston & Blakely)
Book 2: An Unexpected Everything (Isabella & Weston)
Book 3: If You Were Mine (Dorian & Harper)

The First Time Series:
Book 1: Good Time Boyfriend (Heath & Devney)
Book 2: Last Minute Fiancé (Luca & Addison)
Book 3: Second Chance Husband (August & Paisley)

The Montgomery Ink: Fort Collins Series:
Book 1: Inked Persuasion (Jacob & Annabelle)
Book 2: Inked Obsession (Beckett & Eliza)
Book 3: Inked Devotion (Benjamin & Brenna)
Book 3.5: Nothing But Ink (Clay & Riggs)
Book 4: Inked Craving (Lee & Paige)
Book 5: Inked Temptation (Archer & Killian)

ALSO FROM CARRIE ANN RYAN

The Montgomery Ink: Boulder Series:
Book 1: Wrapped in Ink (Liam & Arden)
Book 2: Sated in Ink (Ethan, Lincoln, and Holland)
Book 3: Embraced in Ink (Bristol & Marcus)
Book 3: Moments in Ink (Zia & Meredith)
Book 4: Seduced in Ink (Aaron & Madison)
Book 4.5: Captured in Ink (Julia, Ronin, & Kincaid)
Book 4.7: Inked Fantasy (Secret ??)
Book 4.8: A Very Montgomery Christmas (The Entire Boulder Family)

Montgomery Ink: Colorado Springs
Book 1: Fallen Ink (Adrienne & Mace)
Book 2: Restless Ink (Thea & Dimitri)
Book 2.5: Ashes to Ink (Abby & Ryan)
Book 3: Jagged Ink (Roxie & Carter)
Book 3.5: Ink by Numbers (Landon & Kaylee)

Montgomery Ink Denver:
Book 0.5: Ink Inspired (Shep & Shea)
Book 0.6: Ink Reunited (Sassy, Rare, and Ian)
Book 1: Delicate Ink (Austin & Sierra)
Book 1.5: Forever Ink (Callie & Morgan)
Book 2: Tempting Boundaries (Decker and Miranda)
Book 3: Harder than Words (Meghan & Luc)
Book 3.5: Finally Found You (Mason & Presley)
Book 4: Written in Ink (Griffin & Autumn)
Book 4.5: Hidden Ink (Hailey & Sloane)
Book 5: Ink Enduring (Maya, Jake, and Border)
Book 6: Ink Exposed (Alex & Tabby)

ALSO FROM CARRIE ANN RYAN

Book 6.5: Adoring Ink (Holly & Brody)
Book 6.6: Love, Honor, & Ink (Arianna & Harper)
Book 7: Inked Expressions (Storm & Everly)
Book 7.3: Dropout (Grayson & Kate)
Book 7.5: Executive Ink (Jax & Ashlynn)
Book 8: Inked Memories (Wes & Jillian)
Book 8.5: Inked Nights (Derek & Olivia)
Book 8.7: Second Chance Ink (Brandon & Lauren)
Book 8.5: Montgomery Midnight Kisses (Alex & Tabby Bonus(
Bonus: Inked Kingdom (Stone & Sarina)

The On My Own Series:
Book 0.5: My First Glance
Book 1: My One Night (Dillon & Elise)
Book 2: My Rebound (Pacey & Mackenzie)
Book 3: My Next Play (Miles & Nessa)
Book 4: My Bad Decisions (Tanner & Natalie)

The Promise Me Series:
Book 1: Forever Only Once (Cross & Hazel)
Book 2: From That Moment (Prior & Paris)
Book 3: Far From Destined (Macon & Dakota)
Book 4: From Our First (Nate & Myra)

The Less Than Series:
Book 1: Breathless With Her (Devin & Erin)
Book 2: Reckless With You (Tucker & Amelia)
Book 3: Shameless With Him (Caleb & Zoey)

ALSO FROM CARRIE ANN RYAN

The Fractured Connections Series:
    Book 1: Breaking Without You (Cameron & Violet)
    Book 2: Shouldn't Have You (Brendon & Harmony)
    Book 3: Falling With You (Aiden & Sienna)
    Book 4: Taken With You (Beckham & Meadow)

The Whiskey and Lies Series:
    Book 1: Whiskey Secrets (Dare & Kenzie)
    Book 2: Whiskey Reveals (Fox & Melody)
    Book 3: Whiskey Undone (Loch & Ainsley)

The Gallagher Brothers Series:
    Book 1: Love Restored (Graham & Blake)
    Book 2: Passion Restored (Owen & Liz)
    Book 3: Hope Restored (Murphy & Tessa)

The Ravenwood Coven Series:
    Book 1: Dawn Unearthed
    Book 2: Dusk Unveiled
    Book 3: Evernight Unleashed

The Aspen Pack Series:
    Book 1: Etched in Honor
    Book 2: Hunted in Darkness
    Book 3: Mated in Chaos
    Book 4: Harbored in Silence
    Book 5: Marked in Flames

The Talon Pack:
    Book 1: Tattered Loyalties

ALSO FROM CARRIE ANN RYAN

Book 2: An Alpha's Choice
Book 3: Mated in Mist
Book 4: Wolf Betrayed
Book 5: Fractured Silence
Book 6: Destiny Disgraced
Book 7: Eternal Mourning
Book 8: Strength Enduring
Book 9: Forever Broken
Book 10: Mated in Darkness
Book 11: Fated in Winter

Redwood Pack Series:
Book 1: An Alpha's Path
Book 2: A Taste for a Mate
Book 3: Trinity Bound
Book 3.5: A Night Away
Book 4: Enforcer's Redemption
Book 4.5: Blurred Expectations
Book 4.7: Forgiveness
Book 5: Shattered Emotions
Book 6: Hidden Destiny
Book 6.5: A Beta's Haven
Book 7: Fighting Fate
Book 7.5: Loving the Omega
Book 7.7: The Hunted Heart
Book 8: Wicked Wolf

The Elements of Five Series:
Book 1: From Breath and Ruin
Book 2: From Flame and Ash

Book 3: From Spirit and Binding
Book 4: From Shadow and Silence

Dante's Circle Series:
Book 1: Dust of My Wings
Book 2: Her Warriors' Three Wishes
Book 3: An Unlucky Moon
Book 3.5: His Choice
Book 4: Tangled Innocence
Book 5: Fierce Enchantment
Book 6: An Immortal's Song
Book 7: Prowled Darkness
Book 8: Dante's Circle Reborn

Holiday, Montana Series:
Book 1: Charmed Spirits
Book 2: Santa's Executive
Book 3: Finding Abigail
Book 4: Her Lucky Love
Book 5: Dreams of Ivory

The Branded Pack Series:
(Written with Alexandra Ivy)
Book 1: Stolen and Forgiven
Book 2: Abandoned and Unseen
Book 3: Buried and Shadowed

About the Author

Carrie Ann Ryan is the New York Times and USA Today bestselling author of contemporary, paranormal, and young adult romance. Her works include the Montgomery Ink, Redwood Pack, Fractured Connections, and Elements of Five series, which have sold over 3.0 million books worldwide. She started writing while in graduate school for her advanced degree in chemistry and hasn't stopped since. Carrie Ann has written over seventy-five novels and novellas with more in the works. When she's not losing herself in her emotional and action-packed worlds, she's reading as much as she can while wrangling her clowder of cats who have more followers than she does.

www.CarrieAnnRyan.com

www.ingramcontent.com/pod-product-compliance
Ingram Content Group UK Ltd.
Pitfield, Milton Keynes, MK11 3LW, UK
UKHW022040270125
4314UKWH00059B/1723